BURT FRANKLIN: RESEARCH & SOURCE WORKS SERIES 595
American Classics in History & Social Science 157

THE CORRESPONDENCE AND PUBLIC PAPERS

OF

JOHN JAY

VOL. II

1781–1782

THE CORRESPONDENCE AND PUBLIC PAPERS

OF

JOHN JAY

FIRST CHIEF-JUSTICE OF THE UNITED STATES, MEMBER AND PRESIDENT OF THE
CONTINENTAL CONGRESS, MINISTER TO SPAIN, MEMBER OF COMMISSION
TO NEGOTIATE TREATY OF INDEPENDENCE, ENVOY TO GREAT
BRITAIN, GOVERNOR OF NEW YORK, ETC.

1781–1782

EDITED BY

HENRY P. JOHNSTON, A.M.

VOL. II

BURT FRANKLIN
NEW YORK

308
F331 C
v.2

Published by LENOX HILL Pub. & Dist. Co. (Burt Franklin)
235 East 44th St., New York, N.Y. 10017
Originally Published: 1890
Reprinted: 1970
Printed in the U.S.A.

S.B.N.: 8337-18479
Library of Congress Card Catalog No.: 73-140983
Burt Franklin: Research and Source Works Series 595
American Classics in History and Social Science 157

Reprinted from the original edition in the University of Illinois
Library at Urbana.

CONTENTS OF VOLUME II.

1781.

CORRESPONDENCE AND PUBLIC PAPERS

OF

JOHN JAY.

———

JAY TO BENJAMIN FRANKLIN.

MADRID, 21st February, 1781.

DEAR SIR :

Your favour of the 15th ult., with the packets mentioned in it, arrived in good order. I regret your long silence, though I am strongly inclined to rejoice in the cause of it : a fit of the gout, it is said, often prolongs life.

Affairs here begin to wear a better aspect. I am promised 3,000,000 rials—that is, 150,000 dollars, which, though inadequate to the demands upon me, is still a great consolation, especially as men who are at the pains of planting and watering trees seldom let them perish for want of a few drops extraordinary.

I scarcely know how to desire you to make further advances on account of our salary, four months of which is now due, and yet I find myself under a necessity of doing it. My expenses here, notwithstanding the most rigid economy, are very great.

Since writing the above, I have had the pleasure of receiving yours of the 27th January, and sincerely congratulate you on your recovery.   The amount of my bill on you shall, agreeable to your request, be considered as part of the 25,000 dollars.   Your reckoning, as to our salaries, corresponds with mine, though we have been losers by the exchange.

As to the residue of the 25,000 dollars, my drafts shall be entirely regulated by my necessities, and I shall be happy if they permit me to leave a considerable proportion of that sum in your hands.   I shall be constrained, however, to call for a part of that sum shortly ; but whether by a bill, or by means of the Marquis, is uncertain.   As to that gentleman's complaint of my reserve towards him, I could make many remarks, which, though proper for your perusal, ought not to go further.

A few days after my arrival here, a person, whom I was told was the Marquis, was introduced to me.   He said he came to pay me a visit by *order of Mr. Grand.*[1]   I did not then know I was indebted to that gentleman for a letter of recommendation to the marquis, it not having come to my hands.   This singularity struck me, though I appeared not to observe it.   The civilities usual on such occasions passed between us, and at parting the marquis gave me a general invitation to dine with him whenever I should find it convenient.   I returned his visit, but as general invitations from strangers pass with us for mere matters of compliment, I declined doing myself the honour of dining with him.   Interchanges of

[1] Banker, at Paris, with whom the American Commissioners deposited their funds.

visits were continued, and the general invitation to dine once or twice repeated. In this line my connection with the marquis remained, until I received the offer of the king's responsibility for a loan, etc. Several reasons induced me to think it expedient to consult the marquis as to the manner of making this offer useful to us. I waited upon him for that purpose. He told me he could not intermeddle in these affairs *without instructions from the court;* but was nevertheless very civil, and expressed a desire of doing me services, etc. As he declined entering into particulars, I did not press it; nor had my ideas of his importance risen so high as to reconcile me to the extraordinary and unnecessary measure of applying to the Court for the instructions in question. I did not, however, let him know my sentiments or intentions on the subject. It seems he had heard of Mr. Grand having been desired by you to make inquiries for money for me, and he advised me to write to him on the subject, which I accordingly did. In his answer of the 21st October, he says:

I am very unhappy to hear you are not benefited on the spot by the facility tendered to you by the Court of Spain, so much more so that the nature of circumstances here does not admit of the least hope of success. Too many attempts, all vainless, have already been made for the good of your credit; adding any more to the number would be destructive to it entirely, at this particular juncture, chiefly when our government is about raising a sum of money much more enticing and advantageous in its conditions. This perplexing situation suggested me an idea I communicated to Dr. Franklin, etc.

Meanwhile it is highly important to avail yourself of the favourable disposition of the Court of Spain, and get it to authorize and charge the Marquis to help you in your finance business. He writes me that without orders he cannot take it upon himself. It will be better for your excellency not to consult him before making the application to government, etc.

You, my good friend, have seen and thought too much of men and things to need any of my remarks on this letter. I replied to it on the 1st November as follows:

" SIR:

" I have had the honour of receiving your letter of the 21st October last. I had flattered myself that a loan on reasonable terms and adequate security might have been effected for the United States in France; but as that Court is raising money on conditions more advantageous and agreeable, I am not surprised at our having little prospect of success.

" The hint you gave Dr. Franklin was a good one, and I hope will be productive of good consequences.

" Your obliging advice relative to the Marquis shall meet with all the attention due to its importance; and if that measure should, on further consideration, appear expedient, it shall be pursued in the manner you recommend."

The marquis repeating his general invitation about this time, I dined with him. He received and entertained me very politely. We parted, to appearances, pleased with each other; but he has not been at my house since, though a great many visits in my debt.

Ever since my arrival, I have been particularly cautious to avoid offending any person of any rank; to endeavour to please all, without becoming the property or sycophant of any. My disagreeable situation was not unknown to him, but the inferences he drew from it proved fallacious. I never find myself less disposed to humility, or improper compliances, than when fortune frowns. I have uniformly been very civil, though not confidential, to the marquis, nor has any thing harsh ever passed between us. He is a man of business, abilities, and observation, and (what is of much importance here) of money. He keeps the most, and indeed only, hospitable house here, and persons of the first rank and fashion are found at his table. His consequence at court is unequal to his desires, and I think to his capacity of being useful. In a word, he has a good share of sagacity, ambition, and pride. I think it probable that we shall yet be on more familiar terms; for though I will never court, I shall with pleasure cultivate, his acquaintance.

The Count de Montmorin continues very friendly. I believe him to be an able minister, and well attached to our cause.

Mrs. Jay desires me to make her compliments to you. I am, dear sir, with sincere attachment and esteem,

Your most obedient servant,

JOHN JAY.

JAY TO EGBERT BENSON.

DEAR BENSON :   MADRID, March, 1781.

Either some very singular fatality must have attended the letters of my New York friends to me, or they have given me abundant reason to complain of them as correspondents ; not one letter to me, dated in our State, has reached me since I left America.

I have written to you from Martinico, from Cadiz, and from this place ; some of these letters, I have reason to think, arrived safe, though several others have probably miscarried.   Your governor is largely in my debt, and so is General Schuyler, whom I always thought a very punctual correspondent.   How am I to account for this?   I cannot persuade myself that neglect is among the causes.   Business seldom continues a good excuse for a year together, and indolence, often a real, is never an admissible, one.

The vulgar proverb, *out of sight, out of mind*, always appeared to me in the light of a vulgar error, when applied to old *friends and companions*. I hope I have not been mistaken, especially as the contrary of that proposition is true with respect to myself.   I never loved or admired America so much as since I left it, and my attachment to my friends in it seems to have increased, in proportion as distance of time and place separated me from them.   The remark that we seldom estimate blessings justly till we are about to lose them for a time, or altogether, is, I believe, frequently true, and perhaps that circumstance has tightened the cords which bind me to my friends and country.   I could carry your recollection back to days that are past, and entertain you with the shades of many departed pleasures, in which we had been partakers. These shades speak a language that I hope your heart understands as well as mine, and I flatter myself that their voice, though not loud, will be sufficient to awaken a remembrance of the sincere attachment and regard, with which I have long been, and still am,

Your affectionate friend and servant,

JOHN JAY.

JAMES LOVELL TO JAY.

March 9, 1781.

SIR :

You will herewith receive gazettes and journals, also a resolve respecting the complete ratification of the articles binding the Thirteen States as a confederated body. The delay of that business appears now like all the other circumstances of our rise and growth, for the present is really the best of all times for that particular event. Our enemies have been ripening themselves for this capital *mentitis.*

We have no letters from you or Mr. Carmichael later than those mentioned in my last, a copy of which attends this.

I am, Sir, your friend and humble servant,

JAMES LOVELL.

JAY TO THE PRESIDENT OF CONGRESS.

MADRID, March 22, 1781.

SIR :

I ought, and wish to write your Excellency a long letter, but not by post. The French fleet is not yet sailed. It will, in my opinion, be late in the summer before the fleet at Rhode Island will be reinforced. This Court has promised me one hundred and fifty thousand dollars. Some clothing is now shipping on account of Congress from Cadiz.

Russia has offered her mediation to England and the States-General. The latter have accepted it. The answer of the former (if given) is not known here. If she should refuse, Russia will probably take part with the Dutch ; if she accepts, she will doubtless be obliged either to agree to terms consistent with the armed neutrality, or continue the war. The consequences of either are obvious.

M. Necker has published a state of the French finances, much to his honour and their credit. Perhaps a complimentary order to translate and publish it would be useful.

Mr. Cumberland will set out on his return, through France, in a few days.

This letter is intended to go by Captain Trask, from Bilboa. I am told he will sail much sooner than had been given out, and that unless my letters go by this evening's post they would arrive too late. Hence I am obliged to write in haste, and say little, there being no time for ciphers. I have received some letters from your Excellency. Their dates shall be mentioned another time.

I have the honor to be, etc.,

JOHN JAY.

JAY TO GENERAL WASHINGTON.

MADRID, 29th March, 1781.

There has long, my dear sir, been something about my heart which urged me to write to you, but I

thought it selfish to diminish your few leisure mo-
ments by an additional correspondent, especially as
your punctuality and attention would probably have
led you to consult my wishes rather than your own
convenience. The time, I hope, will come when the
return of tranquillity will give me an opportunity of
conversing with you on several interesting subjects.
I have, however, concluded to allow myself the pleasure of writing you a few lines now and then. Indeed,
I ought to have recollected that while I was giving
myself credit in my own mind for self-denial, you
might have been charging me in yours for inattention ; and, therefore, that it might have been more
prudent, and perhaps not less generous, to have
troubled you with letters than with inducements to
suspect that my heart, like a feather, would, with
equal ease, stick to or quit any man on whom the
breath of whim or interest might blow it on or off.

The firmness and delicacy observed in the case of
Major André is exceedingly admired here. I am
happy Colonel Beverley did not succeed in renewing
his acquaintance with you. You have really been
very fortunate in having so long resisted the attacks
of open enemies, and escaped the snares of secret
ones.

I take the liberty of sending you a cask of Packa-
retti, the favourite wine of our late friend, Don Juan,
whose death I much lament. His place will, I believe, be soon filled by a gentleman who will probably
deliver you a letter of introduction from me.

Mr. Harrison, a very worthy kinsman of your secretary, is shipping from Cadiz the clothing taken by Admiral Cordova, and presented by France and Spain to Congress. I have desired him to send you invoices of each parcel.

Mrs. Jay has more than usual health, and seems as much interested in your health and safety as if you was her own father, as well as that of her country. Be pleased to present our best wishes to Mrs. Washington, and when you write to your honest friend, Colonel Harrison, remember me to him. I hope Arnold has not spoiled his mill-dam. God bless you, my dear sir.

> I am, with perfect esteem and regard,
> Your friend and servant,
> JOHN JAY.

JAY TO BENJAMIN FRANKLIN.

MADRID, April, 1781.

DEAR SIR:

Notwithstanding my repeated and earnest applications to the Count de Florida Blanca, I have as yet been able to obtain only $34,880 of the $150,000 expressly promised me in December last. He has, on the contrary, assured me that this promise cannot be complied with in less than six months. It therefore became necessary to communicate my embarrassments to the Ambassador of France, and to request his friendly aid and interposition. You will perceive, by the enclosed account, that the bills I have accepted and what still remain to be paid (exclusive of those at two months' sight, for the payment of which you

authorized me to draw upon you) amount to $231,-
303 ; of which

$89,083 will be payable this month,		
96,288	"	in May,
18,027	"	June,
9,025	"	July,
15,086	"	August,
3,794	"	September.

$231,303

The Ambassador was very sensible of the pernicious
consequences which would follow a protest of these
bills, and, I must do him the justice to say, interested
himself warmly in endeavouring to extricate me from
that necessity. He has had different conferences
with the Count D. F. B. on the subject, and yesterday he promised the ambassador positively to pay
the $89,083 which will be due in April, in the course
of six months, in six equal payments, reckoning from
next May ; but as this money still left me without
relief as to the April bill, he engaged the Marquis
d'Aranda to advance the sums necessary to pay them,
and which I shall accordingly receive from him.
Thus, my dear sir, I have been, as it were, reprieved
by the kind offices of the French Ambassador from
protesting any of the bills due this month ; but every
ensuing month will bring with it new dangers and
solicitudes, and particularly the month of May, in the
course of which I shall be called upon for no less than
$96,288. I am in a cruel situation, and without the
least expectation of succour, except from France. I

therefore think it necessary to inform you of the delicate state of our affairs here by express, and to entreat you to use your utmost endeavours to provide me, by his return, with funds adequate to the bills accepted, and which at *present* amount to $142,220, without including either those which may yet arrive, or the $89,083 due this month, and for the payment of which I expect to reimburse the Marquis d'Aranda with the money promised by the Minister in the monthly payment before mentioned.

The Marquis d'Aranda, whom I saw yesterday at the French Ambassador's, has further agreed, at the Ambassador's request, to furnish me with the further sum of $142,220 as I shall have occasion for it, provided Mr. Grand will accept his drafts to that amount. It is therefore of the last importance that arrangements for this purpose be immediately taken with that gentleman, and that I receive, by the return of the express, his order on the marquis to furnish me at least with the sum of $142,220, without which it will be impossible for me to pay these bills.

The Ambassador will also write by this courier, and I have little doubt but that your Court will generously interpose on this, as they have on several other occasions, to prevent events prejudicial to America in particular, and the common cause in general. I am also constrained to add that our situation here is daily becoming more disagreeable from the want of our salaries. To be obliged to contract debts and live on credit is terrible. I have not, to this day, received a shilling from America; and we should indeed have been greatly distressed had it not been for your good offices. Endeavour, I beseech you, to provide us with supplies on this account, and deliver me, if possible, from the many disagreeable sensations which such a variety of unpleasant circumstances naturally creates. Remember that new bills are still arriving.

Be pleased to communicate this letter to Mr. Laurens, who, I am persuaded, will cheerfully afford you all the aid in his power.

I have directed the courier to wait your orders, and then return without further delay.

I am, dear sir, your friend and humble servant,

JOHN JAY.

P. S.—You will perceive, from the enclosed account, that I shall be under the necessity of drawing upon you for ten or twelve thousand dollars, on account of the twenty-five thousand, before it will be possible to hear from you on the subject.

JAY TO GENERAL SCHUYLER.

MADRID, April, 1781.

DEAR SIR:

This is the fourth letter I have written to you since my arrival. I am still in doubt whether any of them have reached you, though as duplicates of some were sent I think it probable. From your punctuality as well as your former attentions I am persuaded if any of them have come to hand they have not been left unanswered. . . .

For general politics I refer you to my public despatches.

I have seen a letter from America which mentions the probability of our dispute with Vermont terminating in an acknowledgment of its independence. What should have given this turn to that business I cannot easily conceive, and unless it will be a means of assuring to New York her possessions to the west I cannot think it very wise. Circumstances unknown to me may have influenced it, and therefore I may probably not have sufficient information to see clearly the policy of this measure. There is no doubt but that much ought to be sacrificed to the attainment of uncontested boundaries, but [efforts] for this purpose should not be made without an almost moral certainty of their effecting that purpose.

I hope our State will profit by the experience they have had and not permit the public peace and interest to be hereafter prejudiced or endangered by the partial politics of self-interested and unfeeling land jobbers.

The cruel devastations committed last campaign on the frontiers of our State gave me much pain, and I cannot forbear thinking there must have somewhere been great neglect. How so important an object could have been left unprovided for I cannot well conjecture.

GOVERNOR CLINTON TO JAY.

Po'keepsie, 6th April, 1781.

Dear Sir,

It is sometime since I have been favour'd with your letter of the 20th June, the third and last that I have had the

honor of receiving since your arrival in Europe. I have addressed three to your Excellency; my last was of the first
of June ult. I am sorry to find neither has been received,
tho' I am not much surprised at the miscarriage as the
opportunities of conveyance did not seem certain or direct.

The particular situation of this State has undergone no
considerable change since you left it except by the desola-
tion of several of the frontier Settlements against which the
British with their savage allies have carried on a barbarous
depredatory war. Most of Tryon County and Scoharie
have been destroyed. They are not however abandoned;
the Inhabitants, having recovered themselves, continue to
improve their farms and assist in the general defence. Your
native County (Westchester) frequently experiences the resentment of the enemy; but seldom unavenged. Its Militia
often unsupported and left alone to resist the enemy have
maintained their Ground beyond the most sanguine expectations. Every man, indeed every boy, is become a Soldier,
and I do not believe a superior spirit of bravery and enterprise ever possessed a people, and I have the Pleasure to
assure you that this description is equally applicable to the
inhabitants of Orange County south of the Mountains.

A State, the seat of War, exposed in every quarter to the
incursions of the Enemy and excluded from Commerce as
we are, you will naturally imagine must be greatly impover-
ished; but of this you will form a juster idea than by any
description I can give you, if you estimate by the same
scale on which our finances began gradually to diminish
before you left America. Our resources as a nation are,
however, yet great. We abound in provisions and the prices
in specie are nearly the same as at the commencement of
the War. The term for which the principal part of our
army were engaged you will recollect expired last Winter.
The Enemy impatiently awaited this period in the fullest
confidence that a dissolution of the American army would

take Place without the Power of recruiting it.   You have I presume seen [the present] establishment of our Army.   The quota assigned to this State is one regiment of artillery and two of infantry, and I am happy in being able to inform you that we, I speak of this State, are nearly complete.   I am not informed of the success of the other States.   In this I have discovered as ready a disposition to enter into the Service as at any time since the beginning of 1777, with this advantage, that every recruit we now engage has the experience and habit of a veteran Soldier.   The situation of our finances is perhaps the only thing in human probability that can distress us.—I am pleased with your plan of trade.   I am persuaded it would have been beneficial to the State and had an happy effect on the temper of the inhabitants ; but for many reasons which I decline mentioning I fear it is too late to make the essay.

Genl. Schuyler is in the Senate and on this account and his own particular desire is left out of the delegation [in Congress].   The Chancellor continues in as a special delegate but has not attended since last fall.   Our friend G. Morris resides at Philadelphia and persues his profession.   I think his election as a Member for the State in Congress, at the next meeting of the Legislature not improbable.   The Controversy with the inhabitants of the Grants is yet undecided, but my last advices from our delegates give me reason to hope for a speedy and just decision.   The completion of the Confederation on which I cordially congratulate you, will facilitate this business.

I beg you to offer my best respects to M^rs. Jay to whom as well as to yourself M^rs. Clinton wishes to be remembered.

Believe me to be with great sincerity

Dear Sir

Your most obed^t. Servant

GEO. CLINTON.

JAY TO THE PRESIDENT OF CONGRESS.

DEAR SIR :   MADRID, 21st April, 1781.

Accept my thanks for your favour of the 18th December, which was delivered to me on the 13th of March last. I am happy to hear that your health permits you to continue in the chair and to sustain the weight of business which the duties of that office impose upon you.

The interesting news of General Morgan's glorious victory and the success of the French in the Chesapeake reached us three days ago, and our joy has been since increased by intelligence which is credited, though not quite confirmed, that the English troops in the East Indies have been defeated in a decisive battle by a prince of the country in alliance with France. This campaign opens much to our advantage, and I hope the blessing of heaven on our arms will bring it to a conclusion equally prosperous.

By the letter from Doctor Franklin, herewith enclosed, and which he was so obliging as to leave open for my perusal, I find he has requested permission to retire on account of his age and infirmities. How far his health may be improved I know not, since the letters I have received from him bear no marks of age. There is an acuteness and sententious brevity in them which do not [bespeak] an understanding injured by years. I have many reasons to think our country is much indebted to him, and I confess it would mortify my pride as an American if his constituents should be the only people to whom his character is known that should deny his merit and services. Justice demands of me to assure you that his reputation and respectability are acknowledged and have weight here, and that I have received from him all that uniform attention and aid which was due to the importance of the affairs committed to me. The affectionate mention he makes of his only descendant on whom the support of his name and family will devolve, is extremely amiable, and flows in a delicate manner from that virtuous sensibility by which nature kindly extends the benefits of parental affection to a period beyond the limits of our lives. This is an affecting subject, and minds susceptible of the finer sensations are insensibly led at least to wish that the feelings of an ancient patriot, going in the evening of a long life early devoted to the public, may enjoy repose in the bosom of philosophic retirement, and may be gratified by seeing some little spark of the affection of his country rest on the only support of his age and hope of his family.

Such are the effusions of my heart on this occasion, and I pour them into yours from a persuasion that they will meet with a hospitable reception from congenial emotions.

I hope the idea of putting your foreign affairs on the footing you mention will not be laid aside. A responsible, able secretary for that department would be more useful than all the committees you could appoint. Mrs. Jay presents her compliments to your Mrs. Huntington. We have had a fine winter—far more mild and temperate than our northern States afford ; and were it not for the extreme droughts and heats of summer, from which I suffered greatly the last year, I should be much pleased with this climate —not so much, however, as to wish to spend [my life] in it.   My eyes and affections are constantly turned towards America, and I think I shall return to it with as much real and cordial satisfaction as ever an exiled Israelite felt on returning to his land of promise.

I am, dear sir, with very sincere regard and esteem,

Your most obedient and humble servant,

JOHN JAY.

JAY TO CHARLES THOMPSON.[1]

MADRID, 23d April, 1781.

DEAR SIR :

On the 30th of January last I had the pleasure of receiving your very acceptable letter of the 12th October, 1780.   The able manner in which it treats the important subject of American finances induced me to give that part of it to the Minister, and to send a copy of the same extract to Dr. Franklin, who, in answer, says : " I thank you for communicating to me the letter of the secretary of Congress on our finances. It gives light which I had not before, and may be useful here."

I wish in my heart that you was not only secretary of Congress, but secretary also for foreign affairs.   I should then have better sources of intelligence than gazettes and reports.

---

[1] Secretary of Congress.

My public letter contains a state of our affairs here. I flatter myself that Congress will never again attempt to form an alliance on principles of equality in *forma pauperis.*

Before their ingenious letter on our right to the Mississippi arrived, it was known in Europe ; and the subject of my last instructions on that head was no secret here before they reached this side of the ocean. I would tell you more, had I now time to write in ciphers ; but the gentleman who is to carry these despatches is waiting for them.

The want of a regular and safe communication between Congress and their foreign ministers gives occasion to various inconveniences. Every letter known or suspected to be for or from me, that gets into the post-offices, is opened, often kept back for a while, and, to my certain knowledge, sometimes suppressed entirely.

Hence it happens that Congress receives from me fewer letters than I could wish, or than their affairs may demand. The expense of private couriers is intolerable, nor can many in that character be found who merit confidence.

The unseasonable arrival of bills, without being preceded by funds, and the train of perplexing consequences resulting from that and other causes not in my power to prevent, have given me some anxious hours, and often rendered my situation uneasy.

It is my business, however, to reflect, that pleasure was not the object for which I came here, and that obstacles should rather excite than repress perseverance.

Be pleased to present Mrs. Jay's and my compliments to Mrs. Thompson, and believe me to be with sincere regard and esteem,

Your most obedient servant,

JOHN JAY.

JAY TO THE PRESIDENT OF CONGRESS.[1]

SIR: MADRID, April 25, 1781.

I have had the honour of receiving your Excellency's letters of the 6th and 17th of October last, with the enclosures. They arrived the 30th day of January last. There is more than reason to suspect that the French Court were apprised of their contents before they arrived, and to believe that the construction of the treaty, by which the navigation of the Mississippi is supposed to be comprehended in the guarantee, does not correspond with their ideas on that subject. This Court continues pertinaciously to insist on our ceding that navigation, nor will they, as yet, listen to any middle line. Whether this be their real motive for declining a treaty with us at present, or whether the bills drawn upon me have inspired an expectation of profiting by our necessities, or whether they flatter themselves with a future majority of Congress on that point, or whether they choose, by continuing free from engagements with us, to be better enabled to improve to their advantage the casualties of the war, are questions which still remain undecided. Indeed, the movements of this Court in general, when compared

---

[1] This letter is in effect Jay's third report to Congress of his progress at the Spanish court. See notes to letters of May 11th and November 6, 1780.

with the great rules of national policy applicable to their situation, are so inexplicable that I should not be surprised if it should appear in future that they had no fixed system whatever.

My last particular letter informed your Excellency that having, in September last, been told that his Majesty could not advance us any money, but could be responsible for a loan to the amount of one hundred and fifty thousand dollars, I determined to continue accepting the bills, to attempt the loan, and, by a representation of my situation to the French Court, endeavour to save the necessity of protesting them for non-payment.

I tried to borrow here on the security of this responsibility, but without the least success. I attempted it in France, but it would not do. I made the like attempt in Holland, and a gleam of hope appearing there I was about improving it, when a letter from America informed me that Mr. Adams was authorized to execute the business which had been committed to Mr. Laurens. I had learned before of his being in Holland, but did not know the object which had called him there. Several letters passed between Messrs De Neufville and myself on the subject of this loan. The following is a copy of my last to them about it :

"MADRID, January 8, 1781.

" GENTLEMEN :

" I have had the pleasure of receiving your favour of the 4th ult. together with the one referred to in it.

" England has, it seems, declared war against the

United Provinces, and that in a style of such eminent superiority as I am persuaded will remind your countrymen that the United Netherlands are not comprehended among the territories depending on the Crown of Great Britain.

" The English Ministry, by charging the States with having acted under French influence, intend to alarm their national pride, and, by making Holland the particular object of their resentment, to sow the seeds of dissensions among them, and render that most important Province obnoxious to the others. The tone of the whole declaration is that of a nation going rather to give correction to disobedient vassals, than to war upon a free and independent people. It could have been assumed only upon a persuasion, that the same supposed timidity, to which they ascribed the long forbearance of the Dutch under multiplied insults and injuries, would, on this ostentatious display of terror, reduce them to the humiliating measure of imploring forgiveness for having acted like freemen, and purchasing peace at the expense of their honour and liberty. Every other nation must expect better things of you, and can never believe, that the present generation will want firmness to assert the rights and vindicate the honor of a Republic, which owes its very existence to the glorious spirit and magnanimity of its ancestors.

" It gives me great satisfaction to hear that Mr. Adams has conversed with you on this subject of a loan, and I am persuaded that business will be much advanced by it. The impropriety of two loans at a time is evident.   My chief motive in proposing one at the time I did was, that no time might be lost, by the absence of Mr. Laurens, in prosecuting a measure which appeared to me highly useful to my country.   I have no views or subjects separate from her, and, provided she is effectually served, I am well content that the honour of doing it should devolve on others. As the management of our affairs in your country is committed to Mr. Adams, I request the favour of you to give him all the aid in your power.   When that gentleman went to Holland, I was ignorant of the business which called him thither; and the first knowledge I had of it was from America, long after Mr. Laurens' capture.   It cannot now be necessary that my name should appear in the affair of the proposed loan, but should it be in my power to be useful, Mr. Adams may rely upon my zealous endeavours to promote that and every other measure for the public good.   Indeed, as matters now stand, delicacy forbids me to interfere further than as a mere auxiliary to Mr. Adams, to whom, and to whose affairs, I beg you to extend the influence of that generous regard for America which has placed you so high in the esteem of,

" Gentlemen, etc.,

" JOHN JAY."

My last particular despatches contained a copy of my letter to Count de Vergennes, requesting his aid. I received from Count de Montmorin an extract of a letter he had received from the Minister on that sub-

proaching demands, the Ambassador made personal application to a rich banker here, and on his personal credit and my consenting that the aforesaid six monthly payments should be applied to the repayment, obtained a loan for me of the whole sum wanted for April. I have passed my note for it, payable as soon as possible, with interest at the rate of six per cent. But this provision not extending beyond April, the fate of the bills payable in the succeeding months still remained dubious. That nothing in my power might be left undone, I sent on the 1st of April an express to Dr. Franklin representing to him my true situation, and the injuries our credit would sustain from the protest of a single bill drawn by order of Congress. I desired him to communicate my letter to Colonel Laurens, to whom I also wrote on the subject. The express returned on the 19th instant, with a letter from Dr. Franklin, by which I am authorized to draw upon him as occasion may require, to the amount of one hundred and forty-two thousand two hundred and twenty dollars, towards paying the bills that become due between May and September.

My endeavors, however, to obtain further aids from Spain, shall not be relaxed. They seem very desirous of having the ships of the line, still unfinished on the stocks at Boston and Portsmouth. I have written to your Excellency on this subject, and have as yet received no answer. When I consider that the state of our finances has so long prevented the completing those ships, and the difficulties heretofore experienced in providing for those in service; when I recollect that the finishing and fitting out those ships will bring money into our country, and probably prepare the way for Spain's building more vessels in it; and lastly, when I consider how much these ships seem to be an object, I am almost prevailed upon to engage positively that Spain shall have at least one of them at prime cost. To exercise a power not clearly within the limits of those confided to me, is a delicate and disagreeable business. This is the first time I ever found myself disposed to hazard it, and yet so many circumstances lead me to think that the public good would be promoted by the sale of these ships, that in case I should be again pressed on this subject I believe I shall run the risk, from a persuasion that though such conduct ought not to be approved or encouraged by Congress, yet that when directed by the purest motives, and for the best purpose, it may obtain forgiveness.

Your Excellency will receive herewith enclosed a copy of the invoice of prize clothing, taken by Admiral Cordova, and presented by the Courts of France and Spain to Congress. The Count de Montmorin was very much an American on this occasion also. Mr. Harrison, at Cadiz, has my orders to ship these goods in different vessels to America; part of them is now on the ocean, and the rest will soon follow. Your Excellency will receive a letter of advice with each parcel from Mr. Harrison, of whom I have a very good opinion. He charges no commission for doing this business, being contented with the satisfaction of serving his country.

I have often mentioned to Congress the necessity of more effectual provision for our captive seamen; for want of money I cannot pay that attention to them which their misfortunes and usefulness demand. I am already greatly in arrears on their account, and Mr. Harrison, unless reimbursed, must soon stop his hand.

Portugal, though overawed by France and Spain, fears and perhaps loves England; her conduct will be determined by future events. The Minister here has promised me to interpose the good offices of his Court with that of Lisbon in our behalf. In time something good may result from it. I have not received a line from Mr. Dohrman; I fear he is obliged to be very circumspect and cautious. The letters herewith enclosed from Dr. Franklin were left open for my perusal, the short stay of my courier not allowing time for copies to be made of the information conveyed in and with them. The intercepted letters will be found interesting. One of them ascertains the price paid Arnold.

I perceive that Dr. Franklin desires to retire. This circumstance calls upon me to assure Congress that I have reason to be perfectly satisfied with his conduct towards me, and that I have received from him all the aid and attention I could wish or expect. His character is very high here, and I really believe that the respectability, which he enjoys throughout Europe, has been of general use to our cause and country.

Your Excellency may rely on my cordially adopting and pursuing any measures that can conduce to the enlargement of Mr. Laurens, and I regret that no occasion has yet offered in which I could do any thing towards the attainment of that desirable object.

Mr. Cumberland is on the road home. I much suspect that he was sent and received, from mutual views in the two Courts of deceiving each other. Which of them has been most successful is hard to determine. I believe, in point of intelligence, England has had the advantage. As to the assurances of the Minister on this subject, they are all of little consequence, because on such occasions Courts only say what may be convenient; and therefore may or may not merit confidence. Time and circumstances will cast more light on this subject.

Whatever we may get from this Court is clear gain. We have no demands upon it, and if we had, are not in a capacity to insist upon them. In my opinion, therefore, it is of the utmost importance to avoid appearances of discontent, and rather to impress other nations with an opinion of the friendship of Spain for us, than otherwise. Indeed, I really believe the King means well towards us, and that the Prime-Minister is also well disposed ; but whether as much can be said of the Minister's confidential and I believe influential secretary, M. Del Campo, is by no means a clear point. It is proper that Congress should know that the gentleman intended to succeed M. Mirales was recommended by M. Del Campo, with whom he has long been on terms of intimacy and friendship.

I have nevertheless no room to doubt of this gentleman's attachment to our cause, though I am inclined to think his conduct will be conformable in a certain degree with the views of his patron. This ought to remain a secret. He is still here, although he expects daily to be despatched.

I represented the case of the Dover cutter to the Ministry here the 22d of June last. In December I obtained a promise that it should be appraised, and the value paid to the captors, and two days ago, I was again assured that measures were taking to bring this matter to a conclusion. *Festina lente* seems to be the first maxim in Spanish politics and operations. It is the fashion of the country and strangers must conform to it.

I congratulate Congress on the victory obtained by General Morgan, and the success of the French in the Chesapeake. The enclosed gazette contains much good news from the East Indies. These events will probably give Lord George Germaine other ideas than those which appear in his intercepted letters.

M. Toscan, who goes to reside as Vice-Consul of France at Boston, will carry this letter to America, and perhaps to Philadelphia. He was ready to set out when my courier returned from France. I was obliged to delay my letters till his arrival, and M. Toscan has been so obliging as to wait till I could complete them.

I have the honour to be, sir, etc.,

JOHN JAY.

JAY TO COLONEL LAURENS.

MADRID, 2d May, 1781.

DEAR SIR:

I have been favoured with your very polite and obliging letter by the return of my courier. None of the letters for me from America which you mention to have been committed on your arrival to the care of Dr. Franklin have as yet reached me.

The nature of the warrant under which your good father is detained is, if I am rightly informed, such as that I fear his enlargement on *parole* will not be easily obtained. Indeed I much doubt its being effected in any other way than that of retaliation. Whether we have among the prisoners any of sufficient importance I am not informed. There were some Parliament men taken with General Burgoyne who might be recalled, though not perhaps imprisoned.

From my idea of the coast and disposition of many parts of Britain and Ireland, I should think it practicable to surprise and take off some ministerial men of consequence in both islands, but of this you are better able to judge than I am.

Your remarks on our pecuniary resources are exceedingly just, and the conclusion you draw from them corresponds perfectly with my sentiments on that head. When I did myself the honour of writing to you last, I had been led to suppose that your residence in Europe would probably be for a considerable time, and therefore wished to provide immediately for the means of deriving advantage to our country and satisfaction to myself from a confidential correspondence with you. Your speedy return to America will disappoint these views, but be assured that the same motives which induce me on this occasion to cultivate your friendship will on all others render me desirous of evincing the esteem and regard with which

I am, dear sir,

Your most obedient and humble servant,

JOHN JAY.

THE PRESIDENT OF CONGRESS TO JAY.

In Congress, May 28th, 1781.

SIR :

Your letter of the 6th of November last, detailing your proceedings from the 26th of May down to that period, has been received by the United States in Congress assembled. At the same time was received your letter of the 30th of November, with the several papers therein referred to.

It is with pleasure, Sir, I obey the direction of Congress to inform you, that throughout the whole course of your negotiations and transactions, in which the utmost address and discernment were often necessary to reconcile the respect due to the dignity of the United States with the urgency of their wants, and the complaisance expected by the Spanish Court, your conduct is entirely approved by them.   It is their instruction that you continue to acknowledge, on all suitable occasions, the grateful impression made on these States by the friendly disposition manifested toward them by his Catholic Majesty, and particularly by the proofs given of it in the measures which he has taken, and which it is hoped he will further take, for preserving their credit, and for aiding them with a supply of clothing for their army. You are also authorized and instructed to disavow, in the most positive and explicit terms, any secret understanding or negotiation between the United States and Great Britain ; to assure his Catholic Majesty, that such insinuations have no other source than the invidious designs of the common enemy, and that as the United States have the highest confidence in the honor and good faith both of his Most Christian and of his Catholic Majesty, so it is their inviolable determination to take no step, which shall depart in the smallest degree from their engagements with either.

Should the Court of Spain persist in the refusal intimated by its Minister to accede to the treaty between the United States and his Most Christian Majesty, or to make it the basis of its negotiation with you, the difficulty, it is conceived, may easily be avoided by omitting all express reference to that treaty, and at the same time conforming to the principles and tenor of it ; and you are accordingly authorised so far to vary the plan of your original instructions. As his Most Christian Majesty however may justly expect, in a matter which so nearly concerns him, and which was brought into contemplation in the treaty he so magnanimously entered into with these States, the strongest marks of attention and confidence, you will not fail to maintain, in the several steps of your negotiation, a due communication with his Minister at the Court of Spain, and to include his interests as far as circumstances will warrant.

You are authorised to acquaint his Catholic Majesty that not only entire liberty will be granted, during the war at least, to export naval stores for the royal marine, but that every facility will be afforded for that purpose.

As Congress have no control over the captains of private vessels, however proper your hints may be of obliging them to give a passage to American seamen returning home from foreign ports, and to send an officer with despatches intrusted to them for foreign Ministers, it is impracticable to carry them into execution, you will therefore continue to provide for these objects for the present, in the best manner you can. As soon as the United States are in condition to establish consuls in the principal ports of the States with which they have intercourse, the difficulty will be removed; or if any other practicable remedy be suggested in the meantime, it will be applied.

The letter, of which you enclose a copy, from Stephen d'Audibert Caille, styling himself consul for unrepresented nations at the Court of Morocco, had before been received through the hands of Dr. Franklin. If you shall have no objection to the contrary, you will correspond with him, and assure him in terms the most respectful to the Emperor, that the United States in Congress assembled entertain a sincere disposition to cultivate the most perfect friendship with him, and that they will embrace a favorable occasion to announce their wishes in form.

The generous and critical services rendered these United States by Messrs Neufville and Son, have recommended them to the esteem and confidence of Congress. You will signify as much to them, and that their services will not be forgotten, whenever a proper occasion offers of promoting their interests.

Your intimation with respect to complimenting his Catholic Majesty with a handsome, fast sailing packet-boat, claims attention; but the variety of public embarrassments will render the execution of it very uncertain.

Congress agree to an extension of Colonel Livingston's furlough, till the further order of Congress, which you will make known to him.

Your letter of the 16th of September last was received on the 4th day of December. No bills have been drawn on you since. That of the 28th of January was received on the 27th day of April; and in consequence of it the sale of the bills already drawn, but then remaining on hand, was countermanded.

By a letter from Mr. Carmichael, dated the 22d of February, and received on the 27th of April last, Congress are informed that you had received despatches from them dated in October. These must have contained their instructions to you to adhere to the claim of the United States to the navigation of the Mississippi. A reconsideration of that subject determined Congress, on the 15th day of February last, to recede from that instruction so far as it insisted on their claim to the navigation of that river below the thirty-first degree of north latitude, and to a free port or ports below the same. On the receipt of this latter instruction, Congress have little doubt that the great obstacle to your negotiations will be removed, and that you will not only be able without further delay to conclude the proposed alliance with his Catholic Majesty, but that the liberality and friendly disposition manifested on the part of the United States by such a cession, will induce him to afford them some substantial and effectual aid in the article of money. The loss attending the negotiation of bills of exchange has been severely felt. A supply of specie through the Havana would be much more convenient and acceptable.

SAMUEL HUNTINGTON, *President*.

ROBERT MORRIS TO JAY.

PHILADELPHIA, June 5th, 1781.

DEAR SIR:

I must freely acknowledge the justice of your charge against me as a bad correspondent, for the force of truth would convict, were I to deny, and perhaps friendship will hardly bear with palliatives; but knowing well your attachment to, and practice of sincerity, I shall honestly tell you I did not like to write on political matters, and in what may be called domestic, you had constantly better information than 't was possible for me to give, having also very ample employment for my time; you will reflect, that all these circumstances combined to make me silent, although not inattentive or forgetful of my friends abroad.

I have three letters from you, dated the 28th May, 16th September, and 19th November last, and feel myself exceedingly indebted to that partiality which prompted you to say many civil things; these are stamped with an unusual value, not because I suffer myself to think they are merited, but because you thought so. We have heard more of you and Mrs. Jay than these letters tell me, and upon the whole have not found much cause to be pleased with your situation. Hers must too often have been very disagreeable; the loss of the little *one* was truly distressing, and your almost constant absence extremely hard. But you must comfort yourself with the reflection that still more cruel things might have happened, had you remained in your own country. Suppose you had been with your father, when some of the enemy's ruffians broke into the house, and after satiating themselves with plunder, they had carried you, my dear friend, a prisoner to New York. Think of the triumph of your enemies, the distress of your friends, and what you must, under such circumstances, have suffered: happy that you have escaped such an event, I will not prolong the idea of it.

Our friend Gouverneur has acquainted you with my appointment to the superintendant of finance; the motives of my acceptance are purely patriotic, and I would this moment give much of my property to be excused; but pressed by my friends, acquaintances, fellow-citizens, and almost by all America, I could not resist. I will therefore most assiduously try to be useful, and if in this I do but succeed, my recompense will be ample. Gouverneur and others have promised me the assistance of their abilities. Congress promise support; if the Legislatures and individuals will do the same, we will soon change the face of our affairs, and show our enemies that their hopes of our ruin, through the channel of finance, is as vain as their hope of conquest.

This campaign, as usual, opens to our disadvantage ; but I expect it will also, as usual, close favourably for us.   The vices and follies of our enemies may justly be counted among the number of our fast friends.   They never fail to work for our relief in the hour of distress ; for at those times the pride, insolence, and tyranny of the British heroes are too insufferable to be borne, even by the peasantry of America.   It affords me much pleasure to find the assistance I have given towards delivering supplies at Havannah, is known and approved by the ministry at the court of Madrid, as a favourable impression there may be serviceable to my administration of the finances, and I hope still to return more important services for those I expect from them to this distressed country.   Adieu, my dear sir ; with sincere affection, I am   Your obedient, humble servant,

ROBERT MORRIS.

JAY TO J. SMITH.[1]

ARANJUEZ, 5th June, 1781.

SIR :

So many letters both for and from me miscarry, that I take this opportunity of informing you, that I have had the pleasure of writing to you by the way of Cadiz, and that I consider myself much obliged by your favour of the 27th February last, which did not come to my hands till long after it must have arrived here. The intelligence communicated by it was no less welcome than interesting.   We wait with impatience for further information respecting the military operations

[1] In the original the address is abbreviated as Js. or Is. Smith.   The correspondent may have been James Smith, of Penna., one of the Signers,

in the southern States.   Lord Cornwallis' expedition
bears some marks of rashness, and I cannot but expect he will have some reason to repent it.   I think
his temper and measures well calculated to enrage
and discipline the southern militia ; if so, his victories
will render his enemies more numerous and formidable than ever.   The ratification of the confederation,
and the firm establishment of civil government in the
different Sates, are circumstances very friendly to
the American cause, and should be viewed by our
enemies as insurmountable obstacles to our again becoming their subjects.   Such, however, is their in-
fatuation and their obstinacy, that there appears
very little reason to flatter ourselves with a speedy
peace, unless this campaign should produce events
greatly to their prejudice.   I hope, therefore, that
our countrymen will not suffer themselves to be
amused with such delusive expectations, but on the
contrary will persevere vigorously and systematically
in preparing to prosecute the war.

I am, sir, your most obedient and humble servant,

JOHN JAY.

GOUVERNEUR MORRIS TO JAY.

PHILADELPHIA, 17th June, 1781.

DEAR JAY:

Although I believe myself thoroughly acquainted with
you, yet I cannot tell whether I ought to congratulate or
condole with you on your late appointment.[1]   Ere this

---

[1] Morris here refers to Jay's selection by Congress, June 13, 1781, as one of
the four new Commissioners to be associated with John Adams in negotiating
a treaty of peace with Great Britain.   His colleagues were Franklin, Laurens,

reaches you, you will have learned, that you are on the part of this country one of five to negotiate peace ; so far you are something : but when you come to find by your instructions that you must ultimately obey the dictates of the French minister, I am sure there is something in your bosom which will revolt at the servility of the situation. To have relaxed on all sides, to have given up all things, might easily have been expected from those minds which, softened by wealth and debased by fear, are unable to gain and unworthy to enjoy the blessings of freedom.   But that the proud should prostitute the very little dignity this poor country was possessed of, would be indeed astonishing, if we did not know the near alliance between pride and meanness : men who have too little spirit to demand of their constituents that they do their duty, who have sufficient humility to beg a paltry pittance at the hands of any and every sovereign, such men will always be ready to pay the price which vanity shall demand from the vain.   Do I not know you well enough to believe that you will not act in this new capacity ? I think I do ; and therefore I will express my concern that you must decline the honour, if that name can be applied to such offices.   Decline, however, with decency, though with dignity.   I mean always if no alteration takes place, which shall be done if I can effectuate it, though I almost despair.

No other Congress will surrender all, as this has, to an ally.   I am more moved on this occasion than I ever have been, and therefore it is possible I may be mistaken ; but I think so strong, so deep an impression cannot be false.

Remember me properly, and believe me, Yours,

GOUVERNEUR MORRIS.

and Jefferson.   It was not until a year later, and several months after the capitulation at Yorktown, that the prospects of a speedy peace were sufficiently promising to authorize Jay's departure from Madrid to meet his associates in Paris.   Meanwhile he endeavored, unavailingly, to complete the vexing Spanish business.

BENJAMIN FRANKLIN TO JAY.[1]

PASSY, June 30, 1781.

SIR:

You acquaint me that bills have appeared, drawn on you in March last, and ask very properly if this can be reconciled to the obvious dictates of prudence and policy. It cannot. And if you are unable to pay them, they must be protested ; for it will not be in my power to help you. And I see that nothing will cure the Congress of this madness of drawing upon the Pump at Aldgate, but such a proof that its well has a bottom.

ROBERT MORRIS[2] TO JAY.

PHILADELPHIA, July 4th, 1781.

DEAR SIR:

The derangement of our money affairs, the enormity of our public expenditures, the confusion in all our departments, the languor of our general system, the complexity and consequent inefficacy of our operations ; these are some among the many reasons, which have induced Congress to the appointment of a Superintendent of Finance. I enclose you copies of their resolutions on that subject, with such other papers as will fully explain to you my appointment and powers.

The use of this office must be found in a progress towards the accomplishment of these two capital objects, the raising a revenue with the greatest convenience to the people, and the expenditure of it with the greatest economy to the public. . . .

While we have neither credit nor means at home, it is idle to expect much from individuals abroad. Our foreign credit must be nurtured with tenderness and attention before it can

---

[1] From Hale's "Franklin in France."

[2] Lately appointed Superintendent of Finance by Congress. This letter was followed by another inclosing his plan for a National Bank. See "Diplomatic Correspondence," viii., 438.

possess any great degree of force, and it must be fed by substantial revenue, before we can call it into active exertion or derive beneficial effects from its application.

All reasonable expectation, therefore, is narrowed down to the friendly interposition of those sovereigns, who are associates in the war. From Holland, we can properly ask nothing; nor is she, I believe, in a capacity to grant it if we did ask. The active efforts of France require all the resources of that great nation, and of consequence the pecuniary aid which she affords us can but little advance the general cause, however it may relieve our immediate distress.

We must then turn our eyes to Spain, and we must ask either loans or subsidies to a very considerable amount. Small sums are not worth the acceptance. They have the air of obligation without affording relief. A small sum, therefore, is not an object to the United States, for they do not mean to beg gratuities, but to make rational requests.

As Congress have empowered you to remove the obstacles, which have hitherto impeded your negotiations, you will doubtless proceed with prudent despatch in forming the important treaties, which are to be the basis of our national connexion. Your own integrity, and the dispositions which you certainly feel, as the true representative of your Sovereign, to gratify the wishes of his Catholic Majesty, will give you just claim to the confidence and friendly support of his Ministers. And on the other hand, his Majesty's known piety and justice, will certainly induce him to facilitate a permanent union between the two countries, and to overturn that power, whose ambition is known, felt, and detested, throughout the habitable globe.

Having a perfect confidence in the wisdom of his Majesty's Ministers, I must request that you will submit to their consideration the reasons, which operate in favor of the advances we expect. In doing this, it will immediately strike you and them, that the enemy carries on the operations against us at an expense infinitely greater than that by which they are opposed.   By enabling us, therefore, to increase our resistance, and redouble our offensive efforts, the British will be reduced to the necessity of increasing their force in America, or of submitting beneath a decided superiority.   Either must be fatal to them.   In the first instance, they will be crushed by the weight of expense; and, in the second, they must, while they lose an actual force, and part forever with the object in contest, feel the increased weight of the American arms, and make head against those resources, applied to a marine, which are now consumed in land operations.

Money ought, therefore, to be supplied to us from the Havana, which will at the same time save the risk of transporting it to Europe, while, as I have already observed, it must, when employed among us, absolutely ruin the common enemy,   For, when once they are driven from the United States, they must, at a considerable expense, defend, or, at a great loss, relinquish the rest of their American possessions; and, in either case, the resources of this country will enable France and Spain to carry on operations for the subjection of the British Islands.

With respect to our finance, I am further to observe, that the resolutions of Congress, of the 18th of March, 1780, have neither been so regularly adopted by the States as was hoped and expected, nor been productive of those consequences, which were intended.   It is unnecessary to travel into the causes, or to explain the reasons of this event.   The fact is clear.   The new money is depreciated, and there is the strong evidence of experience to convince us, that the issuing of paper, at present, must be ineffectual.   Taxation has not yet been pursued to that extent, which was necessary.   Neither is it reasonable to expect that it should. Time has been required under all governments to accustom the people by degrees to bear heavy burdens. The people of America have so patiently endured the various calamities of the war, that there is good reason to expect they will not shrink at this late hour from the imposition of just and equal taxes. But many arrangements are necessary to this purpose, and, therefore, an immediate pecuniary assistance is the more necessary to us. Our debts, under which I comprise, as well those of the individual States, as those of the Union, are but trifling, when we consider the exertions which have been made. The debt I have already mentioned on certificates is heavy, not from the real amount, but because it is beyond what the supplies obtained were reasonably worth, and because it impedes taxation and impairs its effects. But the amount of other debts is so small, that a few years of peace would bring it within the bounds of a revenue very moderate, when compared with the wealth of our country. You well know the rapid increase of that wealth, and how soon it would relieve us from the weight of debts, which might be in the first instance very burdensome. There can, therefore, be no doubt, that we shall be able to pay all those, which it may be necessary to contract. But, as I have already observed, our great difficulty is the want of means in our people, and of credit in our government.

It gives me, however, very great pleasure to inform you, that the determined spirit of the country is by no means abated, either by the continuance of the war, the ravages of our enemy, the expense of blood and treasure we have sustained, or the artifices, falsehoods, and delusions of an insidious foe. These last become daily more and more contemptible in America, and it appears equally astonishing, that they should longer attempt them here, or boast the success of such attempts in Europe. Uniform experience has shown the futility of their efforts, and the falsehood of their assertions. I know they take the advantage of every little success to vaunt the prowess of their troops and proclaim hopes of conquest, which they do not feel. But those, who know anything of our history or situation, must have the utmost contempt for all these gasconades. It is impossible they should make impression upon any but weak minds, and I should hardly have thought of mentioning them, but I learn by letters from Spain, that men, who are uninformed, have been led into misapprehensions from circumstances, which were here considered as trivial and even favorable.

I could hardly have supposed that our enemies had still the folly to repeat, as I am told they do, that there is an English party in America. Bribes and deceit have induced some wicked and weak men to join them ; but when we consider the sums they have expended, and the falsehoods they have used, our wonder is not, that they have got so many, but that they have gained so few. The independence of America is considered here as established ; so much so, that even those of equivocal character accustom themselves to cherish the idea ; for the doubt is not now, whether an acknowledgment of it will take place, but when that acknowledgment will be made. Our exertions also, in the present moment, are not so much directed to establish our liberties, as to prevent the ravages of the enemy, abridge the duration and calamities of the war, and faithfully contribute to the reduction of a power, whose ambition was equally dangerous and offensive to every other.

All reasonings on this subject must be deeply enforced, by paying attention to what has happened in the Southern States. The progress of the enemy, while in appearance it menaced the conquest of that extensive region, tended only, in effect, to exhaust him by fruitless efforts, so that at length a handful of men have rescued the whole from his possession. The attack on Virginia (if the piratical incursions there can deserve that name) has been equally futile. The commanders may indeed have enriched themselves by plunder, and many worthy families have been distressed; but what is the consequence ? Indignation and resentment have stimulated even the weak and indolent to action. The wavering are confirmed, and the firm are exasperated, so that every hour, and by every operation, they create enemies, instead of gaining subjects.

Our armies, though not very numerous, are powerful. The regular troops are so much improved in discipline and the habits of a military life, that they are at least equal to any troops in the world. Our militia are becoming more and more warlike, so as to supply the wants of regular troops, when the enemy (taking advantage of that convenience, which their ships afford them) transfer the scene of action from one place to another. The number of the British diminishes daily, and of consequence, our superiority becomes daily more decisive. The greatest plenty of subsistence is to be had for our armies, and the prospects from the present harvest are beyond all former experience. I wish I could add, that clothing and military stores were as abundant as those other requisites for war. This is not the case ; our soldiers, indeed, are well armed, and, in some degree, they are clothed. We have also ammunition abundantly sufficient for the common operations of the field. But many of our militia are unarmed, and the sieges, which will be necessary to expel the enemy, must make a heavy deduction from our military stores.

The proposed siege of New York will soon be commenced, and would undoubtedly be successful, if we could maintain a decided superiority at sea. This must depend on contingencies, which are not in our power, nor perhaps in the power of any human being. I am not without hopes, even if we should not possess that superiority; but the expense will, from the want of it, be very considerably enhanced, and this is a circumstance which I cannot but deplore, for I repeat it again, the want of money can alone prevent us from making the greatest exertions. What our exertions have already been, our enemies themselves must acknowledge, and while from insidious views, they assert that they could not make an impression on us with ninety thousand soldiers and seamen, we are certainly authorised to conclude from this confession, that these States form a considerable balance in the scale against them.

I am now, therefore, again led to reiterate my request of a considerable sum of money from Spain; for I also again repeat, that small sums are not worth our acceptance, and I may add, they are unworthy the dignity of his Catholic Majesty. There can be no doubt, nor will the Spanish Ministry deny, that there is a considerable risk in transporting their money from the new world to the old, besides, that when expended there, it necessarily runs through the different channels of commerce, to feed the wants and invigorate the forces of the enemy. There is, therefore, a double policy in expending a part of it here, where it can not only be brought with safety and despatch, but be employed to an immense advantage, when compared with its effects in Europe. If it be asked, what advantages Spain will derive in particular during the war, and what recompense can be made her after the peace? I answer, that the weakening more the common enemy by a given sum, is in itself a great advantage, and that to do this, by sparing the blood of Spanish subjects, is an advantage still greater. I add, that when relieved from the enemy, we may assist her in the reduction of the Floridas and Bahamas, and, perhaps, of Jamaica. We shall then, also, be in a situation to secure Nova Scotia, thereby depriving Great Britain of her principal resource for ship-timber, and enable us to furnish that essential article to the navy of Spain, on cheaper and better terms, than it can be had elsewhere. On this last subject, I have further to observe, that there is hardly anything in which the maritime power of Spain is so much interested;

for if we do not possess that country, it will be impracticable to furnish those supplies of masts and spars, which both France and Spain may stand in need of; so that, of consequence, their positive and absolute strength at sea will be the less, while that of the enemy is positively and absolutely greater. The comparative inferiority, therefore, will be still more considerable. Nor is this all. A marine requires men, as well as ships. The fisheries and collieries are two pillars, which support the marine of Britain, so far forth as seamen are required. But it is evident, that the fisheries could not long continue in her hands, if she were deprived of Nova Scotia. Here again, we are also to consider, that there is an immense difference between that patient resistance, whose opposition must at length weary the enemy into granting our independence, and those vigorous active operations, which may wrest from them their present possessions. Money is necessary for the latter, and I can say with confidence, that money alone is necessary.

But to return. The advantages which will flow to Spain at a peace, from giving effectual aid to our finances now, will be, in the first place, the common compensation of repayment, should his Catholic Majesty prefer loans to subsidies. The having expelled the English from the Bay of Mexico, and having, by that means, prevented the contraband commerce, so destructive to his revenue, will be another striking advantage, which cannot have escaped the penetration of his Ministers. But this is not all. The opening a port in East Florida, on the shores of the Atlantic, under proper regulations and restrictions, would enable us to carry on a commerce very advantageous to Spain, because we could furnish all such supplies of provisions, &c. as their possessions might stand in need of, and in return, take at port, cocoa, logwood, Nicaragua wood, and, indeed, any other commodities, which his Catholic Majesty should find it for the advantage of his dominions to permit the exportation of. Our commerce with Spain is also, in itself, a very considerable object. At this moment, we take from thence wine, oil, fruit, silk, cloth, &c. And after the conclusion of the war, our remittances of wheat, corn, fish, and naval stores, will be of very great consequence to the commerce of that country. Another article of commerce will be the building of ships, which can be had on cheaper and better terms here than elsewhere ; and there can be no doubt but that the construction of ships in this country is equal, if not superior, to that in any other. Even now, ships might be built on his Majesty's account, though by no means so cheaply as in times of peace ; besides that, as there is now no seasoned timber in the country, such ships would not be durable, and, therefore, it might, perhaps, be imprudent to get any more than are immediately necessary.

To all the other advantages, which would arise to his Catholic Majesty, I may add, (although that is not so properly within my department,) the security, which his dominions would derive from our guarantee. This is an advantage, which must be the more evident from a consideration of what might have happened, had this country continued in union with Great Britain, and had great Britain pursued those schemes of universal empire, which the virtue and fortitude of America first checked, and which it is the object of the present war to frustrate. Our enemies do, I know, allege, that our weakness is unable to withstand them, and that our force is dangerous to Spain. The serious refutation of such absurd contradictions would involve an absurdity. It may not, however, be improper to observe, that the attention of this country, for a century past, has been, and for a century to come, most probably will be, entirely turned to agriculture and commerce. We must always, therefore, be useful neighbors, and never dangerous, except to those who may have views of dominion. Spain can never be in this predica-

Your own good sense will suggest to you many other most forcible arguments, as well as the proper time and manner of applying them. It is necessary to mention, that the sum of five million dollars may, perhaps, be sufficient for our present emergencies; but if a greater sum can be obtained, we shall thereby become more extensively useful. Whatever the grant may be, it will be proper that it be sent hither in some Spanish ships of war from the Havana, or advanced to us there; in which latter case, we will devise the means of bringing it away. Whether to ask for subsidies, or loans, as well as the terms on which either are to be obtained, these, Sir, are objects, which you are fully competent to determine upon. I have only to wish that your applications may meet with that success, which I am confident you will not fail to merit. As the means of facilitating your views, I shall apply to the Minister of his Most Christian Majesty here, to write on the same subject to the French Ambassador at Madrid. The generous conduct of France gives just ground of reliance on her friendly assistance; and you are too well convinced of this, not to act in the most perfect harmony with the servants of that Court, especially on an occasion so important as the present. I need not stimulate your activity, by observing how precious is every moment of time in those affairs, on which the fate of Empires depends; nor need I suggest the importance of a treaty, and particularly a subsidiary treaty with Spain, in that moment, when the judgment of Europe is to be passed on the fate of America. For, however impracticable it may be to subdue us, it is undoubtedly of moment to hasten the approach of that period, when the acknowledgment of our independence shall give the blessings of peace to so many contending nations. To spare the present lavish effusion of blood and treasure, is a serious object with those, who feel, as you do, the emotions of benevolence; and I am confident, that the patriotism, which has inspired your conduct, will and enterprising officer, and the journals of Congress contain ample evidence of it. I sincerely lament his situation, and regret that my own does not put it in my power to afford him relief. The far greater part of the money which the public demands require here, I draw from you. The amount of the bills drawn upon me by Congress far exceeds that of the funds prepared for their payment, and the debts already incurred on account of distressed American seamen still remain unpaid. It would not be delicate in me to advance money to Colonel Talbot, and then request the favour of you to replace it, especially as his situation places him more immediately under your care than mine. All that I can therefore do with propriety is to make you acquainted with his case. He has served his country zealously, and has a right to her care; gratitude as well as policy dictates it. I fear too little attention has in general been paid to our captive seamen. I often hear of many entering into the enemy's service for want of bread, and for ill treatment not retaliated; even those who have had the good fortune and address to escape are frequently obliged, in seeking opportunities to return home, to wander about from place to place, friendless, penniless, ignorant of the language of the strangers through whose land they pass, making known their wants only by the voice of distress, and subsisting on the wretched husks cast to them by the frugal hand of charity. Nor is this all: although their misfortunes, on finding American vessels bound home, ought to recommend them to their brethren, yet it too often happens that masters of American vessels inhumanly refuse (unless paid passage-money) to carry home these unfortunate people, though offering to do duty without wages as sailors during the voyage.

I am, dear sir, with sincere esteem and regard,
Your obliged and affectionate servant,
JOHN JAY.

JAY TO BENJAMIN FRANKLIN.

MADRID, 13 July, 1781.

DEAR SIR :

I have received your favor respecting the Pump at Aldgate.[1]

I have since (two days ago) received letters from Congress assuring me that no further bills shall be drawn upon me.

These despatches have given me so much business that I am obliged to desire Mr. Carmichael to write to you the news, and to assure you without further addition to this letter, that I am most sincerely, your aff. obliged friend and servant.

JAY TO CAPTAIN SILAS TALBOT.[2]

MADRID, 14th July, 1781.

SIR :

Although I have not had the pleasure of your acquaintance, I am not a stranger to your merit.

On receiving your favour of the 11th ult., I sent a copy of it to his Excellency Dr. Franklin, and warmly recommended your case to his attention. I am per-

---

[1] See *ante*, Franklin to Jay, June 30, 1781. From Hale's "Franklin in France."
[2] Prisoner of war in England. See Jay to Franklin, July 9, 1781.

suaded he will do all in his power for your relief, and that the distinguished manner in which you have served our country will always be considered as giving you a title to her care and protection.

Not being authorized by Congress to provide for American prisoners in England, I could not justify undertaking it, and therefore referred your application to Dr. Franklin, within whose department that business appears to me to fall.

I shall always be ready as an individual to contribute to the relief of my distressed countrymen, and should now give you proof of it ; but as your case and that of your fellow-prisoners ought to be, and probably are, provided for by the public, I think assistance should there be asked and denied, before it can become the duty of private benevolence to supply public omissions.

If the application to Dr. Franklin should be fruitless, I shall then consider myself bound, as a good American, to contribute towards the relief of a fellow-citizen, who has so nobly fought in the cause of our country ; and I shall in that case desire Mr. Williams, at Nantz, who forwarded your letter to me, to advance you fifty dollars on my private account ; which sum you will repay to me whenever you may be in circumstances to do it, for should misfortune delay or prevent your being in that situation, it would be more agreeable to me to advance you a farther sum, than to demand the repayment of this.

I am, sir, with real esteem,

Your most obedient and very humble servant,

JOHN JAY.

JAY TO DE NEUFVILLE AND SON.

MADRID, 16th July, 1781.

GENTLEMEN :

Three days ago I had the pleasure of receiving a letter from you without date, but which from its contents cannot be of an old one.

It gives me pleasure to be informed by it that the flame of patriotism begins to extend itself through the United Provinces, and I hope the force of it will be directed against every obstacle that opposes the honour and interest of the Republic.

The more privateers you fit out the better ; a warlike and enterprising spirit will thereby be diffused through your seamen, and the commercial resources of the enemy injured.   The instructions given them are well devised.   The sooner a mutual intercourse is established between our two countries the sooner will your people perceive the value of a connection, and having once experienced the advantages of it, will not easily be persuaded to neglect the measures proper to perpetuate and encourage it.

I had heard before that the *Carolina* frigate built at Amsterdam was a very fine vessel.   This shows your ability to assert your rights on the ocean and by vigorous exertions to render your flag as respectable as it formerly was.

I thank you for your kind congratulations on the anniversary of our independence, and am happy that it was celebrated at Amsterdam.   If I am not much mistaken the time will come when that day will be considered as one of the most important in modern history.

By a vessel lately arrived at Cadiz from Philadelphia I have received a letter from Congress by which I find that the copies of our letters respecting your accepting their bills, etc., which I transmitted to them, had arrived safe.   Congress, in their letter to me on this subject, express themselves in the following words, viz. :

"The generous and critical services rendered these United States by Messrs. Neufville and Son have recommended them to the esteem and confidence of Congress. You will signify as much to them and that their services will not be forgotten whenever a proper occasion offers of promoting their interests."

I am happy in thus having an opportunity of conveying to you the sense entertained by America of your attachment to the cause of freedom, and I assure you that I am, with sincere regard and esteem, Gentlemen,

Your most obedient and very humble servant,

JOHN JAY.

JAY TO FREDERICK JAY.

MADRID, 31st July, 1781.

MY DEAR BROTHER,

We have heard (though not from you) that a number of armed robbers have paid you a visit, and taken from the family their money, plate, etc.; it is also said that they behaved towards our father, Peter, and Nancy, with more decency and respect than people of that class generally observe.   I am very sensible of the distress which this misfortune must have occasioned ; my having, however, in two of my former letters, which I hope have arrived safe, desired you to draw upon me for one hundred pounds sterling, in two sets of bills of fifty pounds each, gives me much consolation ; should this not be adequate to your exigencies, you may draw upon me for thirty pounds sterling more. While I have any thing, a share of it shall be appropriated to the wants of the family. I thank God that, by means of economy, I shall be able to afford them some assistance from time to time, and in some measure mitigate the calamities brought upon them by the war, and the transmutation of their gold into paper.

On the 25th of June last, Mr. Harrison, at Cadiz, shipped at my request, and on my account and risk, by the *Black Prince*, Captain John Robertson, bound from thence for Philadelphia, one bale marked J. Jay, to be delivered to Mr. Robert Morris, and containing $67\frac{3}{4}$ Spanish yards of coarse cloth, and $70\frac{1}{2}$ yards of baize for lining.

If this arrives safe, it will help to keep your servants warm next winter. A Spanish yard is somewhat less than an English one. Miss Katy Livingston writes me, that one little parcel of salt I sent you was then safe in Mr. Morris' custody, and that she had by letter informed you of it. I have since sent another parcel of a dozen or fifteen bushels. I think you would do well to write to Mr. Morris now and then, and enclose to him such of your letters for me as you may intend to go by vessels from Philadelphia.

On considering the state of the family, I am really at a loss to see how the number of it can be considerably reduced. As to the old servants, who have expended their strength and youth for the family, they ought and must be taken good care of, while we have the means of doing it ; common justice, and I may say gratitude, demands it.

Upon the whole I believe it will be best, considering the age, infirmities, and various afflictions of our good old father, not to press him upon these, nor indeed any other points that may not be very important, but by leaving his mind as much as possible undisturbed, and endeavouring daily to soothe and quiet his cares, to render the evening of his days as calm and composed as the complication of perplexities which surround him will permit.

I am told Peggy behaved like a Roman matron, and in her conduct toward the robbers showed great firmness and presence of mind.   Present to her my commendations on the occasion.

I flatter myself that my father's fortitude did not forsake him, and therefore that, though he lost money, he did not lose health by those rude visitors.   Your letter made me happy by assuring me that his strength continued as when I left him.   God grant that I may find it the same on my return.   I really regret Nancy's [1] ill-health ; it should be better if my prayers and wishes could avail.   You must endeavour to keep up each other's spirits, and oppose misfortunes with manly firmness and cheerful resignation.

We are all well.   Remember us affectionately to all the family.   I am, dear Frederick,

Your very affectionate brother,
JOHN JAY.

---

[1] Mr. Jay's blind sister.

JAY TO HIS FATHER.

MADRID, 1st Aug., 1781.

DEAR SIR,

Several letters I have received from Jersey and Philadelphia mention your having been robbed in April last by a number of armed men. It is said they behaved with uncommon respect to you, and humanity towards Peter and Nancy. If this be true, they deserve credit for the manner in which they executed their purposes. The loss sustained on that occasion must have been the more severely felt, as the situation of the country, and the injuries you had suffered from the enemy, and the depreciation of the paper money, rendered it difficult for you to repair it. I thank God, however, that you lost nothing but property—your lives were spared. I beseech you not to permit an improper degree of delicacy to prevent your deriving such succours from me as may from time to time be convenient. I assure you, the reflection that my absence may be the means of rendering the situation of the family less distressing, makes me more reconciled to it than I otherwise should be. You have denied yourself much for the sake of your children; and I am much mistaken if some of them have not inherited dispositions somewhat similar to those of their parents. Had you been less attentive to my education, I should not have been as and where I am. Economy will enable me to give you aid, for though I shall spare no expense here which my situation may require, yet a tax upon avoidable pleasures, amusements, and luxuries, will produce a little fund that may and shall be useful to you. In my letter to Frederick I have been more explicit on this subject. I am much embarrassed by not hearing oftener from the family; but two letters from Fady have come to my hands and none from James. Fady and Peggy would do well to enclose their letters for us to Miss Katy Livingston, at Philadelphia, from whom we have received at least twenty letters, under cover at the same time to Mr. Robert Morris or some other member of Congress in whom Fady may have confidence and who will immediately deliver his letter to Miss Katy. The enclosed is a French letter from Peter. My love to all the family. I am, dear sir,

Your dutiful and affectionate son,

JOHN JAY.

JAY TO BENJAMIN FRANKLIN.

St. Ildefonso, 20 August, 1781.

DEAR SIR,

Seven vessels have lately arrived at Nantes and L'Orient from America, two of them directly from Philadelphia, and but one letter brought by them has as yet reached me. It gives me reason to expect them by every post, as well as to suppose that dispatches of an important nature have arrived on them for you. My correspondent informs me that certain measures relative to peace were preparing in Congress, and refers me for particulars to public letters on that subject which have not yet come to hand. He also gives me to understand that France possesses the fullest confidence of America, and that if the former perseveres in her integrity and does not sacrifice too much to a premature peace, she will be amply repaid for the expenses of the war by an alliance which our countrymen are sincerely desirous of rendering in every respect advantageous to her.

I cannot forbear considering the approaching winter as a very critical season. It is said that Russia and the Emperor have offered their mediation, and that it will be accepted. It is further said that France wishes for peace. For my own part I fear that France has very little to expect from the friendship of these mediators, and unless appearances deceive me, every nation in Europe, except Prussia, wishes better to England than to France. It appears to me expedient to delay the progress of this mediation, and in the meantime to endeavour strenuously to form a close defensive alliance between France, Spain, Holland, and America. If France and Spain could be prevailed upon to adopt this idea *speedily* and heartily, I am persuaded that the Dutch might, in their present temper, and to obtain certain guaranties, easily be brought into the measure. Such a quadruple alliance, followed by a vigorous campaign, could give us a peace worth our acceptance. As to the present campaign, I do not expect great things from it. My expectations from the expedition against New York are far from sanguine ; it depends on too many contingencies not to be very uncertain. I wish to see some great stroke struck, some great plan wisely concerted and vigorously executed. Had a French fleet of decided superiority to the enemy been on our coast early in the spring, and co-operated with General Washington throughout the summer, Halifax, New York, and Charleston would before winter have changed masters, and then we should have been ripe for peace.

As to this Court, I do not apprehend that they are tired of the war, or that they have the least objection to another campaign— they want Jamaica, they want Gibraltar, and Mahon would be a trump card in their hands. If their activity was equal to their perseverance, and they possessed the talent of drawing forth and using all their resources, they would be very formidable. But take Spain as she is, if she could once be prevailed upon to pass the Rubicon, that is, to acknowledge and engage to support our independence, she would give Great Britain a mortal wound, and render essential assistance to the common cause. How far France views the affair in the same light I know not, nor can I clearly comprehend the policy of the system she seems to hold relative to it.

The Embassador is well attached to the American cause, and has such proper views of its importance, as well as the manner of supporting it, that I have often wished him at Versailles. There is, nevertheless, a sort of mysterious reserve about him on this subject; nor am I informed whether any and what steps have been taken by him and his Court to influence Spain to an alliance with us. I have, however, full confidence in the friendship of France, and the late aids she has granted to America give us reason to rely on the King and his principal ministers.

There is some reason to hope that this Court begins to think more seriously of a treaty with us than heretofore. A few weeks will enable me to judge better of their views. In politics I depend upon nothing but facts, and therefore never risk deceiving myself or others by a reliance on professions which may or may not be sincere.

The Duke of Crillon is still at sea. I am tempted to wish that expedition had not been undertaken. If it fails it will do harm, and I see little prospect of its succeeding.[1] You are several letters in my debt, and I wish to know whether one relative to Mr. Vaughan ever reached you.

As I have reason to think this letter will go unopened to your hands, I have written with less reserve than usual. In a former letter I informed you that Mr. Toscan carried your letter for Congress which was committed to my care in April last. I mean the one in which you requested leave to retire, and mentioned your wishes respecting your grandson. Your letter to me upon that occasion also contained an intimation which demanded my warmest acknowledgments. I have since waited for a good opportunity of informing you of the part I acted in consequence of it. It appeared to me most expedient to avoid taking any measures to induce Congress to adopt your proposition, so far as it respected me, for though the change would be agreeable to me, I did not wish to give occasion to debates on a subject which could only affect my personal concerns, especially, too, as

---

[1] Reference to the attack on Minorca which, however, proved successful.

the policy of the measure did not, on the whole, appear to me unquestionable.   For these reasons I did not give hint of the plan to any of my correspondents, but confined myself to the following paragraphs respecting you in a public and a private letter to the President of Congress :

" MADRID, 25 April, 1781.

" The letters herewith enclosed from Doctor Franklin were left open for my perusal, the short stay of my courier at Paris not allowing time for copies to be made of the information conveyed in and with it.

" I perceive that Dr. Franklin desires to retire. This circumstance calls upon me to assure Congress that I have reason to be perfectly satisfied with his conduct towards me, and that I have received from him all the aid and attention I could wish or expect. His character is very high here, and I really believe that the respectability he enjoys throughout Europe has been of general use to our cause and country." [1]

Thus, my dear sir, you will find that the long silence I have observed upon this subject did not result from inattention ; on the contrary, it will always give me pleasure to have opportunities of being useful to you and yours.

Be pleased to inform your grandson that Mrs. Jay has received and is much pleased with her watch and buckles.   I have not time to write to him by this courier.   Assure him of my attention, and present to

---

[1] From Jay's letter of April 21, 1781, printed on pages 17 and 18.

him my thanks for the obliging manner in which he has executed our little commission. I shall do myself the pleasure of writing to him in a few days.

With great and sincere esteem and regards, I am, dear sir,

Your most obedient servant,

JOHN JAY.

BENJAMIN FRANKLIN TO JAY.

VERSAILLES, Sept. 4, 1781.

DEAR SIR:

I received a few days since a very obliging letter from you. I have it not with me here, and therefore cannot mention the date. I shall answer it particularly by the next opportunity. This serves chiefly to cover the communication of two letters which I have received—one from Mr. Adams relative to the proposed mediation, the other from merchants who possess Congress drafts of a late date. . . .

I just now hear that Mr. Adams is very ill. I think it would be of service if you and I could meet. Cannot you make a trip to Paris? Or will you meet me at Bordeaux? Mr. Laurens is not likely to be at liberty to join us; and it is perhaps a question whether Mr. Jefferson will cross the seas. He refused the appointment of coming with me; and I should not wonder if Mr. Adams should return before the treaty commences, in which case the business will rest much with us two.[1] I have many reasons for desiring to converse with you besides the pleasure it would give me.

With great and sincere esteem, I am, Dear Sir,

Your most obedient and most humble Serv't,

B. FRANKLIN.

---

[1] Franklin had intended to resign his diplomatic commission and so expressed himself to Congress, (see Jay to President Huntington, April 21, 1781) but did not carry out his resolution. In a personal letter to Jay, dated April 12,

JAY TO WILLIAM BINGHAM.

St. Ildefonso, 8th September, 1781.

Dear Sir:

Among other letters brought by Major Franks, I had the pleasure of receiving one from you, dated in July last. From the few of mine that have reached you, it appears they have been very unfortunate, and, with many others, have probably perished in the ocean.

I am therefore to repeat my congratulations on the happiness you derive from the most delicate of all connections with one of the most lovely of her sex. As I am always pleased to find those happy who I think deserve to be so, it gave me very sensible satisfaction to hear that you had both made so judicious a choice, notwithstanding the veil which that sweet fascinating passion often draws over our eyes and understanding. Be pleased to present my compliments and best wishes to Mrs. Bingham, and to add

---

1781, he hoped that in the event of his retirement the latter would be his successor at Paris. In this he writes:

" Negotiations for peace are talked of. You will see all I know of them in a letter of mine to Congress which I leave open for your perusal, and desire you to forward with your next despatches. I give you the opportunity of perusing that letter for another reason: I have in it desired a dismission from the service, in consideration of my age, etc., and I wish you to succeed me here. No copy of the letter is yet gone from France, and possibly this which I send you may arrive first; nor have I mentioned my intention to any one here; if therefore the change would be agreeable to you, you may write to your friends in Congress accordingly. This thought occurred to me on hearing from the Princess Masserano, that you and Mrs. Jay did not pass your time agreeably there; and I think you would find this people of a more social turn, besides that I could put you immediately into the society I enjoy here, of a set of very amiable friends. In this case Mr. Carmichael might succeed you in Spain. I purpose to recommend these changes myself in another letter."

and accept those of Mrs. Jay, who never speaks of Martinico without expressing how much we are indebted to you for the agreeable manner in which we passed the time we stayed there.

Your representation of the state of our affairs is flattering, and affords reason to hope that the enemy will soon cease to deceive themselves and others by groundless expectations of conquest.

Peace and the negotiations for it are the prevailing topics of conversation here, and perhaps in America also. I hope, however, that our countrymen will not suffer themselves to be too much influenced by prospects which may prove no less delusive than they are pleasing. To prepare vigorously for war is the only sure way of preparing for a speedy and valuable peace.

The Duke de Crillon is in possession of every part of Minorca except Fort St. Philip, which, unless pressed by want of provisions or ammunition, will not, I suspect, soon or easily change masters.

I should mention some other public intelligence, but before this letter can possibly come to your hands as Major Franks will go from hence to Paris, it will cease to be new in America.

It is natural for you to expect that my letters should now and then contain some traits of this country, its manners, goverment, and principal characters. With respect to the three first, I make it a rule to be perfectly silent in all my letters. The latter is a very delicate subject, and men should be well acquainted with a character before they attempt to describe it.

Much injustice is often done by taking reports as facts, and forming opinions of men from the suggestions which may arise from envy or interested partialities. Though not very old, I have lived too long to credit all I hear; and having been deceived by fair as well as unpromising appearances, they have ceased to decide my judgment of men.

Whenever you write to me, which I hope will be often, recollect that your letters will, in nine instances out of ten, be inspected before they reach me ; write nothing, therefore, that you would wish concealed. But as this necessary precaution may sometimes restrain you from communicating what you may think interesting for me to know, I cannot omit this opportunity of giving you a cipher, viz., Entick's New Spelling Dictionary, printed at London in 1777, which you will easily find at Philadelphia ; I bought mine at Bell's book-store. Add twenty to the number of the page, and ten to that of the word you use. Distinguish the first column by a dot over the first figure, and the second column by a dot over the second figure. For instance, the word *duration* is the first word in the first column of the 139th page, and must be thus written, 159 11. Again, the word *beauty* is the tenth word in the second column of the 60th page, and must be thus written, 80 20. But as it may often happen that you may want to write names or words which you will not find in the dictionary, use the following alphabet in such cases :

a b c d e f g h i j k l m n o p q r s t u v w x y z
n m l k i h f i e d c b a l y v x t u r p w s z o y

The design of this alphabet is obvious; use n for a, m for b, etc.

I must now remark that you will have it in your power to give me advices of such matters as, though often interesting, I am seldom favoured with by any of my correspondents, I mean the state of parties, the views of leading individuals, and such intelligence respecting our friends and others as, though I might wish to know, ought not to be public, and can only be safely communicated in cipher.

Send your leters for me, under cover, to His Excellency the Count de Montmorin, the Ambassador of His Most Christian Majesty at this Court.

I fear you will find a correspondence of this kind a little troublesome, but I know your industry, talents, and disposition to oblige, and therefore, though my letters may not always afford an adequate compensation, I flatter myself you will not decline it, especially as you may be assured of the utmost prudence and secrecy on my part.

Be pleased to remember us to all our friends in your circle.

With sincere regard and attachment,

I am, dear sir, Your most obedient servant,

JOHN JAY.

JAY TO THE PRESIDENT OF CONGRESS.

SIR : ST. ILDEFONSO, 20th Sept., 1781.

Your Excellency's favour of the 5th July past, with the papers therewith enclosed, were delivered to me on the 29th ult. by Major Franks, whom the procrastination of the Minister still obliges me to detain.

The new commissions with which Congress have honoured me argue a degree of confidence which demands my warmest acknowledgments; and which, so far as it may be founded on an opinion of my zeal and integrity, they may be assured will not prove misplaced.

At the commencement of the present troubles I determined to devote myself, during the continuance of them, to the service of my country, in any station in which she might think it proper to place me. This resolution, for the first time, now embarrasses me. I know it to be my duty, as a public servant, to be guided by my own judgment only in matters referred to my discretion; and, in other cases, faithfully to execute my *instructions* without questioning the policy of them. But there is *one* among those which accompany the commissions, which occasions sensations I never before experienced, and induces me to wish that my name had been omitted.

So far as personal pride and reluctance to humiliation may render this appointment disagreeable, I view it as a very unimportant circumstance; and should Congress, on any occasion, think it for the public good to place me in a station inferior and subordinate to the one I now hold, they will find me ready to descend from the one, and cheerfully undertake the duties of the other. My ambition will always be more gratified in being useful than conspicuous; for, in my opinion, the solid dignity of a man depends less on the height or extent of the sphere allotted to him, than on the manner in which he may fulfil the duties of it.

But, sir, as an American, I feel an interest in the dignity of my country, which renders it difficult for me to reconcile myself to the idea of the sovereign independent States of America, submitting, in the persons of their ministers, to be absolutely governed by the *advice* and *opinion* of the servants of another sovereign, especially in a case of such national importance.

That gratitude and confidence are due to our allies is not to be questioned; and that it will probably be in the power of France almost to dictate the terms of peace for us, is but too true. That such extraordinary extent of confidence *may* stimulate our allies to the highest efforts of a generous friendship in our favour, is not to be denied; and that *this instruction* receives some appearance of policy from this consideration, may be admitted.

I must, nevertheless, take the liberty of observing, that however our situation may, in the opinion of Congress, render it necessary to relax their demands on every side, and even to direct their commissioners ultimately to concur (if nothing better can be done) in any peace or truce not subversive of our independence, which France may be determined to accede to, yet that this instruction, besides breathing a degree of complacency not quite republican, puts it out of the power of your Ministers to improve those chances and opportunities which, in the course of human affairs, happen more or less frequently unto all men. Nor is it clear that America, thus casting herself into the arms of the King of France, will advance either her interest or reputation with that or other nations.

What the sentiments of my colleagues on this occasion may be, I do not as yet know ; nor can I foresee how far the negotiations of the ensuing winter may call for the execution of this commission. Thus circumstanced, and at such a distance from America, it would not be proper to decline this appointment. I will, therefore, do my best endeavours to fulfil the expectations of Congress on this subject ; but as, for my own part, I think it improbable that serious negotiations for peace will soon take place, I must entreat Congress to take an early opportunity of relieving me from a station where, in character of their Minister, I must necessarily receive and obey (under the name of *opinions*) the directions of those on whom I really think no American minister ought to be dependent, and to whom, in love for our country, and zeal for her service, I am sure that my colleagues and myself are at least equal.

I have the honour to be, etc.,

JOHN JAY.

P. S.—I had an interview last evening with the Minister. Nothing was promised or denied. A person is to be named on Sunday to confer in earnest, as it is said, with me about the treaties. I do not despair, though having so many bills to pay, and no money, perplexes me extremely. The treasury of Spain is very low; much of the money for the expenses in this war costs them between thirty and forty per hundred, by mismanagement and want of credit. This ought not to be public. His Excellency still looks at your ships on the stocks, but I shall, without refusing, not consent to their changing masters.

J. J.

EGBERT BENSON TO JAY.

DEAR SIR:

You will observe I have deferred my letter till the last day of the month, in hopes that I should have had it in my power to communicate intelligence as agreeable as it would have been important.

When I wrote last Genl. Washington with the allied army was in the lower part of West Chester County, waiting, as it was generally supposed, the arrival of the French Fleet from the West Indies in order to commence operations against New York. I had scarcely dispatched my letter, when we were informed that the whole Army was moving into Jersey, and the arrival of Count De Grasse in the Chesapeake a few days after unfolded the design of this movement, and it was then discovered that the capture of Lord Cornwallis with his Army in Virginia was its object. Our Army made a rapid march to that State and reached the head of Elk, where they embarked the 8th Inst., and at this time they have compleatly surrounded his Lordship, who occupies Gloucester and York, the former on the north and the latter on the south side of York River. His strength is estimated at 6000 regulars and 2000 negroes; indeed it is the only operating Army of the Enemy on the Continent, as they have not more than competent garrisons at New York, Charleston, and Savannah—the only places they now hold within the territory of the United States. Whether this change, from the supposed intended plan of operations for the Campaign was the effect of choice or necessity, I will not determine, but should the present enterprise prove successful it must inevitably produce consequences decisive in our favor. This movement of the Army reflects the highest honor on our General as neither the Country nor the Enemy at New York, knew his design till he had crossed the Delaware. Cornwallis was certainly unapprised of his intentions, or he would doubtless have seasonably retired to South Carolina. Gen¹. Washington's force, French and Americans, is at least 15000 regular troops and Count De Grasse has with him in the Chesapeak, including the Squadron heretofore at Rhode Island, 35 Ships of the Line, and the British have about 20 at New York; so that there is scarcely a possible relief for Cornwallis. On Monday next our new Legislature meet, and the election of Delegates will be as interesting as any other business of the session. It is difficult to form even a remote guess who will be elected, tho' I think it probable there will be a change, not so much from a dislike to the persons who compose the present delegation, as to meet the wishes of the inhabitants of that part of the State which is not within the power of the Enemy, who have expressed their uneasiness that the State should be represented wholly by refugees. Possibly before this reaches you Mʳ. Robt. R. Livingston may have informed you that he is appointed by Congress Minister for foreign affairs. Should Mʳ. Livingston accept this appointment and resign the Chancellorship I imagine it will in the first instance be offered to Mʳ. Duane.

Your Father and the rest of the Family here are in *Statu quo*. Master Jay, the solace of his Grandpapa, is still here.

My best respects to Mʳˢ. Jay.

I am sincerely yours

EGBᵀ. BENSON.

POUGHKEEPSIE, Sept. 30ᵗʰ, 1781.

JAY TO THE PRESIDENT OF CONGRESS.[1]

St. Ildefonso, October 3, 1781.

Sir :

My letter of the 25th of April last, by Mr. Toscan, informed Congress that, on the 30th day of January preceding, I had the honour of receiving their letters of the 6th and 17th of October, 1780, the latter of which states particularly and ably the right of the United States to the free navigation of the river Mississippi, and enumerates the various reasons which induce them to decline relinquishing it.[2]

Among these reasons is the guarantee contained in the treaty with France. I hinted to Congress that it was more than probable that the contents of this interesting letter were well known to the French Court before it came to my hands. I am well persuaded that this was the case. Shortly after receiving it, I took occasion to converse generally with the Ambassador on the subject of the Spanish pretensions to that navigation, and remarked, as it were, inadvertently, how unreasonable it was for them to expect that we should relinquish a territorial right which both justice and the guarantee of France enabled us to retain. The thought did not appear new to him, but he strongly combated this construction of the

---

[1] This communication to the President of Congress forms what may be described as the third extended report from Jay on the progress of the Spanish negotiation. It again emphasizes the fact that delay was the studied policy of the Court at Madrid. See notes on previous reports in vol. i., under dates of May 11 and June 7, 1780.

[2] These letters appear in the *Secret Journal of Congress*, vol. ii., pp. 323, 326.

treaty, and endeavoured to explain it away by observing that the guarantee could not comprehend claims whose objects we had never possessed, etc., etc. I mention this only to show how improper it would have been for me to have communicated this part of your Excellency's letter to the Spanish Minister. It could have answered no good purpose, because, as France would have disputed this construction, Spain could, with propriety, have refused to admit the force of any argument drawn from it ; and it might have done much mischief, not only by bringing on an unseasonable explanation between France and us, but also between Spain and France.

If I had given the Spanish Minister a copy of every other part of this letter, except those paragraphs which contain the reasoning in question, the omission might in future have been urged by France, who, I verily believe, has a copy of that whole letter, as an argument for my having yielded that point as not tenable ; and, though my opinion might not be of much consequence, it appeared to me most prudent to avoid doubts about it. For my own part I really did, and do, think that this guarantee does comprehend the navigation in question, though I also think that no question should be raised about it at present. So circumstanced, I thought it most advisable to make no written communications of any parts or part of this letter, but from time to time to press every argument contained in it in the course of conversations with the Spanish Minister, except those drawn from the guarantee.

This last instance appeared to me to be really cruel ; for if he had intended to withhold the necessary supplies, he ought to have given me notice of it, and not by keeping up my expectations to within a few days before the holders of the bills were to call upon me for their money (and the bills of April amounted to eighty-nine thousand and eighty-three dollars) reduce me to such imminent danger of being obliged to protest them.   Speaking on this subject with the French Ambassador, he intimated that the Court expected I should have made them some further overtures respecting the Mississippi.   I told him I had no authority to make any others than what I had already made. He replied that the Minister believed I had.   At that time I had received no letters, public or private, which gave me the least reason to suspect that Congress had passed the resolution of the 15th of February last, and it was not before the 18th of May that a letter I then received from Mr. Lovell enabled me to understand the reason of the Minister's belief.   I then recalled to mind his frequent assurances of frankness, and of his speaking without reserve, often adding that he was well informed of our affairs, and had minute information of what was passing at Philadelphia. There can be no doubt but that some copies of the President's letters to me have fallen into his hands, and that he supposed I had received others, though this was not in fact the case.   Hence it appears that the double miscarriage, if I may so call it, of these letters had an unfavourable influence on our hopes of pecuniary aids, for it is highly probable that in this instance they were so critically withheld on purpose to extort overtures from me, which the Minister, though mistaken, had reason to believe I was in a capacity to make.

Your Excellency will perceive from this, how important it is that your letters, to and from your Ministers, be transmitted in a manner not subject to these inconveniences.

It was not, as I said before, until the 18th of May, that Mr. Lovell's letter, enclosing a copy of the resolution of Congress of the 15th of February, reached me. It was brought to Cadiz by the *Virginia*, and it is remarkable, that none of the journals, or gazettes, nor the letter from Congress, which Mr. Lovell gave me reason to expect, ever came to my hands. But as all the papers brought by the *Virginia* passed through the hands of the Governor of Cadiz, and afterwards through the Post-office, the suppression of some of them may be easily accounted for.

As Mr. Lovell's letter did not appear to be official, nor the copy of the instruction of the 15th of February authenticated, I was much at a loss to determine how far it was to be considered as a measure finally concluded upon, and this difficulty was increased by another, viz., whether my having no letter on the subject from the President was to be imputed to the miscarriage of it, or to a reconsideration of the instruction in question ; for I recollected, that resolutions had in some former instances been reconsidered, and either altered or repealed a few days after their date ; for these reasons it appeared to me imprudent immediately to hazard overtures on the ground of this instruction.

The next day, the 19th of May, I thought it expedient to wait upon the Minister, and again renew the subject of our proposed treaty, expecting that if he was acquainted with the contents of my letter, something might drop from him in the course of conversation, which would lead me to judge of what he might or might not know on that subject, and others connected with it.

He received me with more than usual cordiality. The conversation turned at first on the situation of the Southern States, the late combat between the fleets in the Chesapeake and General Greene's retreat. He appeared to apprehend much danger from what he called the delicate situation of our army there, and the blockade of the reinforcement intended for it, under the Marquis de la Fayette. I endeavoured to remove such of his fears as appeared to be ill-founded, and (though without leaving room to suppose that the operations of Spain were indispensable to our safety) represented to him the good policy and probable success of France and Spain's seriously turning their attention and force to the expulsion of the enemy from America. I then repeated what I had often before remarked to him, respecting the influence which the hesitations and delays of Spain in forming a treaty with us must naturally have on the hopes and fears of Britain. I announced to him formally the completion of our confederation by the accession of Maryland, and after dwelling on the advantages which the States and their allies might expect from it, I endeavoured to impress him with an opinion that a cordial union between France, Spain, Holland, and America, supported by vigorous measures, would soon reduce the enemy to the necessity of listening to reasonable terms of peace.

The Count replied, generally, that he was very minutely informed of the state of our affairs. That the good disposition of Congress towards Spain had not as yet been evinced in a manner the King expected, and that no one advantage had hitherto been proposed by America to Spain, to induce the latter to come into the measures we desired. That the views of Congress were such as would not permit his Majesty to form a treaty with the States, but that the King was an honest man, and I might again and again assure Congress, that he would never suffer them to be sacrified to Britain, but on the contrary would with constancy maintain the friendship he had professed for them ; that Britain had in vain attempted to deceive Spain ; that Mr. Cumberland had been sent here for that express purpose, but that, however possible it might be for Britain to vanquish, she would never be able to deceive, Spain ; that he wished Congress had been more disposed to oblige the King. He knew indeed that opposition in sentiments must necessarily prevail in public bodies, but that he hoped for the best ; that I ought to preach to them forcibly, for that he thought a good preacher (*un bon prédicateur*) would do much good, thereby intimating, as I understood it, that Congress were not sufficiently apprised of the importance of Spain and the policy of complying with her demands.

To all this I briefly remarked, that his Excellency's knowledge of American affairs must convince him that it was not in their power to give his Majesty other proof of their attachment than what they had already done, and that if he alluded to the affair of the Mississippi, I could only add one remark to those which I had often made to him on that head, viz., that even if a desire of gratifying his Majesty should ever incline Congress to yield to him a point so essential to their interest, yet it still remained a question whether new delays and obstacles to a treaty would not arise to postpone it.

The Count smiled, said he always spoke frankly, and that whenever I should announce to him my having authority to yield that point, I might depend on his being explicit and candid, but as matters stood at present, he could say nothing on that head. He then informed me that M. Gardoqui would set out for America the beginning of June. He said it might be in my power to furnish some useful hints and observations relative to the objects and conduct of his mission, adding that he reposed full confidence in me, and wished that I would also consider whether there were any particular reasons which might render it advisable either to hasten or retard his going.

I suspected there was too much meaning in all this to admit of my entering into these discussions without time for further reflection ; and, therefore, without seeming to avoid it, I told the Count I was happy to hear that M. Gardoqui was so near his departure ; that I considered myself much honoured by his requesting my remarks relative to it, and that I was sure Congress would draw agreeable conclusions from his mission ; that I should write by him to Congress, and as they would expect to learn from me the precise character in which they were to receive and consider him, it became necessary that his Excellency should favour me with that information, as well to enable me to transmit the proper advices to Congress, as to make the remarks which he had done me the honour to request ; that I conceived this to be the more indispensable, because if M. Gardoqui should carry no public testimonials from this Court to Congress he could only be considered by them as a private gentleman, and all his intercourse with Congress would of consequence be subjected to all the inconveniences resulting from it.

This topic carried the conversation off the delicate ground to which the Count had led it. He admitted the propriety of my being exactly apprised of the nature of M. Gardoqui's commission, said that as yet it was not decided, and therefore for the present could only give me his opinion of what it would probably be.

He observed that circumstances did not render it proper that he should go as Minister, though perhaps it might be proper to give him contingent powers ; that it was the common practice where Courts sent to each other persons charged with their affairs, in a character below that of Minister, to give no other credentials than a letter of advice from the Minister of the Court sending to the Minister of the Court receiving the person in question ; that the same practice was about to be pursued by Spain towards Prussia, and had been observed in other instances, therefore he believed the like method would be adopted in this case ; that if it should be purposed to give M. Gardoqui a letter authenticating his being an agent of Spain, it would be either to the President or the Secretary of Congress, and asked me which of the two would be the most proper.

Whether he really was uninformed on this point, or whether he asked the question merely to try my candour, cannot easily be determined. I told him honestly, that Congress had no Secretary or Minister of State for general purposes, nor for foreign affairs particularly, and that neither the President nor Secretary of Congress could regularly be considered in that light ; that there was a committee of Congress whose appointment came near to that of Secretary for Foreign Affairs, but that I had heard Congress were about establishing a more proper and regular mode of conducting the affairs committed to that committee, and had perhaps already done it ; that therefore it was difficult for me to give his Excellency a clear and decided opinion on the subject, and the more so as the letters which I daily expected to receive from the President, and which probably contained exact information relative to this very matter, had not yet come to my hands. He seemed very well satisfied, and extended his civilities so far as to say that if at any time the warmth of his temper had led him into any harshness of expression he hoped I would forget it. I told him, that was the fact, and that I did not recollect any part of his behaviour to me which required that apology. He desired me to wait upon him again on the Wednesday next.

As to the instructions of the 15th of February, I had every reason to wish that it had been a secret to the Ministry. The propriety of them is a subject without my province. To give decided opinions of the views and designs of Courts always appeared to me hazardous, especially as they often change, and as different men will often draw different conclusions from the same facts. This consideration has constantly induced me to state facts accurately and minutely to Congress, and leave them to judge for themselves, and be influenced only by their own opinions.

I could not forbear, however, seeing the danger to which the proviso contained in that instruction exposed me. I have no reason to flatter myself that, more fortunate than others, the propriety and policy of my conduct will not be drawn, at least impliedly, into doubt. If I should, on a persuasion that this cession would be unalterably insisted upon by Spain, yield that point, I am certain that many little half-created doubts and questions would be cast into and cultivated in America. If, on the other hand, I should be of opinion that this point could be gained, and the event prove otherwise, it would soon be whispered what rich supplies and golden opportunities the United States had lost by my obstinacy.

I permitted my mind to dwell on these considerations merely that I might, by the utmost degree of circumspection, endeavour to render the uprightness and propriety of my conduct as evident as possible.

My only difficulty arose from this single question : Whether I could prudently risk acting on a presumption, either that Spain did not already or would not soon be acquainted with the contents of this instruction. If such a presumption had been admissible, I should, without the least hesitation, have played the game a little further, keeping this instruction in my hand as a trump card, to prevent a separate peace between Spain and Britain, in case such an event should otherwise prove inevitable. Had Spain been at peace with our enemies, and offered to acknowledge, guarantee, and fight for our independence, provided we would yield them this point (as once seemed to be the case), I should, for my own part, have no more hesitation about it now than I had then. But Spain being now at war with Great Britain, to gain her own objects, she doubtless will prosecute it full as vigorously as if she fought for our objects. There was and is little reason to suppose that such a cession would render her exertions more vigorous, or her aids to us much more liberal. The effect which an alliance between Spain and America would have on Britain and other nations would certainly be in our favour, but whether more so than the free navigation of the Mississippi is less certain. The cession of this navigation will, in my opinion, render a future war with Spain unavoidable, and I shall look upon my subscribing to the one as fixing the certainty of the other.

I say I should have played this game a little further, if the presumption before mentioned had been admissible, because it has uniformly been my opinion, that if after sending me here Congress had constantly avoided all questions about the Mississippi, and appeared to consider that point as irrevocable, Spain would have endeavoured to purchase it by money, or a free port, but as her hopes of a change in the opinion of Congress were excited and kept alive by successive accounts of debates and intended debates on that question, and as Congress by drawing bills without previous funds had painted their distress for want of money in very strong colors, Spain began to consider America as a petitioner, and treated her accordingly. But as by the intervention of Dr. Franklin our bills for near six months were safe, and as after this resolution of the 15th of February there was reason to expect that the subject of it would not soon be resumed in Congress, I should, in case I could have depended on this instruction being and remaining a secret, have thought it my duty to have given the United States a fair trial for the Mississippi, or at least for a free port near it. With this view I should have appeared to give myself no concern about the bills, applied for no aids, made no offers, and on all proper occasions have treated an alliance with Spain as an event which, though wished for by us, was not essential to our safety, and as the price demanded for it appeared to us unreasonable, it was not probable we should agree.   I think we should then have been courted in our turn, especially as the Minister was very desirous of having our men-of-war on the stocks, and that thus dealing with them on terms of equality would have produced some concessions on their part, as inducements to greater ones on ours.   I am persuaded in my own mind that prudent self-respect is absolutely necessary to those nations who would wish to be treated properly by this Court, and I have not the least doubt but that almost any spirit will prosper more here, than that of humility and compliance.   I had no doubt but that this plan of conduct would have been perfectly consistent with that part of the instruction which orders me to make every possible effort to obtain from his Catholic Majesty the use of the river aforesaid, etc.   For whatever might have been, or may be, my private sentiments, they shall never in mere questions of policy influence me to deviate from those of Congress.

But, on the other hand, there being abundant circumstantial evidence to induce a firm persuasion that the Ministry were well acquainted with the contents of this instruction, this plan would have been idle. The moment they saw that the cession of this navigation was made to depend upon their persevering to insist upon it, it became absurd to suppose that they would cease to persevere.   All that remained for me therefore to do was, in the next conference, to break this subject as decently as possible, and in such a manner as would account for my not having mentioned this instruction at our last meeting.

On Wednesday evening, the 23d of May, I waited upon the Count, agreeably to his appointment. The Count seemed a little hurried in his spirits, and behaved as if he wished I had not come. He asked me rather abruptly if I had any thing particular to communicate to him, and whether I had received any further letters. I told him I had received some private ones from L'Orient, but that none from the President of Congress had as yet reached me, though I had reason to expect one by that opportunity, as well as by the vessel lately arrived at Cadiz. I informed him of my having received from Mr. Harrison a copy of his memorial to the Governor of Cadiz, complaining that letters brought for him by the *Virginia*, from Philadelphia, had been stopped at the gates, on pretence that they must, agreeably to an ordinance for that purpose, be put into the Post-office and charged with the like postage as if brought from Spanish America. He said he had not yet received a copy of the memorial, but that there was such an ordinance, and that it was highly proper the admission of letters into the kingdom, especially in time of war, should be under the direction of government ; that letters from North America rendered new regulations necessary, and that he would turn his thoughts to this subject and do what should appear equitable. This was another proof of what I before suspected, and looked like an indirect apology for opening my letters.

It surprised me a little that he said nothing of the remarks he had desired me to make on M. Gardoqui's going to America, especially as he had appointed this meeting for that purpose. To give him further time, I started a new subject, and begged he would take the earliest opportunity of completing the business of the Dover cutter. Notwithstanding all that had before passed between us about this affair, he affected to be very ignorant of it, and asked me a number of questions. I recapitulated the circumstances of the capture, my several applications to him on the subject, his promise finally to order the prize to be appraised, and the value to be paid to the captors, the arrival of one of them at Madrid, etc., etc. He replied, with some degree of quickness and perplexity, that it was not a lawful prize, the crew not having authority to do what they did ; that he had sent to the Canaries for particular information respecting the value, etc. ; that two of the packet boats had been taken ; that he would pay some gratuity to the captors, and wished I would give him another state of the whole case in writing, to refresh his memory, which I promised to do, and have since done.

He then resumed the subject of the letter, which I expected from Congress. He expressed his regret at its not having arrived, said he was preparing instructions for M. Gardoqui, who would certainly depart in June, and that until I could give him precise information of the disposition of Congress, he could not enter into any further conversations on the subject of the proposed treaty. I joined in regretting the miscarriage of my public letter, and the more so as my private ones gave me reason to expect instructions which would enable me to comply so far with his

Majesty's views as that I hoped no further delays would intervene to prevent a perfect union between Spain and the United States ; that my correspondence had given me to understand that Congress viewed the speedy accomplishment of this union as very important to the common cause ; and, therefore, if Spain would consent forthwith to come into it, in that case they would gratify his Majesty by ceding to him the navigation of the Mississippi, below their territories, on reasonable terms.

He replied that he earnestly desired to see all difficulties on this point removed, but that the treaties subsisting between Spain and other nations, as well as the particular policy and determination of Spain, rendered it necessary that she should possess the exclusive navigation of the Gulf of Mexico. After a variety of other remarks of little importance, he made a very interesting observation, which will help us to account for the delays of the Court, viz. : that all these affairs could with more facility be adjusted at a general peace than now, for that such a particular and even secret treaty with us might then be made as would be very convenient to both ; that he nevertheless wished to know exactly the views and intentions of Congress, but that I must wait for the arrival of my letters, and that he would in the meantime finish M. Gardoqui's instructions, whose going to America, he did not doubt, would make a useful impression on the English Court. I was beginning to reply to what he said when he interrupted me, by mentioning his not having time at present to prolong the conference.

Throughout the whole of this conversation, the Count appeared much less cordial than in the preceding one ; he seemed to want self-possession, and to that cause I ascribe his incautiously mentioning the general peace as the most proper season for completing our political connections. I had, nevertheless, no reason to suspect that this change in his behaviour arose from any cause more important than those variations in temper and feelings which they who are unaccustomed to govern themselves often experience from changes in the weather, in their health, from fatigue of business, or other such like accidental causes.

As I had not as yet received any letter from the President, either by the *Virginia* or the vessel lately arrived at L'Orient, nor by Colonel Laurens, who, I was informed, had brought letters for me, I concluded it would be most prudent to wait ten days, or a fortnight, before I proceeded to act on the copy of my instruction received from Mr. Lovell, expecting that such other letters as might then have arrived in France or Spain for me would reach me in the course of that interval, if at all. And I determined, in case I should receive none, to proceed, without further loss of time, to make a formal overture to the Minister for a treaty on the ground of this instruction. It happened, however, that the Minister was so occupied during the remaining time that the Court stayed at Aranjues, by the expedition preparing to sail from Cadiz, under the Duke of Crillon, and other matters, that it was impossible to engage a moment of his

attention to American affairs. The removal of the
Court to Madrid necessarily consumed some time,
and as soon as they were well settled there I wrote
the Count the following letter, none of the letters
expected from America having come to my hands :

TO THE COUNT DE FLORIDA BLANCA.

SIR : MADRID, July 2, 1781.

When Congress were pleased to order me to
Spain, with the commission of which I have had the
honour of presenting a copy to your Excellency, I left
my country with the most sanguine expectations that
the important objects of it would be speedily accomplished. The proofs they had received of his Majesty's
friendship for them, the interests of a common cause,
and the information they had received from persons
whom they conceived in capacity to give it, all conspired to infuse these hopes.

On my arrival, your Excellency gave me to understand that the realizing these expectations would turn
on one point, and I have uniformly since been informed that this point was the navigation of the
Mississippi below the territories of the United States,
in which Congress desired to retain a common right,
but of which the maxims of policy adopted by his
Majesty required the exclusive use.

I have now the honour of informing your Excellency that Congress, in order to manifest in the most
striking manner the sincerity of their professions to
his Majesty, and with a view that the common cause
may immediately reap all the advantages naturally to

be expected from a cordial and permanent union between France, Spain, and the United States, have authorized me to agree to such terms relative to the point in question as to remove the difficulties to which it has hitherto given occasion.

Permit me, therefore, to hope that his Majesty will now be pleased to become the ally of the United States, and for that purpose authorize some person or persons to adjust with me the several points of compact necessary to form a union which, by being founded on mutual interest, may be no less satisfactory than it certainly will be important to both countries.

Your Excellency will oblige me exceedingly by putting it in my power to give Congress early, explicit, and, let me add, agreeable information of his Majesty's pleasure and intentions on the subject of this letter.

I have the honour to be, etc.

JOHN JAY.

Although it was sufficiently evident that the Court of France could not, for the reasons assigned in my letter to Congress of the 6th of November, 1780, openly and warmly interpose their good offices to bring about this treaty, it nevertheless appeared to me most prudent to behave on this occasion towards the Ambassador as if I knew nothing of those reasons, and therefore sent him a copy of the aforegoing letter to the Minister, enclosed in one of which the following is a copy :

TO THE COUNT DE MONTMORIN.

MADRID, July 2d, 1781.

SIR :

I have the honour of transmitting to your Excellency herewith enclosed a copy of a letter I have this day written to his Excellency the Count de Florida Blanca. I have thereby informed him of my being authorized to remove the objections hitherto made by the Court of Spain to a treaty of alliance with the United States, and again requested that the measures necessary for the purpose may now be taken.

Permit me to request that the favourable interposition of our kind and generous ally with his Catholic Majesty may be exerted to commence the proposed negotiation, and bring it to a speedy and happy conclusion.

The confidence justly reposed by America in the amity and assurances of his Most Christian Majesty forbid me to urge this request by any arguments (persuasives being indelicate, when not warranted by doubts of inclination). I am happy in reflecting that his instructions on this subject are committed to the execution of a Minister, from whose attachment, as well as from whose talents and address, the American cause may expect to derive advantage.

I have the honour to be, etc.

JOHN JAY.

The instructions above alluded to are those which Count de Vergennes, in his letter to me of the 13th of March, 1780, assures me should be sent to their

Ambassador here. I must confess to Congress that I very much doubt his ever having received any other instructions than generally to favour the treaty, and to manage his interference in such a delicate manner as, without alarming the pride of Spain, to give both parties reason to think themselves obliged.

The French Ambassador sent me no answer to this letter, which, in my opinion, gives a greater degree of probability to my conjectures. I must, nevertheless, do him the justice to say that I have great reason to believe him to be in sentiment, and with sincere attachment, a friend to our cause ; and that he considers the honour and interest of France deeply concerned in the success and support of it.

On the 11th of July, having received no answer from the Minister, I waited upon him. He told me he had received my letter, but that the short time the Court would remain at Madrid, and the multiplicity of business that he was obliged to despatch, would not admit of his attending to our affairs till after the arrival of the Court at St. Ildefonso. He then informed me that a vessel had arrived at Cadiz, which had brought despatches for me, and that his courier had brought them to Madrid. He then delivered me a number of letters, among which was one from his Excellency the President, of the 28th of May last.

I need not observe that all these letters bore evident marks of inspection, for that has uniformly been the case with almost every letter I have received.

I do not recollect to have ever received a letter that gave me more real pleasure. When I considered that almost the whole time since I left America had afforded me little else than one continued series of painful perplexities and embarrassments, many of which I neither expected nor ought to have met with ; that I had been engaged in intricate and difficult negotiations, often at a loss to determine where the line of prudence was to be found, and constantly exposed by my particular situation to the danger of either injuring the dignity and interest of my country on the one hand, or trespassing on the overrated respectability and importance of this Court on the other ; I say, sir, that on considering these things, the approbation of Congress gave me most singular and cordial satisfaction.

I was also happy to perceive from this letter that the plan of my late letters to the Minister and French Ambassador, of the 2d of July, above recited, happens to correspond exactly with the views of Congress respecting the manner of conducting this negotiation.

It appearing to me that the communication I was directed to make to this Court could not be better made than in the very words of this letter, which seemed exceedingly well calculated for the purpose, I recited them in a letter, which I wrote two days afterwards to the Minister, viz. :

TO THE COUNT DE FLORIDA BLANCA.

Sir :   Madrid, July 13, 1781.

I have now the honour of communicating to your Excellency a copy of certain instructions I have just received from Congress, dated the 28th of May, 1781, and which were included in the despatches which your Excellency was so obliging as to deliver to me the evening before the last, viz. :

" It is their instruction that you continue to acknowledge, on all suitable occasions, the grateful impression made on these States by the friendly disposition manifested towards them by his Catholic Majesty, and particularly by the proofs given of it in the measures which he has taken, and which it is hoped he will further take, for preserving their credit, and for aiding them with a supply of clothing for their army.

" You are also authorized and instructed to disavow, in the most positive and explicit terms, any secret understanding or negotiation between the United States and Great Britain, to assure his Catholic Majesty that such insinuations have no other source than the insidious designs of the common enemy, and that as the United States have the highest confidence in the honour and good faith, both of his Most Christian and his Catholic Majesty, so it is their inviolable determination to take no step which shall depart in the smallest degree from their engagements with either."

It gives me pleasure to observe that these instructions confirm, in the fullest manner, the assurances and professions I have heretofore made to your Excellency respecting the sentiments and dispositions of the United States, and I flatter myself that his Majesty will be pleased to consider the assurances they contain as receiving unquestionable proofs of sincerity from the offer I have already made to confirm them by deeds no less important to the interests than, I hope, consistent with the views and desires of his Majesty.

I cannot omit this occasion of presenting my congratulations on the success of his Majesty's arms at Pensacola. This event cannot fail of being followed by important consequences to the common cause, and may perhaps induce the enemy to expect greater advantages from concluding a reasonable peace, than continuing to protract an unrighteous war.

Having understood, shortly after receiving my letters from your Excellency, that the Court had also received despatches from Philadelphia, I presumed that the communication of any gazettes from thence, which indeed contain all the intelligence I have, would be useless, and therefore did not send them : but on considering that it was possible that the papers I had might be of later date than those which your Excellency might otherwise receive, I now take the liberty of enclosing two, which contain accounts somewhat interesting. If they should be new to your Excellency, I beg that their not being sooner sent will receive an apology from the abovementioned circumstance ; and that your Excellency will remain assured of the perfect respect and consideration with which I have the honour to be, etc.

JOHN JAY.

I also took the earliest opportunity of mentioning to the Ambassador of France that my letters from

America gave me reason to believe that our union was daily growing more warm and intimate, and that Congress, in writing of their affairs here, had expressed themselves in the strongest terms of attachment to his Most Christian Majesty, and not only approved of my communicating freely and confidentially with his Ambassador here, but also directed me in express terms to endeavour, in the course of my negotiations, to include and promote the interests of France.

The Ambassador was much pleased. He told me his letters assured him that the best understanding subsisted between the French and American troops, and that much good might be expected from the increasing harmony and intercourse between the two countries.

The Court removed to St. Ildefonso without the Minister's having either given any instructions to M. Gardoqui, answered my abovementioned letters, or taken the least notice of my late representations to them about the Dover cutter, etc.

The events of the campaign were as yet undecided, and little money in the treasury.

On the 21st of July the Minister wrote me the following note, in which there was ample field left open for procrastination.

[Translation.]

" The Count de Florida Blanca presents his compliments to Mr. Jay, and has the honour of acquainting him that he has duly received his two letters of the 2d and 13th instant. The short stay of the Court at Madrid allowing time only to despatch the most pressing business, the Count de Florida Blanca has not been able to take into consideration the points which form the object of the above-mentioned letters. He proposes, therefore, to do it at present, in order to render an account thereof to the King, and in the meanwhile he has the honour to repeat to Mr. Jay the assurances of the most perfect esteem and consideration.

"St. Ildefonso, July 21, 1781."

On the 4th of August I arrived here. I did not see the Minister till the 8th, he being, as I was told, from home. He had made no communications to the King. He had been sick ; he had been busy, and was so still. I requested to be informed when it would be most convenient to him to confer with me on the subject of my late letters, and to give me such information relative to his Majesty's intentions as he might be prepared to communicate to me. He answered that he could not then fix a time, being exceedingly hurried by pressing business. He asked how long I proposed to stay ; I told him till the Court removed. He then promised to take an early opportunity of conferring with me on the subject of our affairs, and promised to send me word when he should be ready to receive me.

I remained in this state of suspense and expectation until the 18th of August, when, having been for a week past very much indisposed with a fever and dysentery, and fearing lest that circumstance might become a ground of delay, I wrote the Count word " that my health would permit me to wait upon his Excellency at any time and place he might do me the honour to name." He replied two days afterwards in a manner which indicated his supposing I had gone to Madrid and had returned. He must have known better, for none of my family had been absent from hence, and one or other of them were almost daily about the palace and gardens.

[Translation.]

"The Count de Florida Blanca is charmed to learn that Mr. Jay has sufficiently recovered from his last indisposition to make the journey from Madrid to this place, and thanks him for his attention in communicating it to him.

"The very pressing business with which he finds himself at present surrounded does not permit him to fix the day for a conference with Mr. Jay, but the moment he shall be a little disengaged he will have the honour to advise Mr. Jay of it.

"St. Ildefonso, August 20, 1781."

On the 22d I sent him a note enclosing a newspaper which contained an account of General Greene's operations, the capture of Fort Watson, etc.

The Count answered this note by another, expressing his thanks for the intelligence, but not a word of a conference.

On the 30th of August Major Franks arrived here with interesting despatches, of which I must not here take notice, lest I interrupt the thread of this letter, which I devote particularly to the affair of our negotiations for a treaty.

There was indeed among these despatches a very sensible letter from Mr. R. Morris to me about money matters, etc., excellently well calculated for being shown entire to the Minister.

I consulted with the French Ambassador on the propriety of giving the Minister a copy of it. He advised me to do it, and much commended the letter. As it might have suffered from being carelessly translated, I had it put into very good French.

I was very glad to see the Major. The nature of the despatches he brought being a secret occasioned speculation, and gave me an opportunity of drawing further advantages from his arrival. His accounts of American affairs were favourable to us, and the manner of his behaviour and conversation has not done discredit to himself nor prejudice to his country.

The Ambassador of France having assured me that the Minister had really been a good deal indisposed, I thought it would be best to write him a letter in a style somewhat adapted to his situation. He certainly appears to be fatigued and worn down by business. He looks as I have seen some members of Congress look after two years' attendance.

TO THE COUNT DE FLORIDA BLANCA.

SIR :   St. ILDEFONSO, September 3, 1781.

When I consider that the delicate state of your Excellency's health demands a greater degree of leisure and relaxation than the various business of your office will permit, it is with great reluctance that I can prevail upon myself to remind your Excellency that since our conference at Aranjues the affairs of the United States at this Court have made no progress.

The short residence of his Majesty at Madrid, I am persuaded, made it necessary to postpone the discussion of these affairs to this place ; and since my arrival here on the 4th of August last I have daily flattered myself with being enabled to communicate to Congress his Majesty's pleasure on the important subjects which by their order I have had the honour of laying before your Excellency.

It has also for some time past been my duty to have requested your Excellency's attention to some other objects, which, though of less public importance, are nevertheless interesting to individuals, as well as to the commercial intercourse of the two countries, but it did not appear to be consistent with the respect due to your Excellency to solicit your attention to new objects while the former remained undespatched for want of time.

It would give me great pleasure to have it in my power to regulate all my applications by your Excellency's convenience, and though I am happy to see the connection between our two countries daily increasing, yet, as that circumstance will naturally render necessary applications to government more frequent, I fear the duties of my situation will often press me to be troublesome to your Excellency.

On Friday evening last I received some important despatches from Congress, which I shall do myself the honour of communicating at any time which your Excellency may be pleased to name. The gentleman who brought them will, after passing on to Paris, return immediately to Philadelphia, and will with pleasure execute any orders which your Excellency may honor him with for either of those places. His stay here will be but short. As soon as I can ascertain the day of his departure, your Excellency shall have immediate notice of it. As Congress will naturally expect to receive by him particular information respecting their affairs here, I cannot forbear expressing how anxious I am to make him the bearer of welcome tidings ; and permit me to hope that your Excellency's sensibility will suggest an apology for the solicitude which appears in this letter.

I have the honour to be, with great respect, etc.

JOHN JAY.

On the 5th, I received the following answer, viz.:

[Translation.]

" The Count de Florida Blanca has been much mortified not to be able to receive the visit of Mr. Jay, not only on account of the too pressing business which has engaged all his time, but also by reason of the indisposition he has suffered, and still suffers.

" Although he be not in a situation to engage in long and serious conferences for the reasons above-mentioned, he will, nevertheless, be charmed to converse a moment with Mr. Jay, one of those leisure evenings when there is no business with the King ; in which case, Mr. Jay may, if he thinks proper, bring with him the officer in question.

" Saturday, for instance, towards eight o'clock, the interview may take place.

" Wednesday, the 5th of September."

Your Excellency will be pleased to observe, that the Minister in the above note intimates a desire that I should bring Major Franks with me. I thought it best to do so ; but lest his presence should be a check upon business, and as it was natural to suppose that the Count would begin by asking him questions about our affairs, I desired the Major to relate to him the impression made in America by that article in the capitulation of Pensacola which permitted the garrison to go to New York. I also desired the Major to retire into the antechamber and leave me alone with the Minister, as soon as the latter should appear to have finished with him.

At the time appointed, viz., the evening of the 8th of September, we waited upon the Minister.

The Count received us very politely. He spoke much of his want of health, and how greatly it incapacitated him for business. He then asked the Major several questions about our military operations. The Major answered them clearly, and, in speaking of the proposed siege of New York, very naturally introduced an account of the surprise and apprehensions occasioned by the permission given to the Pensacola garrison to join that of New York. The Count confessed it was ill done ; said it was very unexpected, and that they ought to have been sent to Europe ; that the like should not happen in future, and that proper orders upon that subject should be despatched to their generals. He then observed that our fears were not altogether well founded, for that those troops were restrained by the capitulation from taking arms against the allies of Spain till exchanged, and could not operate against our troops without also operating against those of France, who were joined with them, and who, it was well known, were the allies of Spain.

The Major replied that it was feared that the enemy would attempt to evade this reasoning by insisting that the French troops in America were only to be considered as auxiliaries to the United States, and that though that argument might be fallacious, yet that in matters affecting America the enemy had invariably neglected good faith whenever they found it convenient.

The Count asked how long the Major would stay here. I told him that I only detained him in expectation of being soon enabled by his Excellency to write something decisive by him to Congress on the subjects under his consideration. He said he hoped in the course of next week to enter into serious conferences with me on those subjects, and that he would give me notice of the day. He offered to give the Major letters to the Spanish Ambassador at Paris, and to do him any other services in his power. He then rose from his chair in a manner indicating indisposition, said he was unable to do business, and that M. Del Campo should inform me when it would be convenient for him that I should see him again. I expressed my regret at his illness, and gave him the French translation of Mr. Morris' letter, adding that I had intended to offer him some remarks on the subject of it. He said he would read it with pleasure. He spoke of Mr. Morris' appointment, and after conversing a few minutes about the good consequences expected from it, and of the services done by that gentleman to Spain, in some business they had committed to his care, we parted.

Thus this conference ended as fruitless as the last.

Eight days elapsed. I heard nothing from the Minister. He was daily at Court, and every evening took his ride.

I repeatedly mentioned and complained of these delays to the French Ambassador. He regretted them, promised to speak to the Minister on the subject, but, I believe, did not. I appeared much dissatisfied, though not with him, and told him that if Major Franks returned to America with no other intelligence than that of repeated delays, it was more than probable that Congress would be much hurt, as well as much disappointed. He had the same fears, and advised me to detain the Major.

It became in my opinion important that the Minister, as well as the French Ambassador, should be seriously apprehensive of my dismissing the Major with letters that would render Congress very little disposed to make sacrifices to this Court. The manner of doing this required some caution. I could think of nothing better than to prepare a letter to the Minister, and send the Ambassador a fair copy of my draft for his consideration and advice.

The following are copies of that letter, and of the one I sent with it to the Ambassador :

TO THE COUNT DE MONTMORIN.

St. Ildefonso, September 16, 1781.

Sir :

The paper herewith enclosed is the draft of a letter which I think of writing to his Excellency, the Count de Florida Blanca.

The subject, as well as the occasion, demands that dexterous and delicate management of which they only are capable who possess an accurate judgment and much experience in affairs of this kind.

I am happy, therefore, that on such occasions I can avoid the risk of committing errors by recurring to your friendly advice. Without compliment, but with sincerity, I am, sir, etc.

JOHN JAY.

TO THE COUNT DE FLORIDA BLANCA.

Whatever may be the issue of the American Revolution, whether that country shall continue independent or be doomed to reunite her power with that of Great Britain, the good-will and affection of the people of North America cannot in either case be unimportant to their neighbors ; nor will the impressions made upon their minds by the benefits or injuries which they may receive from other nations in the course of their present struggles ever cease to have a certain degree of influence on their future conduct.

Various circumstances led Congress at an early period to suppose that the Court of Spain had wisely and generously determined to take a decided part in their favour. The supplies granted to them by his Catholic Majesty, soon after the British armies became numerous in America, spoke this language in strong terms, and the assurances repeatedly given me by your Excellency, that his Majesty would firmly support their cause, and never consent to their being reduced to the subjection of Britain, left no room to doubt of his friendly disposition and intention towards them.

Many obvious considerations prompted Congress to desire that an intimate connection might speedily be established between the two countries by such treaties as would take from the enemy every prospect of success, and secure to Spain and the United States the permanent enjoyment of mutual advantages and reciprocal attachment. With this view Congress were pleased to send me to Spain, and the first letter I had the honour of receiving from your Excellency gave me reason to believe that the object of my mission was not displeasing to his Majesty; unavoidable and long delays were, nevertheless, created by differences respecting a certain important right which America wished to retain. So strong, however, was the reliance of Congress on his Majesty's assurances of support, and such was their disposition to render the proposed treaties consistent with his inclinations, that they have since agreed to remove the only obstacle which seemed to prevent his Majesty from realizing those assurances by substantial aids and an open declaration of his intentions.

But unfortunately for America, and perhaps for the general cause, the delays in question have not ceased with the cause to which they were ascribed, and although the confidence reposed by Congress in his Majesty's assurances will not permit them to doubt of his determination to support their independence, yet the silent inattention with which their offers to remove the former obstacle to a treaty have long lain unanswered, must appear to them as being very singular. Your Excellency has indeed repeatedly promised me to name a time when I should have an opportunity of conferring with you on that and other subjects submitted to your consideration, but it constantly happened that the expectations excited by these promises proved abortive.

Knowing that Congress would expect to receive, by the return of Major Franks, particular information respecting their affairs here, I was anxious to send them some intelligence more welcome than I have reason to think a detail of delays and procrastination would be, at a season when they would be indulging the most flattering expectations from the measures they had taken to gratify his Majesty. For this reason I informed your Excellency that I should detain Major Franks for the present, and your Excellency promised me on the 8th instant that you would appoint some time in the ensuing week for entering into a serious conference about these matters, and that M. Del Campo should give me notice of it. That week, however, has passed away without having been witness to any such notice or conference.

I think your Excellency will do me the justice to acknowledge that the utmost respect, delicacy, and patience have been observed in all my transactions with your Excellency, and therefore I cannot forbear hinting that my constituents are at least entitled to that species of attention which the most dignified sovereigns usually pay to the friendly propositions of such States as solicit either their aid or alliance in a decent manner, viz., a candid answer.

I am sensible that Spain possesses a higher degree on the scale of national importance than the United States, and I can readily admit that the friendship of this Court is of more immediate consequence to America, than that of America to the Spanish Empire. But as his Catholic Majesty and his Ministers doubtless extend their views beyond the present moment, it would ill become me to remark how essential it is to the happiness of neighboring nations that their conduct towards each other should be actuated by such passions and sentiments only as naturally tend to establish and perpetuate harmony and good-will between them. Most certain it is, that in whatever manner the negotiations between Spain and North America may terminate, various good or evil consequences will in future naturally and necessarily flow from it to both.

There is good reason to believe that the apparent indecision of Spain, relative to an open acknowledgment of the independence of the United States, has inspired other nations with doubts and conjectures unfavorable to the American cause, and on the other hand it is more than probable that, if his Catholic Majesty would be pleased to declare to the world that the United States were his allies, and that he had given his royal word to support their independence, Holland and many other nations would follow his example.

On such an event, also, it might not be difficult to form a permanent alliance between France, Spain, the Dutch, and the United States, and thereby not only prevent a separate peace between the Dutch and English, but effectually reduce the latter to reasonable terms of general pacification.

The limits of a letter forbid my enlarging on these topics. The eyes of America, and indeed of all Europe, are turned towards Spain. It is in the power of his Catholic Majesty to increase his friends and humble his enemies. I will only add my most sincere wishes that the annals of America may inform succeeding generations that the wisdom, constancy, and generous protection of his Catholic Majesty, Charles the Third, and of his Minister, the Count de Florida Blanca, are to be ranked among the causes that insured success to a revolution which posterity will consider as one of the most important and interesting events in modern history.

John Jay.

The Ambassador called upon me in the evening to answer my letter.

He observed that the delays of which I complained were not singular, but that others, and even himself, experienced the like ; that he had reason to believe this Court were really disposed to treat with us, though the time when might be doubtful ; that the remarks made in the draft of my intended letter were but too just ; that he feared they would give offence ; that, at any rate, he thought I had better postpone it, and for the present write one less pointed and more laconic. We had much conversation on the subject, unnecessary to repeat. It ended in my consenting to pursue his advice.

It is observable, that he did not offer to return me the draft of this letter, though I had agreed to suppress it.

The letter which, agreeable to the Ambassador's advice, I substituted in the place of the other, is in these words, viz. :

TO THE COUNT DE FLORIDA BLANCA.

SIR : ST. ILDEFONSO, September 17, 1781.

A reluctance to despatch Major Franks without transmitting by him to Congress the information they expect to receive, on the subject I have had the honour of submitting to your Excellency's consideration, has induced me hitherto to detain him, especially as I was encouraged to hope that your Excellency would have found leisure last week for entering into serious conference with me on those important points. The same reluctance prevails upon me to detain him another week, and I think it my duty to inform your Excellency that he will set out on Saturday next.

I need not remark to your Excellency that if the letter I may then write by him should not contain the desired intelligence, Congress will naturally be led to apprehend that their expectations of forming an intimate union with Spain were not well founded.

I have the honour to be, etc.,

JOHN JAY.

On the 19th I received the following answer :

[Translation.]

" The Count de Florida Blanca would have been charmed to have had it in his power to have a long conference with

Mr. Jay, if his ordinary indispositions had not prevented him ; he will, therefore, have the honour to see him this evening about eight o'clock, if Mr. Jay will give himself the trouble of waiting on him, either alone or with Major Franks, and in communicating to the King the result of their conference, he will endeavour to prevail on his Majesty to name some other person to confer with Mr. Jay in case of need, in order to avoid, as much as possible, the embarrassments which Mr. Jay has hitherto experienced.

" Wednesday, 19th of September, 1781."

I waited upon the Count at the time appointed. The following is a copy of my notes of that conference :

Notes of a Conference held at St. Ildefonso, on Wednesday Evening, the 19th of September, 1781, between his Excellency, the Count de Florida Blanca, and Mr. Jay, agreeably to the Appointment of the Former.

The Count introduced the conference by asking for Major Franks, and why Mr. Jay did not bring him with him. Mr. Jay answered that as Major Franks was not charged with the transaction of any business with his Excellency, and had, at a former interview, answered such questions relative to American affairs as the Count had thought proper to ask him, Mr. Jay did not think his attendance on this occasion necessary, as he supposed his Excellency meant to enter at present into the discussion of the matters referred to in Mr. Jay's last letter.

The Count then proceeded to enumerate the various obstacles arising from his ill health, the multiplicity

of business, which had so long subjected Mr. Jay to
the delays he had hitherto experienced, and which,
for his part, he could not but regret ; that, agreeable
to his promise made to Mr. Jay soon after his arrival,
and frequently afterwards repeated, he had attempted
to commit to paper his sentiments on the various
points on which the proposed treaties must turn, and
although he had made some progress in it, he had,
for the reasons above mentioned, been obliged to
leave it imperfect ; that daily experience convinced
him that his official business was too extensive and
various to admit of his application to other objects,
especially as his indisposition often rendered it impracticable for him to pay a due attention to it ; that
he, therefore, conceived it necessary that some person,
duly authorized to confer with Mr. Jay on these subjects, should be appointed by his Majesty ; that he
intended on Sunday next to recommend this measure
to the King, to whom he would, at the same time,
communicate the copy of Mr. Morris' letter to Mr.
Jay, which the latter had given him ; that, in order to
the putting of this matter in proper train, it would be
expedient for Mr. Jay previously to commit to paper
his ideas of the outlines of the proposed treaties, and
particularly to state the propositions he might think
proper to make relative thereto ; that he had been informed that the treaties between France and America
had been preceded by the like measures, for that the
American Commissioners had first offered a plan of
propositions, and then M. Gerard was appointed to
confer with them before those treaties were drawn

into the state they now appear, and finally concluded ; that the like proceedings were rendered particularly necessary in this case, by the variety and importance of the points necessary to be adjusted between Spain and America; that in forming political connections between nations, constant regard must be had to their reciprocal interests, and care taken, by previous arrangements, to avoid the inconveniences which would result from any clashing of interest ; that three great points presented themselves as requiring great attention in forming the proposed connection between Spain and America.

1st. The aids requested by America, as stated in Mr. Morris' letter, were very considerable ; that it would be necessary on the part of Spain to determine what pecuniary aids it might be in their power to grant, either by loan or subsidy, as well as the time, place, and manner of payment ; for that great punctuality was requisite in such transactions, as well that the royal engagements might be properly fulfilled as that Congress might not be subjected to inconveniences and disappointments ; that, on the part of America, it must be ascertained what compensation they should make, as well as the time and manner of doing it ; and that it might be well to consider how far such compensation might be made in ship timber, or other productions of that country ; that a compensation would be indispensable, for that the King, being only the guardian of his dominions, would not think himself justifiable in dispensing with the just rights of his people.

2dly. That the commercial concerns of the two countries was another point which would call for very accurate and important regulations. That so far as this commerce would respect the United States and old Spain, the difficulty would not be very great ; for that such commerce being in a considerable degree permitted to other nations, America ought also to participate in the benefits of it. But with respect to the Spanish dominions in America, as all other nations were excluded from any direct commerce with any part of them, the United States could not reasonably expect to be on a better footing than other nations, and particularly the French, who were the near allies of Spain.

3dly. That with respect to the proposed treaty of alliance, Mr. Jay must be sensible that the several engagements which would thereby be rendered necessary between the parties, the matters of boundary, and the navigation of the Mississippi, would give occasion to several important articles, which ought to be maturely considered and well digested. To this end, he wished that Mr. Jay would immediately turn his thoughts on these subjects, and offer him such a set of propositions as might become the basis of future conferences between him and the person whom he expected his Majesty would appoint.

The Count then took occasion to observe that he had long wished Mr. Jay had offered him such propositions, but that his Court had as yet received from Congress nothing but good words and fair assurances, and that though his Majesty had given them some

little aids, yet they had discovered no disposition, by
acts, to acknowledge them. Mr. Jay reminded his
Excellency of his having, at a very early day, undertaken to commit to paper the outlines of the proposed
treaties, and that the constant expectations of his per-
fecting it had restrained Mr. Jay from offering any
thing of the like nature on the subject. That he could
conceive of nothing in the power of Congress to do,
which could more fully evidence their disposition to
gratify his Majesty, than their having offered to
recede from their claims to the navigation of the
Mississippi, though the preservation of it was deemed
of the highest importance to their constituents. The
Count admitted the propriety of both these observations, and said he hoped that the delays which had so
long embarrassed Mr. Jay would soon be terminated.

Mr. Jay expressed his anxiety to be enabled to
communicate to Congress some decided intelligence
respecting the aids they might expect from this Court ;
to which the Count replied that the sum requested
was great, the expenses of the kingdom very extensive,
and the means of obtaining the sums necessary to defray them subject to many difficulties ; that he would, as
he had before mentioned, communicate Mr. Morris'
letter to the King, and, until that was done, he could
not be in capacity to say any thing further on the
subject ; that as the appointment of a person to confer with Mr. Jay would rest with his Majesty, he could
not say who in particular it would be, but he hoped
and was persuaded that it would be some person well-
intentioned towards America ; that he was the more

formal propositions on the several points stated in this conference. But it would not have been proper for me to desire further time.

On the 22d of September, I sent him the following letter and propositions :

SIR, ST. ILDEFONSO, September 22, 1781.

I have the honour of transmitting, herewith enclosed, the propositions requested by your Excellency on Wednesday evening last.

I have endeavoured to render them as short and simple as possible, and I flatter myself that the unreserved frankness with which they are written will be no less agreeable to your Excellency than I am sure it is consistent with the desire and disposition of my constituents.

As the issue of this measure will in a great degree ascertain the expectations which Congress entertain from their negotiations here, and as they flatter themselves with receiving information on this subject by the return of Major Franks, they will doubtless excuse my detaining him another week, unless your Excellency should sooner be enabled to communicate to me his Majesty's pleasure relative to the proposed treaty.

Permit me to entreat your Excellency, therefore, to enable me to transmit by him such intelligence to Congress as may relieve them from their present distressing doubts and uncertainties.

I sincerely hope it may be such as may make them happy in a prospect of soon seeing an intimate and lasting union established between France, Spain, and the United States, a union which, by being raised on the solid foundation of mutual interest and reciprocal advantages, may secure to each the blessings of uninterrupted tranquillity.   This generous policy pervades the treaties already formed between his Most Christian Majesty and the United States, and I am happy in being persuaded that the magnanimity of his Catholic Majesty's conduct towards my country, on this and other occasions, will furnish materials for some bright pages in the American annals.

I have the honour to be, sir, etc.

JOHN JAY.

Here follow the propositions alluded to, and sent enclosed in the preceding letter :

ST. ILDEFONSO, September 22, 1781.

As the time allowed Mr. Jay for offering such propositions as may become the basis of the proposed treaty between his Catholic Majesty and the United States of North America is very short, he should fear the consequences of haste and inaccuracy, if he were not persuaded that the candour with which they will be received will secure him from the inconveniences to which these circumstances might otherwise expose him.

Mr. Jay presumes that it is not expected he should offer a plan of a treaty drawn at length, but only general propositions, which may be so modified and enlarged as, on due consideration and discussion, may appear expedient. With this view, he begs leave to present the following as the basis of a treaty of amity and alliance, viz. :

PROPOSITIONS.

I.

There shall forever subsist an inviolable and universal peace and friendship between his Catholic Majesty and the United States, and the subjects and citizens of both.

II.

That every privilege, exemption, and favour, with respect to commerce, navigation, and personal rights, which now are or hereafter may be granted by either to any the most favoured nation, be also granted by them to each other.

III.

That they mutually extend to the vessels, merchants, and inhabitants of each other all that protection which is usual and proper between friendly and allied nations.

IV.

That the vessels, merchants, or other subjects of his Catholic Majesty and the United States shall not resort to or be permitted (except in cases which humanity allows to distress) to enter into any of those ports or dominions of the other from which the most favoured nation shall be excluded.

V.

That the following commerce be prohibited and declared contraband between the subjects of his Catholic Majesty and the United States, viz. :

All such as his Catholic Majesty may think proper to specify.

REMARKS. On this proposition Mr. Jay can offer nothing but an assurance of his being ready to concur in every reasonable regulation that may be proposed.

VI.

The United States shall relinquish to his Catholic Majesty, and in future forbear to use, or attempt to use, the navigation of the river Mississippi from the thirty-first degree of north latitude—that is, from the point where it leaves the United States—down to the ocean.

REMARKS. The impression made upon the United States by the magnanimity of his Majesty's conduct towards them ; the assistance they hope to receive from the further exertions of the same magnanimity ; the deep wound which an alliance with so great a monarch would give to the hopes and efforts of the enemy ; the strong support it would afford to their independence ; the favourable influence which the example of such a King would have on other nations ; and the many other great and extensive good consequences which would result at this interesting period from his Majesty's taking so noble and decided a part in their favour, have all conspired in prevailing upon Congress to offer to relinquish in his favour the enjoyment of this territorial and national privilege, the importance of which to their constituents can only be estimated by the value they set upon his Majesty's friendship.

By this proposition the United States offer to forego all the advantages and conveniences which nature has given to the country bordering on the upper parts of that river, by ceasing to export their own, and receiving in return the commodities of other countries by that only channel, thereby greatly reducing the value of that country, retarding its settlement, and diminishing the benefits which the United States would reap from its cultivation.

Mr. Jay thinks it is his duty frankly to confess that the difficulty of reconciling this measure to the feelings of their constituents has appeared to Congress in a serious light, and they now expect to do it only by placing in the opposite scale the gratitude due to his Catholic Majesty, and the great and various advantages which the United States will derive from the acknowledgment and generous support of their independence by the Spanish monarchy at a time when the vicissitudes, dangers, and difficulties of a distressing war with a powerful, obstinate, and vindictive nation renders the friendship and avowed protection of his Catholic Majesty in a very particular manner interesting to them. The offer of this proposition, therefore, being dictated by these expectations and this combination of circumstances, must necessarily be limited by the duration of them, and consequently that if the acceptance of it should, together with the proposed alliance, be postponed to a general peace, the United States will cease to consider themselves bound by any propositions or offers which he may now make in their behalf.

Nor can Mr. Jay omit mentioning the hopes and expectations of Congress, that his Majesty's generosity and greatness of mind will prompt him to alleviate, as much as possible, the disadvantages to which this proposition subjects the United States by either granting them a free port, under certain restrictions, in the vicinity, or by such other marks of his liberality and justice as may give him additional claims to the affection and attachment of the United States.

VII.

That his Catholic Majesty shall guarantee to the United States all their respective territories.

VIII.

That the United States shall guarantee to his Catholic Majesty all his dominions in North America.

Lastly.

As the aforegoing propositions appear to Mr. Jay the most essential, he omits proposing those less and subordinate ones, which seem to follow of course. He therefore concludes this subject with a general offer and propositions to make and admit all such articles as, in the course of this negotiation, shall appear conducive to the great objects of the proposed treaty.

REMARKS. Nothing on Mr. Jay's part shall be wanting to expedite the happy conclusion of this business by adhering constantly to the dictates of candour, frankness, and unsuspecting confidence.

He is ready to receive the treaty between the United States and his Christian Majesty as a model for this, or with such alterations as, founded on the principles of reciprocity, may be more agreeable to his Catholic Majesty, it being his earnest desire to arrive at the important objects of his mission in any way his Majesty may be pleased to prefer.

The subject of aids, either by subsidy or loan, as may be most convenient to his Majesty, will require a particular convention, but as the manner, extent, and terms depend on his Majesty's pleasure, it is impossible for Mr. Jay, without some knowledge of it, to offer propositions adapted thereto. All that he can at present say on that subject is, that Congress are ready to do every thing in their power. He will not, however, endeavour to conceal their incapacity to do much in the way of compensation while the enemy shall continue to make the United States the theatre of war and the object of their predatory operations. But when those obstacles shall cease, it will be in their power, as well as their inclination, to make retribution and render important services to his Majesty. Mr. Jay will therefore continue to decline attempting to induce his Majesty to take any measures, however favorable to his country, by delusive promises or rash engagements ; but, on the other hand, he is ready to enter into such reasonable ones as he may have good reason to say shall be faithfully and punctually performed.

A particular treaty, regulating the conduct to be observed by his Catholic Majesty and the United States towards each other during the war, also appears to Mr. Jay important to both, but as the proper plans and articles of such a treaty can only result from a free conference on the subject, he can upon this occasion only express his readiness to concur in every provision which may be calculated to give energy and success to the operations and objects of both.

JOHN JAY.

Your Excellency will be pleased to observe, that among my remarks on the sixth proposition I have limited the duration of the offer contained in it. I did this from a persuasion that such limitation was not only just and reasonable in itself, but absolutely necessary to prevent this Court's continuing to delay a treaty to a general peace. Besides what the Minister dropped upon this head in his conference with me at Aranjues, I think it probable that they still wish to adhere to that idea. To me they appear desirous of avoiding the expense that the aids which a treaty we should expect would render unavoidable, and which at present would not be very convenient for them. They wish to see our independence established, and yet not be among the first to subscribe a precedent that may one day be turned against them. They wish not to exclude themselves by any present engagements from taking advantage of the chances and events of the war, not choosing on the one hand, in case we sink, that we should be fastened to them by any particular ties, nor on the other hand, in case we survive the storm, to be so circumstanced as not to make the most of us. I think it is their design, therefore, to draw from us all such concessions as our present distress and the hopes of aid may extort, and by protracting negotiations about the treaty endeavour to avail themselves of these concessions at a future day, when our inducements to offer them shall have ceased. As this would evidently be unjust, I think the limitation in question can give them no offence, and I hope Congress will be pleased to communicate to me their sentiments on the subject.

I must also remark that, after what has passed, and considering how well they are acquainted with my instructions, it would not only have been useless but absurd to have made these propositions otherwise than agreeably to those instructions.

Congress may at first view be a little surprised at the extent of the fifth proposition, but when they compare it with the second, I am persuaded they will find it sufficiently restrained.

In forming these propositions, it was my determination to leave them so free from disputed, or disputable points, as that no plausible pretexts for delay should arise from the face of them. I am well apprised, nevertheless, that in the course of the negotiation it will be impossible for me to prevent their practising as much procrastination as they may find convenient. Almost the only hope I have of their seriously doing business arises from their fearing that the instruction respecting the Mississippi will be recalled the moment that either any very decided successes on our part in America may render a treaty with Spain of less importance to us, or a general treaty of peace give us different views and prospects.

These are my conjectures and opinions. Perhaps they may prove erroneous ; as facts accompany them, Congress will be enabled to judge for themselves. I will add that, from every thing I can hear, the King is honestly disposed to do us good, and were he alone to be consulted in this business, I believe it would soon be concluded.

On the 23d of September the foregoing propositions were to be laid before the King. I heard nothing further from the Minister until the 27th, when he sent me the following note :

[Translation.]

" Although the last letter of Mr. Jay, accompanied with a certain plan, was transmitted on Saturday in the evening to the Count de Florida Blanca, and although he could not inform himself of their contents until translated from the English, he nevertheless did not fail to render an account thereof to the King in his despatch of Sunday. His Majesty having then shown himself disposed to appoint some person to confer with Mr. Jay, it is become necessary to prepare a suitable instruction, and present it to the King for his approbation. The Count de Florida Blanca flatters himself that he shall be able to arrange this affair before the departure of the Court for the Escurial, and in the meanwhile he has the honour to transmit to Mr. Jay a passport for Major Franks.

" Thursday, September 27, 1781."

I have been given to understand, though not officially, that M. Del Campo, the Minister's Secretary,
is the person who will be appointed to confer with
me, and though that gentleman is constantly about
the Minister, yet it seems that a set of formal instructions are to be prepared for him. When the Minister
will be able to find either time or health to complete
them is uncertain.

There is reason to believe that still less progress
would have been made in this affair had Major Franks
not have arrived. I regret his detention, but hope
the reasons assigned for it will be deemed sufficient ;
I am perfectly satisfied with him.

Notwithstanding Congress had given me reason to
expect that the plan of drawing bills upon me had
been laid aside, I have now bills to the amount of
between seventy and eighty thousand dollars to pay,
and no funds provided. What am I to do ? Dr.
Franklin writes me that, so far from being able to
give me further aids, he does not expect to have it in
his power even to pay our salaries in future.

From the facts stated in this letter, Congress will
perceive that this Court neither refuse nor promise
to afford us further aid. Delay is their system ; when
it will cease I cannot conjecture, for that is a question
which I doubt whether they themselves have as yet
determined.

I am indebted largely to Mr. Harrison for money
advanced by him to distressed seamen. He ought to
be paid, and it is so far from being in my power to
do it that I have been reduced to the mortifying
necessity of desiring him for the present to hold his

hand. A great many of this valuable class of people are confined in English gaols, without other means of obtaining their enlargement than by entering into the enemy's service. They complain bitterly of being neglected by their country, and, I really think, not without reason. Retaliation ought to be practised, and if we have not a sufficient number of marine officers and seamen in our power to make the objects of it, why would it be improper to substitute landsmen?

As to Portugal, I have more than once spoken to the Minister on the subject. He admits the justice of our being treated by that as by other neutral nations. He has promised to interfere in our behalf, but nothing efficacious has yet been done. To send an agent there could do no harm and might do good; I am therefore for it. The Ambassador of France thinks with me that, before that step is taken, it ought to be confidentially communicated to this Court, and I am persuaded difficulties will arise from it. I shall do my best.

M. Gardoqui's departure is uncertain. He is still attending the orders of the Court. I doubt his receiving them till the campaign closes, and perhaps not then.

I do not despair of seeing some good result, finally, from all this complication of political solecisms. It would not surprise me if we should in the end be the gainers by them. My greatest fears are about the fate of the bills. If protested, for want of payment, they will become the source of much evil.

I have the honour to be, etc.,

JOHN JAY.

JAY TO THE PRESIDENT OF CONGRESS.

MADRID, 10th October, 1781.

SIR :

Major Frank delivered me the despatches committed to his care the 30th of August. He set out for France the 5th inst. My letters by him to your Excellency will account for his remaining here so long. I also beg leave to refer to them for other more interesting particulars.

Congress will doubtless be informed that I have refused to accept some of their bills. As the enemies of America in Europe had with some success endeavoured to render the credit of our paper suspected, it appeared to me expedient to state the reasons for these refusals very particularly, and I caused them to be recited at large in the protests. I have sent copies of them to Doctor Franklin and Mr. Adams, that in case these transactions should be represented to our disadvantage either in France or Holland they might be enabled to set the matter right. I now send copies to Congress to prevent their being alarmed at any general report that may arrive in America of my having refused to accept their bills drawn upon me. Our merchants would in my opinion do well to write their indorsements on bills, at length, and in their own handwriting. There is reason to believe that the enemy often turn blank indorsements to good account.

Mr. Gardoqui is here. More ships of the Spanish Flota which carried the treasure are arrived at Cadiz. Trenches are not yet opened against Fort St. Philip at Minorca. Another expedition is preparing at Cadiz ; its destination is uncertain.

I have the honour to be, with great respect and consideration,

Your Excellency's most obedient and
very humble servant,
JOHN JAY.

His Ex'y, Thos. McKean, Esq.,
    President of Congress.

KITTY LIVINGSTON TO MRS. JAY.

PHILADELPHIA, Oct. 18, 1781.

I purpose sending this letter to my dear sister by Mr. Ridley, a gentleman who leaves town to-morrow morning for the Chesepeek, to take passage in the Frigate that will sail with the important intelligence of the capture of Cornwallis's army—an event that in all human probability must soon crown with success the allied arms.

This gentleman is a particular friend of Mr. and Mrs. Morris's, (indeed it is only to know Mr. Ridley to esteem him). Mr. and Mrs. Morris esteem themselves very fortunate in having so valuable an acquaintance to commit the care of their two eldest sons to, who are going to Europe for their education, to be placed at a school Dr. Franklin and Mr. Morris's other friends shall think most expedient for them. They are very promising boys ; their present dispositions and future advantages flatter their friends that they will return solidly prepared for their country's utility, and their own future happiness.

Before this can reach my dear friends they will have felt the emotions arising from the late joyful accounts of our success to the Southward. Gen. Greene is gaining immortal honour, for *true Glory consists in overcoming difficulties*, and history perhaps does not furnish an instance of more or as many as that great man has had to encounter with. His, poor, ragged, proud, independent army, as he styles them, not only do what men can do, but what before men were not thought equal to. The consequence of that great general's defeats have always been those of victory. America does not know its treasure. General Greene's talents would not probably have been so conspicuously great but for the opportunity and occasion of them in the Carolinas ; and many Americans there may be whose abilities want only the same exertions to equal his. But a truce to politics, lest you infer with the Colonel that as it's a favorite subject with me, I expect it to be part of your letters—but anything else cannot fail of giving me more pleasure ; situations, clymates, fashions, manners, etequete, etc., etc., will afford me more entertainment, tho' I do not mean to dictate to a sister who never was at a loss for a subject to entertain her friends with.

Your friends in this State, Jersey, and New York are well ; they are too many to enumerate. Mrs. Morris I have the pleasure to inform you, enjoys uninterrupted health ; at present her spirits are much affected ; the cause I have already mentioned—Mr. Morris is closely engaged in his herculean labors from which a change in his health is much to be apprehended . . . Mr. Jay will receive the picture he did me the honour to solicit, with, or soon after this, as Mr. Morris sends it by Mr. Ridley. To hear frequently from my friends is essential to the happiness of your

Affectionate Sister.

ROBERT MORRIS TO JAY.

PHILADELPHIA, Oct. 19th, 1781.

DEAR SIR :

I believe Kitty Livingston has availed herself of this good conveyance by Matthew Ridley, Esq. to write you very fully, and of course she will have told you all the news both domestic and political. Mrs. Morris has also written to Mrs. Jay and no doubt apprises her of that esteem and affection in which she holds both her and you. I need not tell you how sincerely I join her in these sentiments. You are often the subject of our conversation, and we never speak of you but with a pleasing remembrance of past time. We anxiously look forward to those hours when we may again enjoy your company, but the keenest wishes are checked when necessity prescribes patience. I will therefore quit this subject and proceed to inform you that some particular circumstances have put me in possession of Kitty's picture taken by Mr. Du Simitiere. It was intended for you and therefore you must permit me to present you with it. Whilst the original is under my roof—the copy has less value, or perhaps you might not have found me so ready to part with it. Don't allow me the merit of being generous in this instance, wherein I hope an opportunity of obliging three persons, for any one of whom I would sacrifice my own gratification. Consequently I resolve this sacrifice into an act of mere selfishness. The portrait goes by Mr. Ridley who will send it to you by the first good opportunity after his arrival in France.

My two oldest sons go with Mr. Ridley in order to receive their education in France. Many considerations which it is needless to enumerate, induce me to this measure, which my judgment approves, but which now that it is to be carried into execution awakens all the tender feelings of a father. Your and Mrs. Jay's sensibility will disclose the situation of Mrs. Morris and myself when I tell you that these two good and well beloved boys leave us to-morrow; they are tractable good boys. I hope they will make good men, for that is essential. Perhaps they may become useful to their country which is very desirable, and if they have genius and judgment, the education they will receive may be the foundation for them to become learned or great men, but this is of most consequence to themselves. Should it fall in your way to notice them I am sure you will do it ; I expect they will be fixed at the schools in Geneva. This parting reminds me, my good friend, that we are but too much the slaves of ambition and vanity to permit the enjoyment of that happiness, which is in our power. I need not part with my children but———

Excuse me from writing on political matters at this time, when I know that you have seen Major Franks and received my cypher. You shall hear from me officially on many points. Chancellor Livingston on this day arrived to take possession of his office, so that I hope you will in future be well informed of all things in the public line, that can be of use for you to know, and I flatter myself that your situation will become far more eligible than it has been.

Gouverneur is with me and a most useful and able adjunct he is. I hope our joint labors will in the end have the desired effect. We have mended the appearance of things very much, and are regaining public credit and confidence by degrees. If our efforts are seconded and supported by the several legislatures as they ought, we need not fear the utmost efforts of our enemies, because we will learn to exert and concenter our own force.

With the most sincere attachment and esteem
     I am
       . My Dear Sir
         Your obedient, humble servant,
           ROBERT MORRIS.

GENERAL WASHINGTON TO JAY.

HEAD-QUARTERS NEAR YORK IN VIRGINIA,
22d Oct., 1781.

SIR :

As the transmission of the inclosed paper through the usual channel of the Department of foreign Affairs, would, on the present occasion, probably be attended with great delay—and recent intelligence of military transactions must be important to our Minister in Europe, at the present period of affairs—I have thought that it would be agreeable to Congress and your Excellency, that the matter should be communicated immediately by a French frigate dispatched by the Count de Grasse.

Annexed to the capitulation is a summary return of the prisoners and cannon taken in the two places of York and Gloucester.

I have added, upon the principles above mentioned a copy of General Greene's report of his last action in South Carolina.

I have the honor to be Your Excellency's

Most obedient and most humble servant,

GEORGE WASHINGTON.

EGBERT BENSON TO JAY.

ALBANY, Oct. 27, 1781.

DEAR SIR:

The great event which I in some measure predicted in my last is come to pass. Cornwallis and his army are captured; we have this moment received the intelligence, and therefore have no particulars. If I had, I should not trouble you with them, as they doubtless will be communicated to you in your public character more authentic and very probably e'er this comes to hand. I mention the news merely to present you my sincere congratulations. What effect this success will have upon our affairs cannot with certainty be determined. I dread that supineness and security too frequently the attendant on prosperity. If instead of this it should produce a spirit of exertion, I think, reasoning as an American politician who judges only from what he hears and sees on this side of the Atlantic, it must be decisive in our favor, and we have reason to hope for the happiest consequences; and among others, which be assured in my estimation is not the least, your return to your friends.

This much for good news. Now for a streak of lean. I have this day heard of my being elected a delegate to Congress for the coming year. This was not wholly unexpected to me, for I left the Legislature sitting at Poughkeepsie when I came from home and several members of the Legislature had intimated their intentions to nominate me unless they saw a prospect of a tolerable unanimity in favour of some other person, who would in any respect answer and who could afford it better. When the matter was put on this footing, duty forbade me declining positively, and I could only express a wish to be excused; it was however stipulated that my attendance in Congress was not to be expected, at all events till after the April term, so that I have a respite for six months, and in the meantime we may have a Peace, or Millenium, or something else may turn up to justify me in a resignation. My colleagues are Messrs. Duane, Floyd, Scott and L'Hommedieu.

I am at this place attending the Supreme Court, for thank God, the streams of Justice, altho' interrupted in their course by the accident of the war, still continue to flow, and, as we have upright judges, with purity. Messrs. Morris, Yates and Hobart remain yet on the Bench, but what with the poverty of the State and the parsimony of the Legislature, the salaries are as incompetent as ever. They have no other inducement to hold their offices now than mere patriotism and an expectation that we may shortly regain the southern parts of the state, when wealth and a liberal spirit may produce allowances more adequate.

The enemy, as usual at this season, have again appeared at our western and northern frontiers. Col. Willet who commands about 600 levies in Tyron County, attacked their main body, which penetrated from the westward, and of about an equal force at Johnstown, and obliged them to retire. Our success consists in the capture of about 60 prisoners, and our loss in the destruction of a few houses at Warren Bush, a settlement about 25 miles from Schenectady in the south circle of the Mohawk. St. Leger who commanded in the attempt on Fort Schuyler in 1777, is with a considerable detachment at Ticonderoga. He remains inactive and shows no disposition to advance further. It is difficult to determine the design of his errand, unless we suppose it is to promote the defection of Vermont. There is more than probable evidence of an improper intercourse between the leaders on the Grants and the Governor of Quebec—whether they seriously mean to attach themselves to the enemy, or whether this is only a manneuvre to excite our fears and by that means compel us to a recognition of their independence is doubtful; but as the people there at large are Whigs, I should rather hope the latter.

The Legislature, I understand, have again taken up the Vermont business, and in my next I will communicate to you the Result. I have hitherto been silent on this subject, waiting for something definitive respecting it, either from Congress or the State for *adhuc sub Judice lis est.*

My month is almost out, and unless I write to-day, I am fearful I shall not have another opportunity, besides a conveyance offers to-morrow for Philadelphia, and I dare not defer my letter till then, and risque the consequence of a court supper on this glorious occasion. I expect immediately a summons to attend Court, so that I have only time to assure you that

I am, *ut alias et pluries,*

Yours sincerely,

EGB^{t.} BENSON.

ROBERT R. LIVINGSTON TO JAY.

PHILADELPHIA, November 1st, 1781.

DEAR SIR:

Your letter to Congress of April last having been read and answered by them, though not so minutely as I would wish, I forbear making any remarks upon it, because I am not yet perfectly acquainted with their sentiments, (and would not wish any which might interfere with them) having just entered upon the office, in consequence of which I open this correspondence, though long since appointed. I beg of you, agreeably to the directions of Congress, to address in future your public letters to me, and to notify the Count de Florida Blanca of this alteration in our system, our unacknowledged situation rendering it improper to do it formally.

Congress have at length completed the organization of their executive departments, by the choice of General Lincoln for their Secretary at War. It is expected that order and system will arise out of this mode of doing business, and the strictest economy.

If the great powers of Europe, with every advantage that settled governments enjoy, feel themselves under the necessity of making foreign loans, can it be expected that a war of six years, in the heart of our country, should not have abridged the resources of a State, which had every necessity for their army to import; which never manufactured for itself; which had no marine; and which, with a number of internal enemies in their bosom, had civil governments to establish? Perhaps it would be impossible to offer a better picture of the resources of this country, and the stability of her funds when they shall be well managed, than by comparing our present debt with the duration of the war and the exertions we have made. For though our enemies may allege, that our debt was relieved by the depreciation of our bills, yet it must be remembered, that that very depreciation was a tax, though an unequal one, borne by the people of these States, and as it has not produced national ruin, it must follow, that the States had sufficient resources to bear this burthen. These resources, though lessened, still remain.

The only object for which Britain continues the war, is the recovery of this country. What better plan of finance then can be adopted by France or Spain, than by timely aids of ships and money to blast this hope, and by a speedy peace to terminate their expenses? If, on the contrary, they wish to linger out the war till Britain is more exhausted, this country affords them the easiest means of doing it.

Armies may be maintained here for one third of the expense that Britain lays out upon hers. This France has experienced. Though her affairs were not perhaps managed with the strictest economy, though her bills were extremely low, her supplies cost at least one third less that the British paid at New York, without taking into account the hire of transports, the seamen employed, paid, and fed in that service, and the number of them that fell into our hands. Be persuaded yourself, and endeavor to persuade others, that if this is a war of finance, which all modern wars are, Britain is most vulnerable in America.

I congratulate you upon the important success of our arms in South Carolina and Virginia, of which I enclose you official accounts. On the returns you will remark a number of British American nominal regiments. These were recruiting in Virginia and North Carolina, and their success will show the truth of what Britain advances with respect to the number of her partisans in America. I will venture to say, that with similar advantages, their recruiting parties would have been more successful in any country in Europe. Besides the troops mentioned in the returns, the enemy lost during the siege near two thousand negroes. Previous to the surrender, they had a naval engagement with the Count de Grasse. The *Terrible*, a British seventy-four, was burnt, so that our affairs here stand upon the most respectable footing imaginable. [In cipher].

But this is a delicate subject, and I quit it till I am more fully acquainted with the views of Congress thereon, for I confess to you, that the sentiments I have hazarded are rather my own, than any that I know to be theirs, and should weigh accordingly with you. The provision trade with the Havana being very considerable and important to Spain, while she has fleets and armies to maintain there, it might be proper to suggest to the Spanish Ministry the advantage of allowing small convoys of frigates, which would enable us to carry it on in vessels of greater burden, and by that means diminish the expense or freight and insurance, both of which, eventually, fall upon Spain. A few frigates would answer the purpose, as the stations of the enemy's ships are almost always known on this coast, and, indeed, they seldom have any out but frigates cruising singly.

Another thought strikes me, which, perhaps, if digested, might be ripened into a plan advantageous to France, Spain, and America. While France keeps an army here, she must draw bills, or export money. She has, for the most part, preferred the former, at the loss of forty per cent. discount. The money of Spain is lodged at the Havana, and cannot be brought to Europe without great hazard ; whereas the risk of sending it here under convoy is extremely small. It may be vested in European bills to such advantage, as to pay the whole expense of transportation, and even an interest, till the bills are negotiated in Europe. This plan affords France a market for her bills, Spain a cheap and easy way of bringing her money home, and America a circulating medium, which enables her to tax with advantage.

As I know the confidence you once had in D[eane] I must caution you against any communication with him. Some letters have been published by Rivington said to be his, which being compared with others received here, bear the marks of authenticity. The enclosed act of Congress informs you of the appointment of Mr. Hanson, of Maryland, to the Presidentship. I shall write very frequently to you, and shall in return expect that you will omit no opportunity of letting me hear from you. A Court Kalendar, if one is printed with you, with notes of your own thereon, might be of some service to us. I shall use our private Cypher as corrected by that sent by M^r. Tocsan till you receive the one transmitted by M^r. Thomson, in which case, as it is less troublesome, be pleased to use that, if you are sure it came safe. I am, dear Sir, with the sincerest regard and esteem

Your most aff. & Hum. Servt.

R. R. LIVINGSTON.

JAY TO DEL CAMPO.[1]

MADRID, November 3, 1781.

SIR :

I have received the letter you did me the honour to write on the 2d instant.

As Mr. [John] Vaughan was favored last spring at Aranjuez with a passport from his Excellency the Count de Florida to go to and reside at Toledo, I omitted to enumerate in my last the circumstances requested in your letter.

The gentleman's father is an Englishman, his mother is an American ; he himself was born I think in England ; he means to become a citizen of and to settle in one of the United States, and is by profession a merchant. He has been a considerable time in France learning the language and acquainting himself with the commerce of that country. From thence he came last spring to Spain, for the same purposes ;

[1] Confidential Secretary to Florida Blanca at the Spanish Court. See p. 29.

he brought with him a warm recommendation from Dr. Franklin ; he spent the summer at Toledo learning the Spanish language ; he visited Ildefonso while the Court was last there, and he is now desirous of going to Cadiz that he may during the winter form proper commercial connections there, and in the spring embark for North America. He has offered to take an oath of allegiance to the United States before me. I advised him to postpone it until he arrived there, as well because I thought it more proper in itself as because I did not conceive myself authorized to administer it.

This is a short but very candid account of what I know of this gentleman. I may indeed add that in my opinion he possesses a good share of understanding and much useful knowledge. I for my part confide in the sincerity of his professions, and shall accordingly do him good office in America by recommending him to my friends there.

Be pleased to accept my thanks for your polite attention. I have the honour to be, with great consideration and respect,

Your most obedient and most humble servant,

JOHN JAY.

JAY TO FLORIDA BLANCA.

MADRID, 16th November, 1781.

SIR :

I find myself constrained to beseech your Excellency to think a little of my situation. Congress flatter themselves that the offer they have made would certainly induce his Majesty at least to assist them with some supplies. The residue of the bills drawn upon me remain to be provided for. Those payable next month amount to 31,809 dollars. Would it be too inconvenient to your Excellency to lend us this sum? Before January your Excellency may probably find leisure to give me an answer respecting our propositions. The time presses. I entreat your Excellency's answer. I can only add, that I am, with great consideration and respect,

Your Excellency's

Most obedient and most humble servant,

JOHN JAY.

JAY TO GOVERNOR CLINTON.

MADRID, 16th November 1781.

DEAR SIR :

The last and indeed only letter I have had the pleasure of receiving from you is dated the 6th April last. I wrote to you on the 28th September last by Major Franks.

If my friends in your State knew how much pleasure it gives me to hear of and receive letters from them, I flatter myself they would give me less reason to complain of inattention.

We have long been in suspense about the real state of our affairs with you, having had no direct and certain intelligence from America since July last. Various reports of good and bad fortune have in the meantime spread through this country. At present

we are told that General Greene has defeated the
enemy to the southward and captured the 19th regiment; that Lord Cornwallis' entrenchments have
been carried by assault and himself killed; that
Digby's squadron has fallen into the hands of Mon-
sieur Barras, and consequently that Graves cannot
make head against De Grasse. God grant that all
this may be true, and that victory may ever support
the standards of justice and liberty.

Fort St. Philip continues besieged by about sixteen thousand French and Spaniards. How long it
may hold out is uncertain.

The approaching winter will give occasion to
various speculations and conjectures respecting the
probability and terms of a general peace. For my
own part I expect at least one more campaign, unless
our successes in America should be much more decisive than I can yet flatter myself that they will be,
considering the advanced season when Count de
Grasse arrived. To all appearance Britain can only
be delivered from her strong delusions respecting
America to render us tributaries by repeated losses
and defeats. It gave me much pleasure to hear that
G. Morris would probably be in your delegation this
fall. Independent of my regard for him, it appears
to me of great importance to the State that every
valuable man in it should be preserved, and that it is
particularly our interest to cultivate, cherish, and support all such of our citizens, especially young and
rising ones, as are, or promise to be, able and honest
servants of the public. Mrs. Jay presents her com-

pliments to you and Mrs. Clinton ; be pleased to add mine, and believe me to be,

> Dear sir,
>> Your friend and servant,
>>> JOHN JAY.

P. S.—Be so kind as to forward the enclosed, and as I scarce ever hear from my father's family, you will oblige me by writing me now and then what you may know or hear of them.

JOHN ADAMS TO JAY.

AMSTERDAM, Novr. 26, 1781.

SIR :

By the last post, I received from L'Orient a set of fresh instructions from Congress, dated the 16th of August, and with the more pleasure as I am enjoined to open a correspondence with your Excellency upon the subject of them.

I presume you have copy by the home vessel ; but as it is possible it may have been omitted, I shall venture to enclose a copy, and hope it may pass unopened. I have communicated it to the French Ambassador here, who says it is "très bien vû ; très bien combiné." I shall take no step in it without his knowledge and approbation. I shall hope for your Excellency's communications as soon as convenient.

The Dutch have an inclination to ally themselves to France and America ; but they have many whimsical fears, and are much embarrassed with party quarrels. In time I hope they will agree better with one another, and see their true interests more clearly. This measure of Congress is very well timed.

By our Act of Submission any two delegates for the time being were authorized, as agents, to manage the matter before Congress and Messrs. Duane, Scott and myself were appointed Commissioners for collecting the proofs. Shortly after the rising of the Legislature in the fall of 1779, we entered on the Business and had it compleated, and the evidence properly digested and arranged, at least a month before the 1st of Feby. following, the day of our leaving; but thro' mistake the Papers did not reach Philadelphia in season and consequently we were reduced to the necessity of requesting another day for our hearing. This you, who have been a Witness of the finesse and delay too frequently prevailing in Congress, can easily imagine was not unattended with Difficulties. After repeated sollicitation, however, another day was appointed when the Parties appeared and were heard, as you will perceive by the Resolutions. Notwithstanding the evidence, in favor of our claim to Connecticut River, was not only clear and full, but even conclusive, yet our Delegates, from an apprehension that a majority would inevitably be against us, thought it imprudent to press Congress for a decision, and conceived it most eligible to leave them to decide whenever they thought proper.

That these apprehensions were well founded was evident from the Behaviour of several of the members. I shall mention an Instance: A delegate from Rhode-Island declared that, altho' from the evidence and on the *merits* we were enitled to a Decision, yet a very great number of the Inhabitants of the State which he represented were interested in Grants, either under New Hampshire or the pretended State, and opposed to our claims, and therefore, as he intended to vote agreeable to what he conceived to be the sense and wishes of his Constituents, independent of any other considerations, he should give his voice against us. He made this Declaration publicly in Congress where *cially*, according to *evidence*, and on *equitable* principles, but not *arbitrarily*, or as Interest or *Expediency* should dictate, and this I take to be the true distinction in the case. If the Individuals in Congress who favor the independency of the Grants, had attended to this distinction, two methods presented themselves for accomplishing this injurious Design, neither of which would have been liable to such fatal objections as the present mode of Procedure, and one of them would have been obligatory on us. The one is for Congress to have declared that should they proceed to decide judicially and should the Decision be against Vermont, it would be difficult if not impossible to carry the adjudication into effect without greatly endangering the general liberties, and therefore request Massachusetts, New Hampshire, and this State to make a partial Sacrifice for the good of the whole, waive their rights, relinquish their claim to the territory in question, consent to its independency and that it should be received into the Union, and apply to the several States for authority in Such case to admit the new State as a member of the Confederation. A fertile mind could have suggested numberless arguments to evince the Policy of this measure ; and as the Eastern States *certainly* and others very *probably* would have approved it, and as it carries with it at least the marks of Candor, I am induced to believe that this State would have come into it also, especially if Congress had declared that as they had engaged, so they would still, if we insisted, decide according to *equity* and endeavor to carry the Decision into effect, but requested us in gentle terms to contemplate the serious Consequences which such an attempt might produce. The other is for Congress to have declared that from the Evidence it appeared that the present Line between this State and Massachusetts, continued to the 45th degree of Latitude, was our eastern Boundary, that Connecticut River was the western Boundary of New Hampshire, and that the present was the true northern Boundary of Massachusetts; there would then have been a vacant Territory which it would have been our interest and that of every other State to recognize as independent and receive into the Union. Altho' we might have complained of this Adjudication as being contrary to evidence, yet being made agreeable to the Submission and having the requisite formalities, it would have been conclusive.

I cannot suppose this last mode of Procedure escaped every member in Congress, but I imagine that, as the Evidence in support of our claim to Connecticut River was incontrovertible, it was deemed more eligible to have recourse to open *Violence* than to palpable *Falsehood.* I am not of this opinion, for if Injustice is the *end*, the *means*, setting aside cruelty, are not very material, and an aberration from the Truth would in this instance have been a kind of pious fraud as it would have prevented the necessity of violating the fundamentals of the Union.

Where this affair will terminate I will not even conjecture, tho' I could form a guess provided every Person of influence in the State possessed a due proportion of that virtue for which you was distinguished and which your friends sometimes called *Obstinacy.* I prize this obstinacy so highly that I shall conclude with a wish that you may ever retain it, and that with respect to *that* and with respect to *you* the adage may be verified—*non animum mutant qui trans mare currunt.*

Yours Sincerely,

EGBT. BENSON.

ROBERT R. LIVINGSTON TO JAY.

PHILADELPHIA, November 28th, 1781.

DEAR SIR:

I wrote so fully to you not long since, that I should not trouble you at this time, if I had not determined to omit no opportunity of letting you hear from this side of the water and enabling you at all times to meet any falsehood the enemy may find it politic to publish.

Since the capture of Cornwallis, nothing very material has happened. The ravaging parties on the northern frontiers have been defeated with great loss by the militia. The armies have taken their stations for the winter quarters; the French, in Virginia and Maryland; our troops, on the Hudson, excepting some detachments under General St. Clair, destined to reinforce General Greene. They have orders to take Wilmington in their way, where the enemy have about six hundred men; it is probable they will not wait the attack. General Greene will have men enough to shut up the enemy, but not to force their strong holds. Want of money cramps all their exertions, and prevents our making a glorious winter campaign. The enemy are all shut up on two or three points of land, which is all they possess of the immense country they hope to conquer; and even these they hold by a very precarious tenure. Disaffection, which has languished for some time past, died when Cornwallis surrendered.

Congress are occupied in taking measures for an active campaign; and they feel themselves satisfied with everything both at home and abroad. [Ciphers.]

Congress have dissolved Mr. Adams's powers to make a treaty of commerce with Great Britain; and, as you know, joined you, Dr. Franklin and Mr. Laurens in his other commission, if England should at length be wise enough to wish for peace.

The Marquis de Lafayette is the bearer of this. He has promised to convey it with safety to you, and to correspond with you in such a manner as to enable you to avail yourself of the knowledge which he has acquired, that may be of use to you. Th resolves of Congress, of which I enclose a copy, show their sense on this subject, and the confidence which they very justly repose in him. His Aid waits for this. Adieu my dear Sir.

Believe me to be, with the highest respect and esteem, &c.
ROBERT R. LIVINGSTON.[1]

JAY TO GOVERNOR CLINTON.

MADRID, December 1, 1781.

DEAR SIR:

I congratulate you on the surrender of Lord Corn-wallis—a most joyful and important event. We are waiting with impatience to hear what effect it has on the British Court, and whether it will abate their pride or excite them to still more vigorous efforts. I hope our country will prepare for the latter.

Adieu. I am yours, etc.,

JOHN JAY.

JAY TO EGBERT BENSON.

MADRID, 8 December, 1781.

DEAR BENSON :

I had yesterday the pleasure of receiving your favor of the 30th October last—the only one that has come to my hands since I left Philadelphia. The letter you mention to have written when General Washington was in Westchester County has mis-carried, and I the more regret it as it probably contained some particulars about my father's family, of whom I hear little except by persons at a distance from them. But two letters from Fady and none

---

[1] American Secretary of Foreign Affairs, Philadelphia.

from James have come to my hands since we parted. You need not be informed how this circumstance operated upon my feelings, nor how much you will oblige me by supplying their omissions. Remember, however, that your letters will probably be inspected before they reach me. I thank you sincerely and cordially for this instance of attention and the intelligence you favor me with.——Thank God! Cornwallis and his army are our prisoners, a most joyful and important event. The news must have arrived in England at the opening of Parliament. We are impatient to know what influence it will have upon the British counsels. In my opinion it will either lead the enemy to think more seriously of peace, or excite them to make the most strenuous efforts for prosecuting the war. I hope and pray that our success may not relax our exertions.

I have had no letter for many months past from R. Livingston, though I have wrote him several. His appointment gives me pleasure ; our State will nevertheless lose an able Counsellor by his absence.

. . . .

I have been informed that my father had been robbed, that he removed his family to Poughkeepsie, and that on the way he lost one of his servants (but which I know not) by an unfortunate accident. I am to this moment ignorant of the particulars except so far as they have been conveyed by report. I wish to know where he lives and how he does ; nobody writes me a syllable about Peter and Nancy. This distressed family are never out of my thoughts or heart. Harry Livingston, Jr., has been so kind as to write a letter to Mrs. Jay, and for which we are much obliged to him. I wish, however, he had been as particular about my father as about my son. You tell me he is the solace of my father. This circumstance makes me regret their parting. So few rays of comfort beam on that good and affectionate parent of mine that it is a pity he should be deprived of those which it seems he derives from the company and prattle of his little grandson. It must not be. You, my good friend, must manage this matter for me. Harry Livingston, I imagine, lives in the neighbourhood. His wife is an excellent woman, and in my opinion a *rara avis in terra*. I believe they both wish me well, and would not refuse to oblige me by taking my son to live with them and treating him as they do their own. In that family he would neither see nor be indulged in immoralities, and he might every day or two spend some hours with his grandfather, and go to school with Harry's children; or otherwise as you may think proper. At any rate he must not live with his grandfather, to whom he would in that case be as much trouble as satisfaction. This is a point on which I am decided, and therefore write in very express and positive terms. Unless objections strike you that I neither know or think of, be so kind as to speak to Mr. and Mrs. Livingston about it. I will cheerfully pay them whatever you may think proper, and I would rather that you should agree to a generous allowance than a mere adequate compensation. In case Mr. and Mrs. Livingston should consent to this, be pleased then to mention it to my father and the family. . . .

I entreat your attention to this subject and beg that you will extend your regard for the father to the son and family of

Your affectionate friend.

JOHN JAY.

Mrs. Jay desires me to assure you of her esteem and best wishes. Remember me to my friends, and when you see Doctor Van Wyck assure him that my father's leaving his farm and neighbourhood does not in the least abate the attachment and gratitude I owe him for his kindness to the family, but that, on the contrary, I shall rejoice in every opportunity I may have of being useful to him and his.

JAY TO GENERAL WASHINGTON.

MADRID, December 9, 1781.

SIR:

On the 7th inst. I had the honour of receiving your Excellency's favour of the 22d of October last, with the copies of the articles of capitulation, returns, and of General Greene's letter mentioned in it. I also received on the same day duplicates of each.

The reasons which induced your Excellency to transmit these papers will, I am persuaded, appear no less proper to Congress than the speedy reception of such welcome and interesting intelligence is agreeable to me.

I congratulate your Excellency and my country on this important event, and permit me to assure you that its having been achieved under the immediate direction of the Commander-in-chief adds to the satisfaction I feel on the occasion. General Greene's conduct merits the commendation and thanks of his country. He has done much with slender means, and will, I hope, be soon enabled to restore every part of the Southern States to the peaceable enjoyment of their liberty and independence.

I have the honour to be, with perfect respect and esteem, your Excellency's most obedient and most humble servant,

JOHN JAY.

JAY TO GENERAL KNOX.

MADRID, 10th December, 1781.

DEAR SIR :

I thank you sincerely for your very friendly letter of the 21st October last, which I had the pleasure of receiving on the 7th inst. I rejoice most cordially with you and every other good American in the important event you communicate, and to which you had both the honour and the satisfaction of essentially contributing.

General Washington has favoured me with copies of the articles of capitulation and returns of the prisoners, etc. It gives me very sensible pleasure to find that he commanded in person on this glorious occasion, and had the satisfaction of bringing deliverance to his native and, consequently, favourite part of America. If Providence shall be pleased to lead him, with safety and success, through all the duties of his station, and carry him home with the blessings of all America on his head, I think he will exhibit to the world the most singular instance of virtue, greatness, and good-fortune united which the history of mankind has hitherto recorded.[1]

The harmony subsisting between the French troops and ours is an agreeable as well as an important circumstance, and I am glad that the Marquis de Lafayette had an opportunity of cutting some sprigs of laurel on one of the enemy's redoubts. He has given strong proofs of attachment to our cause and country, and as military glory seems to be his mistress, he has my best wishes that she may be as constant to him as he has been to us.

General Greene has deservedly acquired great reputation. He has nobly surmounted a variety of difficulties, and his country has fortunately found resources in his talents and perseverance which the peculiar situation of the Southern States rendered no less seasonable than important.

---

[1] The original draft of this letter contains the following sentences crossed out. Jay probably regarded them as too pronounced, but as conveying his views at the moment they have their place here :

" I confess to you that my pride as an American is a little qualified by those articles of the capitulation which respect the *honours* granted to the garrison, for, though these matters are in themselves of no great importance, yet it appears to me that the former conduct of Lord Cornwallis rendered this retaliation very proper.

" The article on the subject of the Tories must meet with general approbation. I suspect, however, that the 8th article has made a way for some to escape. The Saratoga Convention permitted them to go into Canada, and the next year they ravaged our frontiers. Policy directs that these people should at least be restrained from doing us mischief, and that, during the war, examples should

This campaign ends gloriously for us. How far British counsels may be changed by these events is as yet uncertain. I am much inclined to think that another campaign will precede a general peace. In my opinion, our country would do well to continue making the most vigorous efforts to render peace more essential to her enemies than herself.

It would give me pleasure to transmit to you some interesting advices from this quarter of the world. The sieges of Gibraltar and Fort St. Philip continue. When they will be terminated is impossible to divine. The Dutch are praying for peace, and neglecting the means necessary to obtain a proper one. The people do not appear to want spirit, but their government and their ruler subject them to numberless embarrassments.

France is full of joy and ardour, and will, I believe, do her best endeavours to make the next campaign active and brilliant. The Emperor is regulating the internal policy of his dominions, encouraging commerce, and extending toleration without suffering himself to be incommoded by ecclesiastical privileges or immunities. He seems to be seriously preparing to be great and formidable ; he undoubtedly possesses the means of power, and, it is said, has talents to use them to advantage. Mrs. Jay desires me to present you her compliments and congratulations. With great regard and esteem,

I am, dear sir, your most obedient and very humble servant, JOHN JAY.

---

be made of some to deter others. I must nevertheless acknowledge that I would, if possible, rather hang ten twisting, equivocating, neutral nothingarians than one Tory taken in arms openly and fairly fighting against us."

MATTHEW RIDLEY TO JAY.

PARIS, December 10th, 1781.

SIR :

I have the pleasure of enclosing you four letters from your Friends in America, committed to my care ; also a picture from Mr. Morris.[1] I arrived from the Chesapeake at Brest in 19 days. I sailed a few days after the capture of Lord Cornwallis, the particulars of which you have doubtless heard from Dr. Franklin, and therefore 'tis unnecessary for me to repeat.

I left Philadelphia the 20th Oct., at which time such of your Friends as I had the honor of being acquainted with were well. Mr. Morris's two oldest sons, Robert and Thomas, came with me. At present I have put them in a *pension;* in the Spring I shall take them to Geneva, where if matters are suitable they are to finish their Education.

For you and your Lady's particular satisfaction I must mention Miss K. Livingston, with whom I have the happiness of being acquainted. She was well, but under great anxiety for her Brother, Mr. John Livingston, who went out in the *Saratoga* and had not been heard of. She was induced to believe that the vessel had been carried to England, and entrusted a Letter to my care for her Brother. I am sorry to add I can hear nothing of him.[2]

The little opportunity I had of cultivating the Honor of your acquaintance when I saw you in Philadelphia scarcely permits me the liberty of asking to hear from you; but when your Engagements permit, the acknowledging the receipt of the letters and Miss Livingston's picture will

---

[1] See letter from Kitty Livingston to Mrs. Jay, Oct. 18, 1781 ; also Robert Morris to Jay, Oct. 19, 1781.

[2] Respecting John Livingston and the *Saratoga* see letter from Kitty L. to Mrs. Jay, July 10, 1780, vol. i., pp. 374–77 ; also reference in note, p. 376, *ibid.* The *Saratoga* was lost at sea with all on board.

oblige me. I forgot to mention that Chancellor Livingston was arrived at Phila. before I left there to act as Minister of Foreign Affairs.

I am with respect for your Lady and self

Sir, your most obedient humble servant,

MATT: RIDLEY.

ROBERT R. LIVINGSTON TO JAY.

PHILADELPHIA, December 13, 1781.

DEAR SIR:

My last letter of the 28th of November, sent by the Marquis de Lafayette, must for the most part have been unintelligible to you, owing to an unfortunate mistake of Mr. Thompson, who delivered me a cypher sent by Mr. Palfrey, which you never received, instead of that sent by Major Franks. The duplicate enclosed is in the last, so that you will no longer be at a loss for my meaning. Since the date of that letter the enemy have thought it prudent to abandon Wilmington, in North Carolina. This port was extremely important to them, not only as it checked the trade of that State, but as it directly communicated with the disaffected counties. For it must be confessed, that though in other parts of the continent they had only well wishers, in North Carolina they had active partisans. These they have left to the mercy of their country, and abandoned as disgracefully as the capitulation of York did those of Virginia. It is not improbable, that when General St. Clair joins the southern army, the enemy will evacuate Savannah, as they are at present extremely weak there; and unless they reinforce from New York, may be attacked with a prospect of success.

Your letter of the 20th of September has been received and read in Congress. They have not been pleased to direct any particular answer thereto, so that you are to consider it as their wish, that you execute the commission with which they have intrusted you.

You will see that I neglect no opportunity of writing. I flatter myself that you will be equally attentive to let us hear from you. It is not without some degree of pain, that we receive our earliest intelligence frequently from the Minister of France. I know you may retort upon us with too much justice, but I hope to give you less reason to do so in the future. I send a packet of newspapers with this. I sent another some time ago. I hope they may reach you. In one of them you will find an ordinance of Congress, which comprises all their resolutions with respect to captures; and forfeits all British goods, which have not been taken, as prizes. Perhaps this may make some arrangements with the Court of Spain necessary; that is, if any prize goods are re-shipped from thence to America.

I am, my Dear Sir, with the greatest esteem and regard, &c.

ROBERT R. LIVINGSTON.

JAY TO JOHN ADAMS.

MADRID, 15th December, 1781.

SIR :

The two last posts brought me your favours of the 26th and 28th ult. It really gives me great satisfaction at length to see a prospect of a regular correspondence between us. The failure of my former attempts had almost discouraged me, though from the frequent miscarriage of letters to and from me I had reason to impute your silence more to that than to any other cause.

I have not received a syllable from Congress, nor from any one of its members, by the vessel which brought you the instructions of the 16th August, but I by no means infer from thence that they did not write, for on more than one occasion I knew that letters for me had been put into the post-office which never came to my hands, and I advise you never to write to me but under the persuasion that your letter will be inspected before I receive it.

As to the instructions, I had neither seen nor heard of them till the receipt of your letter. They appear to me to be wise, and I shall be happy to see the object of them fully and speedily attained.

As to the prospect of my negotiations here, I can only inform you that, though the last offer of America was made so long ago as July last, the Court has not yet found it convenient to give me an answer. I would give you a particular history of delays, but it would be useless. I would also communicate to you my conjectures as to the real causes of them, but by the post it would be improper. In a word, it is not in my power to write any thing of importance but what I ought not to write by such a conveyance unless in cipher. Delay is and has long been the system, and when it will cease cannot be divined. M. Del Campo, the Minister's first and confidential Secretary, has been appointed near three months to confer with me, and yet this appointment was not announced to me till last week. I have not yet had a conference with him ; he has been sick, and it seems has not sufficiently recovered to do business, etc.

It will not be necessary to send me copies of the commission and instructions you mention. The originals intended for me were brought by Major Franks in September last. I think it probable that duplicates for me accompanied those you have received, and I am the more inclined to this opinion from having lately received a packet directed to Secretary Thomson, in which I found nothing but his cipher, endorsed in his handwriting, but no letter or line from him or other. It was committed to the care of Mr. Barclay, our consul in France; he sent it to me by the post, and on comparing the date of my letter come from L'Orient with the time I received it, I found it was thirteen days on the way; it had evident marks of inspection.

I am very much of your opinion, and for the same reason, that peace is yet at a distance, and therefore that I cannot soon expect to have the pleasure of seeing you, which I much desire for many reasons.

As to Gibraltar and Minorca, it is difficult to conjecture when or in what manner the operations against them will terminate; for my own part I think their fate will remain in suspense for some time yet.

The Dutch certainly do not want spirit, and I ascribe their want of vigour more to the embarrassment they experience from the nature of their government and the Anglican connections of the ruling family than to any other cause. A national convention under the protection of France would in my opinion be the most effectual remedy for these evils. General Greene's late action does great honour to him as well as to the American arms. This and the sur-

render of Lord Cornwallis are most joyful and interesting events. I am anxious to know what influence
they will have on the British counsels.

If the alliance in agitation should promise to take
effect and draw near to a conclusion, it would have
much influence here and elsewhere. You shall have
immediate advice of the first change that may happen
in our affairs here.

My expectations are not very sanguine, but I confess to you that it would not surprise me if the various
delays practised should in the end prove much more
advantageous than injurious to our interests.

I have the honour to be, with great respect and
esteem, your Excellency's most obedient servant,

JOHN JAY.

JAY TO ELBRIDGE GERRY.

MADRID, 9th January, 1782.

DEAR SIR :

I should have much wondered what could have
detained my letter, mentioned in yours of 20th
September last, so long from you had not my correspondence been strangely interrupted ever since my
arrival.

Your constitution [Massachusetts] gives me much
satisfaction. It appears to be upon the whole wisely
formed and well digested. I find that it describes
your State as being in *New England* as well as in
America ; perhaps it would be better if these distinc-
tions were permitted to die away.

Your predictions respecting the fate of Lord Cornwallis have, thank God, been verified. It is a glorious, joyful, and important event. Britain feels the force of that stroke and other nations begin to doubt less of the continuance of our independence. Further successes must prepare the way for peace, and I hope that victory will stimulate instead of relaxing our exertions.

Although myself and my family have most severely suffered by the Continental money, I am resigned to fate. Provided we preserve our liberty and independence I shall be content under their auspices ; in a fruitful country and by patient industry, a competence may always be acquired, and I shall never cease to prefer a little with freedom to opulence without it.

Your account of the plenty which abounds in our country is very flattering and ought to excite our gratitude to the hand that gave it. While our governments tax wisely, reward merit, and punish offenders, we shall have little to fear. The public has been too much a prey to peculation. Economy and strict accounts ought to be and continue among the first objects of our attention.

I have not heard any thing for a long time respecting our disputed lines. In my opinion few things demand more immediate care than this subject, and I differ from those who think that such matters had better be postponed till after the war. At present a sense of common danger guarantees our union ; we have neither time nor inclination to dispute among ourselves. Peace will give us leisure, and leisure often finds improper occasions for employment. I most sincerely wish that no dispute may survive the war, and that on the return of peace we may congratulate each other on our deliverance and the prospects of uninterrupted liberty, without finding ourselves exposed to differences and litigations which never fail to make impressions injurious to that courage and confidence which both our interest and our duty call upon us to cultivate and cherish.

Mrs. Jay charges me to present her compliments to you.

I am, dear sir, with great and sincere esteem, your most obedient and very humble servant,

JOHN JAY.

MARQUIS DE LAFAYETTE TO JAY.

VERSAILLES, Jan. 30, 1782.

DEAR SIR:

On my departure from America I have been intrusted with dispatches[1] for you which it had been recommended to me to forward by a safe opportunity. I dare not send them by post, and still less will I put them in the hands of Spanish expresses, but as there is no private person going towards Madrid I will make use of the first French Courier that will be despatched to M. de Montmorin.

As every piece of intelligence is of course contained in the enclosed letter I will only add that a small expedition of the enemy from Canada had been checked by the gallantry of Lt. Col. Miller and that after the evacuation of Wilmington and a little rally of Gen. Greene against a fort in Carolina, the enemy are now confined to Penobscot, New York, Charleston and Savannah. That they may be driven from

---

[1] See R. R. Livingston to Jay, Nov. 28, 1781.

all or at least from one of the two important places, and that before further assistance may be obtained from hence, is the ardent wish of my heart.

Whether a communication between you and me may be productive of advantages to America or of some personal *agrément* to you, I shall ever consider myself happy and honoured by a Correspondence with Mr. Jay for whom I entertain the highest respect and whom I beg to be convinced that my attachment is not less sincere than the regard I have the honour to be with,

Dear Sir, your most obedient and humble servant,

LAFAYETTE.

I beg my best Compliments may be presented to my friend Carmichael and my best respects to Mrs. Jay.

MRS. JAY TO HER FATHER.

MADRID, 31st Jan^ry, 1782.

The great distance that separates me from dear Papa makes me solicitous to inform him of such things as would amuse him, or at least give him an account of this part of his family, and with those intentions I have frequently taken up my pen; but there is an ingenuousness in my disposition which often disposes me to more frankness than prudence justifies, and for want of caution have been obliged by prudential reasons to suppress some letters after they were written. I have at this instant in my desk an interesting one that was written last June containing eighteen pages; nor should I now have mentioned those letters had I not feared that the long silent interval between the last and present might have occasioned the revival of that old idea that being out of sight you had lost my remembrance—the most unorthodox idea that can present itself in minds that affection, gratitude and esteem unite. Accept my thanks for your obliging favor of the 21st of Aug^st; it was handed to me on the 31st of Nov br, and would have contributed greatly to my satisfaction as the former instances of your attention had done, had not my feelings been alarmed by the paragraphs relative to my dear unfortunate brother. It 's true my feeling were a little relieved by your letter to Brockholst mentioning the probability of his capture, but even that ray of hope has been greatly obscured by the unsuccessful inquiries of our friends in Europe. The many distressing incidents that have arisen in our part of the world in consequence of the cruel war that has been prosecuted against us are sufficient to contrast the former goodness of Providence to our Country and to raise our gratitude for the prospect which the happy conclusion of this Campaign has opened to peace and independence. Our once haughty foe now finds himself deprived of great part of his empire, dignity, and the confidence of many of his subjects.

The late brilliant enterprise of the French against St. Eustatia has acquired for the Marquis De Bouillé great encomiums and the subsequent conduct of himself and officers has added greatly to their honor.

The 6th of Febry Count De Montmorin, the French Embassador, will give a very splendid entertainment at his house in celebration of the birth of the Dauphin, and you may judge whether or not it is likely to be elegant when I tell you that it is said that the ten thousand dollars allowed by his Court for the occasion will be insufficient to defray the expence that will be incurred. Your attention to my dear little boy increases my gratitude, and makes me wish you may one day be repaid by his own amiable conduct, being sensible that a generous mind is most agreeably rewarded when it perceives that its benefits have been useful.

Please to remember me to my dear Mama and brother William, and believe me to be, my dear Papa, with great sincerity,

Your very dutiful daughter,

SARAH JAY.

To Gov. Livingston.

ROBERT R. LIVINGSTON TO JAY.

PHILADELPHIA, February 2d, 1782.

DEAR SIR,

Having heard that a vessel is soon to go to Cadiz from Baltimore, I embrace the opportunity to send a quadruplicate of my last letter, and to add thereto the little information which this inactive season affords. Nothing passes here between the armies; they are cantoned at a distance from each other. The enemy is secure from attack by the nature of their situation; and we by our numbers, our success, and the apprehensions of Sir Henry. We turn our faces therefore to the south, and expect from the enterprize of General Greene an activity, which the season will not admit of here.

I had a letter from him of the 13th of December, which contains the latest advices. His camp is at Round O. He writes in high spirits, and assures me he is preparing for the siege of Charleston, which he is not without hopes of carrying even before any foreign assistance can arrive. I must confess for my own part, notwithstanding the natural coolness of General Greene, that I believe he is much too sanguine on this occasion; for I have no conception that his means are adequate to so important an object, more especially as troops have since the date of his letter sailed from New York, as I suppose for Charleston.

The governments of Georgia and Carolina are again established, and their legislatures are now sitting. The detestation of the people for the British can hardly be conceived. General Greene's letter expresses it in the following words; "The tyrants of Syracuse were never more detested than the British army in this country; even the slaves rejoice, and find a kind of temporary freedom from oppression on the return of their masters."

I congratulate you upon the capture of St. Eustatia and St. Martin's. The enterprise does the highest honor to the abilities and spirit of the Marquis de Bouillé; and his disinterested generosity is finely contrasted with the sordid avarice of the British commanders.

Order and economy have taken place in our finances. The troops are regularly clothed and fed at West Point, and most of the other posts, at the moderate rate of nine-pence a ration when issued, so that the innumerable band of purchasing and issuing commissaries is discharged. The hospitals are well supplied in the same way, and small advances of pay are made to the officers and men. Upon the whole, they were never in so comfortable a situation as they are at present. Our civil list formed upon plans of the strictest economy, after having been many years in arrear, is now regularly paid off; and the departments, in consequence of it, filled with men of integrity and abilities. Embargoes and other restrictions being removed, our commerce begins to revive, and with it the spirit of industry and enterprise; and what will astonish you still more is, that public credit has again reared its head. Our bank paper is in equal estimation with specie. Nothing can be more agreeable than to see the satisfaction with which people bring their money to the bank, and take out paper; or the joy mixed with surprise with which some, who have hesitatingly taken bank bills for the first time, see that they can turn them into specie at their option.

Whether Spain wishes for peace or war, it is certainly her interest to push the enemy where they are most vulnerable, and where she can do it with the smallest expense to herself, and the greatest to her enemy. Every additional man she enables us to maintain here, forces Britain to lay out four times as much in procuring, transporting, and feeding another to oppose him. It has been acknowledged in the British House of Commons, that every man in America costs the nation annually one hundred pounds sterling. Though this may appear exorbitant, yet whoever reflects on the first expense of raising and transporting a regiment, and the additional charge of sending over recruits to make up deficiencies, and that of sending provisions to an army and its innumerable dependants three thousand miles, will think it deserves some degree of credit. It is obvious then as nations are only strong in proportion to the money they can command, that every thousand men we oblige the British to maintain here must make a diminution of their strength in some other quarter, equal to three times that number.

Enclosed you have copies of two original letters from Mr. Deane, in which he acknowledges others that Rivington has published, which speak a still more dangerous language. No doubt is entertained here of his apostacy, or of his endeavor to weaken the efforts of the United States, and to traduce the character of the people and their rulers, both in Europe and America. You will doubtless use every means in your power to destroy the ill effects, which his calumnies may have had upon the minds of people with you. I enclose you the gazettes, and again entreat you to let us hear from you more frequently, and to leave letters at all times at Cadiz, and in the hands of our Consul in France, so that no vessel may sail without bringing us some intelligence. The last letter we had from you is dated in September, near five months ago. I dare say this has been owing to some accidental cause, and I only mention it, that you may guard against it by writing more frequently in future, as the silence of our Ministers excites more uneasiness here than you can conceive. Pray send me, when no other subject presents itself, and you have leisure, a sketch of the government of Spain, and the present state of its trade, marine, military establishments, commerce, revenues, and agriculture.

I could also wish to have the Madrid Gazette, and Mercury, and the Court Kalendar of this year. I have the pleasure of informing you, that your friends here are well, and as numerous as ever.

I am, my dear Sir, with those sentiments of esteem and friendship, which I shall always feel for you, your most obedient humble servant,

ROBERT R. LIVINGSTON.

JAY TO ROBERT R. LIVINGSTON.

DEAR SIR :

MADRID, February 6, 1782.

The Secretary of the Minister of State sent me yesterday morning your favour of the 13th of December last, accompanied by various papers.

These are the first letters or papers of any kind that I have as yet had the pleasure of receiving from you since your appointment, and they must for the present remain unintelligible for the want of your cipher. The one mentioned to have been enclosed with these papers is missing, and the other never came to hand.

On the 29th of November last I received a packet, in which I found enclosed a set of ciphers endorsed by Mr. Secretary Thomson, and nothing else. Mr. Barclay had sent it by the post, under cover, to a banker here. It had evident marks of inspection, but I acquit the banker of any hand in it.

A letter of the 18th ult., from Mr. Joshua Johnson, at Nantes, mentions the arrival there of the brig *Betsey*, from Philadelphia, and that she brought letters for me, which were put into the post-office by the captain. I have not yet seen them.

There are letters in town, brought by the Marquis de Lafayette to France ; but I have not yet received a line by or from him.

We must do like other nations; manage our correspondences in important cases by couriers, and not by the post.

I have not written you a single official letter, not having been ascertained of your having entered on the execution of your office. I have, indeed, sent you by more than one opportunity my congratulations on your appointment.

You may rely on my writing you many letters, private as well as official, and as I still have confidence in Mr. R. Morris' cipher, I shall sometimes use it to you.

A duplicate of my letter of the 3d of October to Congress, which goes with this, renders it unnecessary for me to go into particulars at present; nothing having since happened but a repetition of delays, and, of consequence, additional dangers to the credit of our bills.

I am, dear sir, etc., JOHN JAY.

JAY TO THE PRESIDENT OF CONGRESS.

SIR : MADRID, February 6, 1782.

My last particular letter to your Excellency was dated the 3d of October last, by Major Franks. I now transmit a duplicate of it by Mr. Stephen Codman, a young gentleman of Boston, who is passing through this city to Cadiz, from whence he will either be the bearer of it himself to America, or forward it by some person of confidence.

From the date of that letter to this day the Minister has found it convenient to continue the system of delay mentioned in it. I have not been able to obtain any thing more than excuses for procrastination, and these excuses are uniformly want of health or want of time.

There is little prospect of our receiving speedy aids from this Court, and Dr. Franklin gives me reason to fear that a great number of the bills drawn upon me must, after all our exertions to save them, be finally protested for non-payment. I have, from time to time, given the Doctor a great deal of trouble on this subject, and I ought to acknowledge that I am under many and great obligations to him for his constant attention to our affairs here.

As soon as I get a little better of the rheumatism, with which I am now and have for some time past been much afflicted, I shall write your Excellency another long and particular letter.

I have just received, through the hands of the Minister's Secretary, a letter from Mr. Livingston dated the 13th of December, marked No. 3. It is in cipher, but I cannot read it, nor a duplicate of No. 2, enclosed in it, for want of a key, which, though mentioned to have been enclosed, is missing. None of his other letters have reached me. A duplicate of Mr. Thomson's cipher, brought by Mr. Barclay, came to me through the post-office with such evident marks of inspection that it would be imprudent to use it hereafter.

Notwithstanding all our difficulties here, I think we should continue to oppose obstacles by perseverance and patience, and my recall should rather be the result of cool policy than of resentment. I am somewhat inclined to think that it may become politic to suspend it on the reply of the Court to a demand of a categorical answer. Unless the Minister's system should change (for they still give me hopes), it might perhaps also be proper for me to consult with Dr. Franklin and Mr. Adams on the subject, and send Congress the result. For this purpose I submit to Congress the propriety of giving me permission to go to France or Holland.

Advantages are certainly to be derived from preserving the appearance of being well here; and such is the general opinion at present. But I am still much inclined to think it advisable to push this Court by a demand of a categorical answer. I doubt their venturing to break with us. The French Ambassador thinks it would be rash, and opposes it. Hence principally arises my suspense.

I have the honour to be, etc.

JOHN JAY.

JAY TO ROBERT R. LIVINGSTON.

MADRID, Feb. 16, 1782.

DEAR SIR:

No letters by the Marquis de Lafayette have as yet reached me. I had the honour of writing to you on the 6th and 13th instant.

We were yesterday informed, and so the fact is, that the Castle of St. Philip surrendered by capitulation to the Duc de Crillon, on the 4th instant. There was no breach made, nor any of the outworks taken.

The garrison are to go to England and remain prisoners of war till exchanged.

I am to go to the Pardo this evening. There I shall learn some further details from the Minister. If I return sufficiently early for the post, they shall be subjoined.

Things look better just at present, but my sky has hitherto been so like an April one that I dare not as yet flatter you or myself with settled fair weather.

I am, dear sir,

With great esteem and regard, etc.,

JOHN JAY.

JAY TO HIS FATHER.

MADRID, 21st February, 1782.

DEAR SIR:

My last letter from Fady was dated in November last. Mr. Benson has been so kind as to give me the most particular and satisfactory accounts of the family which I have received since I have been in Spain. I am glad that you are near neighbours, for I am persuaded that you will find him disposed to do every thing in his power to manifest the regard which he entertains for us all. He informs me that you intended to keep Peter with you during the winter. I am happy that he affords you satisfaction, and that nothing in my power might be wanting to promote it. I have written to Fady and to Mr. Benson that Peter must not leave you.

I have now the pleasure of informing you that Sally was last evening safely delivered of a daughter, whom we mean to call Mary. They are both remarkably well, and Sally desires me to assure you of her very affectionate regard. Be pleased to remember me to all my brothers and sisters. Peter Munro is perfectly well. A limner is now employed in taking his picture in miniature, which I shall send you by the first good opportunity. Your affection for every branch of your family demands this mark of attention from me, and be assured that one of my first wishes has been to have more frequent and better opportunities of evincing the gratitude and affectionate regard with which I am, dear sir,

Your very dutiful son,

JOHN JAY.[1]

JAY TO GOVERNOR CLINTON.

MADRID, 23d Feb., 1782.

DEAR SIR:

My last to you was written on the 16th November, since which I have not had the pleasure of hearing from you.

I congratulate you on the successful issue of the last campaign, to the brilliancy of which the late surrender of Fort St. Philip, at Mahon, has much contributed.

Your hemisphere brightens fast, and there is reason to hope another vigorous campaign will be followed by halcyon days.

---

[1] Jay's father lived but a short time after this date, his death occurring April 17, 1782. See letter from Frederick Jay, April 20th.

Mr. Benson writes me that your judges are industriously serving their country, but that their country had not, as yet, made an adequate provision for them. This is bad policy, and poverty cannot excuse it. The bench is at present well filled ; but it should be remembered, that although we are told that Justice should be blind, yet there are no proverbs which declare that she ought also to be hungry. Assure these gentlemen of my esteem, and believe me to be, dear sir, with sincere attachment,

Your friend and servant,

JOHN JAY.

JOHN ADAMS TO JAY.

AMSTERDAM, Feby. 28th, 1782.

SIR :

I have the pleasure to inform you that Friesland has taken the provincial resolution to acknowledge the Sovereignty of the United States of America, and to admit their Minister to an audience, and have instructed their deputies in the Assembly of their High Mightinesses at the Hague to make the motion in eight days from this.

The States of Holland have also taken my last requisition and transmitted it to the several cities, and to-morrow it is to be taken into consideration in the regency of Amsterdam. Dort has made a motion in the States of Holland to acknowledge American independence and admit me to an audience. Their High Mightinesses have encouraging news from Petersburg and from the East and West Indies ; so that at present there are appearances that our affairs will go well here and come to a speedy treaty. If anything should delay it, it will be the example of Spain ; but I don't believe that will a great while. One thing is past a doubt ; if Spain should now make a treaty with you, this republic would immediately follow the example, which, if anything can, would accelerate the negotiations for peace.

By the 10th article of the treaty of alliance between France and America the parties agree to invite in concert other powers to make common cause and accede. Permit me to suggest an idea. Suppose you write to the French ambassador at Madrid and request him to join you in an invitation to the King of Spain.

Excuse this freedom ; you will judge whether it will do.

I should be exceedingly obliged to you for the earliest intelligence, whether there is any prospect with you or not.

With great esteem and respect, I have the honor to be, Sir,

> Your most obedient and humble servant,
>
> J. ADAMS.

JAY TO FLORIDA BLANCA.

SIR : MADRID, 2 March, 1782.

. . . .

It is with great pain that I hear his Majesty is displeased with the silence of Congress respecting the return on their part to the friendship of Spain, and particularly in not having offered to comply with the propositions made by your Excellency, relative to the ships building in New England.

Permit me to observe to your Excellency that the long and constant expectation of Mr. Gardoqui's arrival in America, with full powers on this subject, naturally induced Congress to postpone coming to any resolutions on them until they would have the pleasure of seeing him. They were well apprised of my ignorance respecting such matters, and therefore could not with any propriety refer to my discretion the entering into any engagements on subjects with which I was totally unacquainted.

I am authorized to assure your Excellency of the readiness of Congress to make every return in their power to the kindness of his Majesty, and there is reason to hope that by the end of the next campaign their abilities may be more proportionate to their wishes than they have hitherto been.

Your Excellency will be pleased to recollect that the propositions of Congress respecting the Mississippi evince a strong desire to oblige his Majesty, and that reason has been given me to hope that their compliance in that instance would be followed by new proofs of his Majesty's good disposition toward us.

I must candidly confess to your Excellency that I now find myself entirely without resources. The Ambassador of France can afford me no assistance, and my only remaining hope arises from reliance in his Majesty's friendship and magnanimity, which your Excellency has so often encouraged me to entertain and confide in.

I have the honour to be, with great respect and consideration, your Excellency's most obedient and most humble servant, JOHN JAY.

JAY TO DR. JOHN BARD.[1]

DEAR SIR :   MADRID, 8 March, 1782.

It was not until the 8th of January that your favour of the 3d of July last reached me. In whatever coun-

---

[1] A noted physician in New York City, both before and after the Revolution.

try or concerns I may find myself employed, I assure you the recollection of former friends and former social hours will always be among the most favourite of my pleasures.

The want of proper information, and the difficulty of obtaining it on such subjects here, led me into a mistake respecting the Algarroba seed I sent you. It seems there are two kinds of it, the one produced by a tree such as I described, and which I have since been told will not bear much fruit; the other is a kind of vetch. I intended to send you the first, but the names being alike, they gave me the last, which, however, is much esteemed here for hogs and poultry, and indeed generally preferred for poultry to other grain. I enclose you some Spanish onion seed, because I have never seen any in our country of more than half the size of many that are daily to be met with in this market. The soil or climate may perhaps occasion this difference, as well as the constant care the Spanish take to water their gardens, which indeed is absolutely necessary, on account of the long droughts that are common in this country. There were six months in the year 1780 in which Madrid did not receive, in the whole, six hours' rain. They have a very simple machine worked by a horse for drawing water from wells dug in the highest part of their garden; it flows into reservoirs, made for the purpose, and is thence led at the pleasure of the gardener.

They have a kind of winter melon here that is most excellent; they are brought to market every day from fall to spring. We have great plenty at present; they preserve them I am told by hanging them up single with bark strings in rooms; but this will not probably succeed so well with you, where there are few rooms without constant fire but what are visited by frost. We have no opportunity of trying here what effect hard frost would have upon them. I nevertheless take this opportunity of sending you some of the seed. Let Mr. Johnson have a share, and assure him of my respect and esteem.

I thank you for mentioning my father's health. I hear so seldom of or from him that the information you gave me was particularly interesting. Mrs. Jay, (who has a little daughter) joins me in desiring our compliments to Mrs. Bard and your good family.

I am, dear sir, with sincere regard,

Your most obedient servant,

JOHN JAY.

P. S.—I don't remember to have seen yellow pinks in America. I have sent for some of the seed; if the messenger returns with any it shall be enclosed. As the seeds I send are from the King's garden, and well paid for, I presume they will prove genuine.

I shall continue sending you such new things of this kind as I may meet with. I am sure that if, on experiment, they should agree with our climate, you will be as much pleased to see them in the gardens of others as in your own. You have my best wishes that your happiness may always be proportionate to your benevolence. I think you would then have as much as man has a right to expect in this world. Adieu.

JAY TO JOHN ADAMS.

MADRID, 18th March, 1782.

SIR :

I had the pleasure of receiving your favour of the 28th ult. a few days ago.

I congratulate you sincerely on the action of Friesland, and the flattering prospect there is that the example of that province will be followed by that of Holland and the others. It would give me great satisfaction to be able to transmit you intelligence equally agreeable, but that is not the case. Prudence forbids me to explain myself, for though I am not even now without hopes, yet I dare not predict when the delays of this Court will terminate.

I thank you for the hint respecting the tenth article. That matter has heretofore been attended to and pressed. I could mention some singular circumstances respecting it, but they must not be committed to the post-office.

The protest of my bills for want of payment will afford you some meditation, and I am persuaded that your discernment will save me the necessity of being particular. That affair and others connected with it have so engaged me that I must take another opportunity of writing more fully to you.

With great esteem and regard,

I am, sir, yours, etc.,

JOHN JAY

JAY TO JOHN ADAMS.

SIR :   MADRID, 15th April, 1782.

Many weeks have elapsed since I received a letter from our country ; but a packet of newspapers, which I think must have been sent from the office of the Secretary for Foreign Affairs, was brought to me by the last post from Bilboa. They contain nothing very interesting. There is a paragraph in one of them, under the Boston head, which mentions the safe arrival of the *Cicero*, Captain Hill, and among other passengers who came in her I find your son is particularly named. As you might not have had any advices of this circumstance, I take this first opportunity of communicating it, and sincerely congratulate you on the occasion.

We hear that affairs with you are very promising, and that the Dutch are on the point of acknowledging our independence. Things here begin to look a little better, but as yet I dare not flatter myself nor you.

ROBERT R. LIVINGSTON TO JAY.[1]

DEAR SIR :   PHILADELPHIA, 16th April, 1782.

Returning from an excursion to the State of New York, I found your letter of October [3rd] which on account of my absence had been committed to a Committee of Congress.

[1] Mr. Sparks' omission of this letter from the Livingston-Jay series in the "Diplomatic Correspondence" was due to the loss of the key to the cipher in which it was written. See vol. viii., p. 14, note, of that work. The Jay Papers fortunately contain Jay's own deciphered copy of the letter as given above. It may be read in connection with Jay's "Propositions" to Spain, which appear in his report to Congress of Oct. 3, 1781, *ante*, pp. 124-26.

They have shown me their report; it will try their sentiments on a very interesting point if it goes thro', but as they
may not suddenly come to a Resolution, and as I have just
heard that a vessel will sail in two hours for Cadiz, I avail myself of it to inform you that your conduct thro' the whole of
your negotiation has been particularly acceptable to Congress.

The condition you have annexed to the proposed cession
is very well calculated to hasten the Spanish Minister [sev-
eral words unintelligible] as we shall have the means of
enforcing it, too valuable to be relinquished. Spain may
flatter herself with the hopes of gaining that at a general
peace by the favor of the mediators which she is unwilling
to purchase of us by the smallest concession. In this, however, I conceive she will find when too late that she has
been led by a partial regard to trifling interests to sacrifice
those of a more extensive and important nature. Spain can
have no claims to the Mississippi but what are derived from
Conquest. Our claims are valid. Those of Great Britain
are at least specious. Both will be opposed to her's at a
general peace, and as she has made the cession of Gibraltar
a preliminary to a peace she can hardly expect that the
mediators, if they gratify her in that, will add other countries to which she has no claim—more particularly as the
right of Britain, next to ours, is incontestably the best that
can be set up; so that there is little doubt that if the negotiation should open when the success of our affairs gives us
importance in the eyes of the mediators they will recognize
our right. If, on the other hand, we should meet with any
reverse of fortune, the claims of Britain will become more
respectable thereby, and the weak claims which Spain may
set up from the conquest of a few inconsiderable posts in a
country of such immense extent, already in part conquered
by us, only serve as arguments of unbounded ambition
without establishing a right.

Sound policy then certainly dictates as a sure means of
attaining this great [advantage] such a vigorous prosecution

of the war as will reduce Great Britain to the necessity of making the mortifying cession which Spain requires, and give more validity to the rights with which we are willing on certain conditions to invest her. Pecuniary aids afforded to us will be the most effectual means of destroying the common enemy and reducing them to accept such terms as Spain may choose to dictate, while the purchase of our rights will enable her to support them with dignity and enable her even to appear at the Congress as a Sovereign power which has supported a distressed ally without availing herself of that distress to deprive her of any rights which she has not paid them an equivalent for. *America considers her independence as placed beyond all doubt.* She begins now to look forward to more important objects. She knows the value of the country which is washed by the Mississippi ; it is also well known to the nations of Europe. By the cession of her right to it she is satisfied that she can procure important advantages in commerce from any of the maritime powers in Europe. Some of the northern potentates, who have means of giving validity to our claims, would consider an establishment, under the restrictions with which we have offered it to Spain, as cheaply purchased by an alliance with us, and a much greater advance of money than we have yet thought of asking from Spain, if our present wants should make it expedient to pursue this idea. Spain has not laid such obligations upon us, notwithstanding our respectful and patient attention to her, as to render us chargeable with the slightest degree of ingratitude in so doing.

You will, therefore, persist in the line in which you now are, declaring explicitly that the cessions you propose are only dictated by your desire to make early and vigorous efforts against the common enemy ; that if they are not accepted so soon and upon such terms as to afford you a prospect of obtaining this desirable end, you will not consider your offer as binding upon you. I am persuaded that in this I speak the sentiments of Congress, and you may deliver them as such.

Your never having spoken of the answer of France, Spain and Great Britain to the proposals of the mediators make me doubt whether you have seen them; that of Spain I have not seen. If I can get the others copied and cyphered before this vessel sails, I will send them to you; if not, I will enclose so much of the answer of France as relates to Spain. I see a use that may be made of it.

No incidents since my last have turned up worth communicating; the enemy are drawing lines across New York Island at Mr. Elliot's, and making every preparation for defence. The Eastern and Northern States and some of the Southern States are using the most vigorous exertions to obtain a respectable force for the opening Campaign. France has lent us six millions of livres for this year. —— of Dollars from Spain is all that is necessary to enable us to make the most spirited exertions. Our army is at present well clad and well fed and as well disciplined as any in the world. The force at West Point by the 20th of May will amount to about ten thousand men and will gradually be increased till September, as the recruits can be collected; so that our operating force there, including the French troops, will amount by the beginning of June to about fifteen or sixteen thousand men exclusive of militia, which may be called in if necessary. I mention this because I know great misrepresentations have gone abroad on this subject.

I have just received a letter from Mr. Carmichael which I shall answer if possible by this conveyance. Be pleased to present my compliments to him and the rest of your family.

I am, Dear Sir, with great esteem and regard, your most obedient humble servant,

ROB. R. LIVINGSTON.

FREDERICK JAY TO JAY.

POUGHKEEPSIE, 20th April, 1782.

DEAR SIR:

My last to you, of the 3d ult., was short and contained very little more than giving you an account of Papa's illness and that he was past recovery.

It gives me pain to inform you that it pleased God to take him from us on the morning of the 17th inst., and was yesterday intered in the vault of Gysbert Schenck, Esqr., at Fish Kill. It is very remarkable that he expired on the same day and month and the very hour that our poor mother did. To give you an account of his illness would only add to your Grief; his greatest complaint was frequent and violent pains in his breast, and ye last attack proved fatal.

Poor Nancy and Peter are much distressed—Nancy especially, but nothing to make them easy and comfortable shall be wanting on my part. I will not forsake them; in a word, ever since and long before our robbery I have had the burthen of the family upon me, and the weight has been almost too heavy for me to bear. However I am determined to do all I can, and shall be happy if what I have done and will still do will be satisfactory. Your not hearing as often from me as you had reason to expect or I would wish, must in a great measure be attributed to the great charge I had upon me, and being under the necessity of attending Papa every other night during his Illness, which commenced early in December, really affected both my body and mind to such a Degree as rendered me almost incapable of doing any thing.[1]

---

[1] In a letter to his brother Frederick, dated Feb. 13, 1782, Jay wrote: " Mr. Benson informs me that the family are now at Poughkeepsie and that my father has resigned the management of it to you. I am pleased with this circumstance, especially as it will now be in your power to make the remainder of his days free from care and consequently as easy and agreeable as age and infirmi-

Sir James left us in the beginning of Feby., and went to Elizabethtown to sollicit some of his Friends in N. Y. to lend him money, and was to have returned in three weeks. He remained in Jersey untill the 15th inst. when a Party of the enemy took him out of his bed at Arent Schuyler's and carried him to N. Y. where he is now confined in Provost. Such another man surely was never born. . . .

Your son [Peter] is still with me, but will in a few days return to Jersey with his Aunt Susan. It gives me pleasure to inform you that he has greatly improved, and if he could speak plain would read as well as any boy of his age ever did. I am sorry you have not given some person direction about his Education; this I hinted to you in my former letters; it will not be to his advantage to remain long at Elizabethtown.

The only articles we have received from you are thirty bushells salt, one bale coarse cloth with Linings, a bale of blankets and some Oznabrigs in all of which you have been greatly imposed upon—the cloth not much superior to brown paper, the Oznabrigs rotten, and the blankets only fit for cradles. I shall write you again shortly. Peter, Nancy and Mrs. Jay join me in assuring you and Sally of our affection and that I am

Yours,

FRED: JAY.

Inform Peter Monro that his mother is very well. Mr. Benson has informed me that you have given him directions about Peter. I am glad of it and will assist him all in my power. Mr. Benson is now in Albany.

F. J.

---

ties will permit. It gives me pleasure to reflect that it is also in your inclination as well as power to be a father to this distressed family, and that Mrs. Jay has now an opportunity of acquiring the reputation of a domestic matron as well as an agreeable woman."

BENJAMIN FRANKLIN TO JAY.

PASSY, April 22nd, 1782.

DEAR SIR :

I have undertaken to pay all the bills of your acceptance that have come to my knowledge, and I hope in God no more will be drawn upon us, but when funds are first provided. In that case your constant residence at Madrid is no longer so necessary. You may make a journey either for health or pleasure, without retarding the progress of a negociation not yet begun. Here you are greatly wanted, for messengers begin to come and go, and there is much talk of a treaty proposed, but I can neither make, nor agree to propositions of peace, without the assistance of my colleagues. Mr. Adams, I am afraid, cannot just now leave Holland. Mr. Jefferson is not in Europe, and Mr. Laurens is a prisoner, though abroad upon parol. I wish, therefore, that you would resolve upon the journey, and render yourself here as soon as possible. You would be of infinite service. Spain has taken four years to consider whether she should treat with us or not. Give her forty, and let us in the meantime mind our own business. I have much to communicate to you, but choose rather to do it *viva voce*, than trust it to letters.

I am ever, my dear friend,
Yours most affectionately,
BENJAMIN FRANKLIN.

BENJAMIN FRANKLIN TO JAY.

VERSAILLES, April 23, 1782.

DEAR SIR :

I wrote a few lines to you from Passy to go by the Post of this day, pressing you to come hither as soon as possible. I have just mentioned it to M. de Vergennes, who is of opinion it will be proper to leave Mr. Carmichael there, that it may not seem as if we abandoned that court.   As I understand a courier is just setting out from hence for Madrid, I add this line to inform you of this particular, having great regard to the judgment of this Minister.   Let me know by a previous line if you conclude to come, and if, as I hope, Mrs. Jay will accompany you, that I may provide for you proper lodgings.

I am with great and sincere esteem,
Dear Sir, your most obedient and
most humble servant,
B. FRANKLIN.

BENJAMIN FRANKLIN TO JAY.

PASSY, April 24th, 1782.

DEAR SIR :

The Prince de Massaran being so good as to desire carrying a letter to you, I sit down to write you a few lines, though I hope soon to see you.

Enclosed I send a copy of one of Mr. Deane's letters ; I shall show you more when you come.

In consequence of a proposition I sent over, the parliament of Britain have just passed an act for exchanging American prisoners.   They have near 1100 in the jails of England and Ireland, all committed as charged with high treason.   The act is to empower the king, notwithstanding such commitments, to consider them as prisoners of war, according to the law of nations, and exchange them as such. This seems to be giving up their pretensions of considering us as rebellious subjects, and is a kind of acknowledgment of our independence.   Transports are now taking up to carry back to their country the poor, brave fellows, who have borne for years their cruel captivity, rather than serve our enemies, and an equal number of English are to be delivered in return. I have, upon desire, furnished passports for the vessels.

Our affairs in Holland are *en bon train ;* we have some prospect of another loan there ; and all goes well here.

The proposal to us of a separate peace with England, has been rejected in the manner you wish, and I am pretty certain they will now enter into a general treaty. I wrote you a few lines by last post, and on the same day a few more by the court courier. They were chiefly to press your coming hither to assist in the affair.

With great and sincere esteem,

I am ever, dear sir,

Your most obedient and most humble servant,

BENJAMIN FRANKLIN.

JAY TO ROBERT MORRIS.

MADRID, 25th April 1782.

DEAR SIR :

Some of my letters to you have, I find, miscarried by the capture of the vessels that were carrying them ; and there is reason to suspect that two others were stopped here, as the letters enclosing them did not reach the persons at the seaports to whom they were directed.

I have heretofore mentioned the receipt of the picture you were so kind as to send me by Mr. Ridley, and the arrival of your sons. I don't know the fate of that letter, and that uncertainty induces me to repeat my thanks for the one, and my congratulations on the other. The estimation in which I hold your friendship, and the marks I have received of it, interest me in every thing which concerns you and yours, and be assured that no opportunity of giving higher proofs of it shall be omitted.

Mrs. Jay's time is much employed in nursing and amusing herself with her little girl. She is writing to Mrs. Morris. We are cheerful, and not unhappy, though distant from our friends, and deprived of the pleasures which result from that free and unreserved conversation which can only be indulged in the company of safe companions, or in a country like ours.

We remove next week to Aranjuez, where I expect again to spend some agreeable weeks. It is a charming place, containing a tract of several miles in circumference, and divided into gardens, meadows, parks, cultivated grounds, and wilds, full of fine trees, fine roads, and fine walks, and watered by a slow winding river, which, if more clear, would be very beautiful. But still, my friend, it is not America. A genius of a different character from that which presides at your hills and gardens reigns over these. Soldiers, with fixed bayonets, present themselves at various stations in these peaceful retreats; and though none but inoffensive citizens are near, yet horsemen with drawn swords, guarding one or other of the royal family in their little excursions to take the air daily, renew and impress ideas of subjection. Power unlimited, and distrust misplaced, thus exacting homage and imposing awe, occasion uneasy reflections, and alloy the pleasing sensations which nature, smiling in such delightful scenes, never fails to excite. Were I a Spaniard, these decorated seats would appear to me like the temporary enchantments of some despotic magician, who, by re-extending his wand, could at pleasure command them to vanish, and be succeeded by galleys and prisons.

Nothing is more true, than that all things figure by comparison. This elegant seat being surrounded by exclusive wastes, appears like a blessed and fortunate island in a dreary ocean. The contrast heightens its charms, and every traveller arrives with a mind predisposed to admire and enjoy them ; but as the first impression wears away, and he begins to recollect the more happy though less magnificent abodes in his own country, the attractions and allurements of this insensibly diminish. I have more than once experienced this, and though not difficult to please or be contented, yet I confess that I find little here that resembles, and nothing that can compensate for, the free air, the free conversation, the equal liberty, and the other numerous blessings which God and nature, and laws of our making, have given and secured to our happier country. I would not be understood to insinuate that good society and agreeable companions are wanting here. They may, perhaps, abound more in some other parts of the world, but they are also to be found here, though an unsocial kind of policy requires unceasing attention to the most austere rules of caution and prudence. The little that I have seen and observed of this people induces me to think that (except the generality of those who compose the highest and lowest orders) they possess many qualities which are praiseworthy ; and that two or three

long and wise reigns would make them a very powerful and an amiable nation.   But as I have not had
sufficient opportunities of mixing with, and personally
knowing many of them, time and further information
may either confirm or alter this opinion.   The evident
suspense and indecision of the court respecting us
has kept many at a distance, with whom I should
otherwise have been on a very familiar footing, and
some of them have been so candid as to tell me so.
This is a kind of prudence which naturally grows out
of a jealous and absolute government, under which
the people have, for many generations, been habitu-
ated to that kind of dependence, which constrains
every class to watch and respect the opinions and
inclinations of their superiors in power.   The prosperous tide of our affairs, however, has for some time
past run so strong, that I think many of our obstacles
here must soon give way.   Shyness will then cease,
and I shall not afterward find it difficult to be received
into more of their houses, and that in the only manner I ever wish to be received into any—I mean, at the
front door, by direct invitation from the masters of
them, and without the precursory good offices of
upper servants and unimportant favourites, whom I
never can submit to court.   Until this period arrives,
I shall continue to cultivate the few acquaintances I
have, and without giving offence to any, endeavour
to increase their number, whenever it may be done
with propriety and to advantage ; but I shall, as heretofore, avoid embarrassing and intruding upon those
who, in the meantime, may think it necessary to be

the King to renew the invitation, not in *general* terms, but in terms expressly declaring that it was given to me as a private gentleman, and was so to be accepted, with the additional favor, nevertheless, of being permitted to bring Mr. Carmichael with me.

The only objection which opposes my accepting it arises from the question, viz., whether a Minister or representative of an independent sovereign can with propriety accept any invitation which, *in the terms of it*, impeaches his title to that character. So far as this question respects the Ministers of independent states and kingdoms in general, your Excellency will agree with me in opinion that it must be answered in the *negative*.

The next inquiry which presents itself is whether the United States of America come so far under that description as to render this reasoning applicable to their Ministers. Every American thinks they do. Whatever doubts this or other Courts may entertain relative to their independence, the United States entertain none, and therefore their servants ought not by word or actions to admit any. For instance, ought General Washington to accept an invitation which *expressly* imposed upon him the condition of laying aside his uniform and appearing at table in the dress of a private gentleman ? I think not !

If this reasoning is just, the impropriety of my accepting this invitation becomes manifest, and all arguments from the expediency of it must cease to operate. For my part I consider it, as a general rule, that although particular circumstances may sometimes render it expedient for a nation to make great sacrifices to the attainment of national objects, yet it can in no case be expedient for them to impair their honour, their dignity, or their independence. As to the temporary advantages which might result from my accepting this invitation, I find them balanced by at least equal disadvantages. There can be no doubt, on the one hand, that my frequenting the Count de Florida Blanca's table on the days appointed for entertaining the Foreign Ministers would impress a general opinion that Spain was about to become our ally; and I readily admit that such an opinion might operate to our advantage in other countries. But, on the other hand, when the Count de Florida Blanca, in order (though perhaps in vain) to save appearances, shall inform those Ministers that I was *expressly* invited as a private gentleman, and had consented to come in that character, they would naturally entertain ideas which would tend to diminish rather than increase their respect for America and American Legations.

It would give me pain if the Count de Florida Blanca should suppose me to be in the least influenced by the promising aspect of our affairs. I flatter myself he will not incline to that opinion when he reflects on the particular circumstances under which the United States declared themselves independent, and under which they afterwards refused to treat with their then victorious enemies on any terms inconsistent with it. Although offence and disrespect are very far from my thoughts, I fear the Count will be a little hurt at my declining the invitation in question. I am persuaded that he meant to do me a favour, and I feel myself indebted for his friendly intentions. But as the considerations mentioned in this letter forbid me to accept it, I wish to communicate that circumstance to him in the most soft and delicate manner, and therefore request the favour of your Excellency to undertake it.

I have the honour to be, with great esteem and respect, your Excellency's

Most obedient and very humble servant,

JOHN JAY.

ROBERT R. LIVINGSTON TO JAY.

PHILADELPHIA, April 27th, 1782.

DEAR SIR:

I informed you in my letter of the 16th instant,[1] that yours of the 3d of October had been received and submitted to Congress in my absence, and, as I had then reason to think, that it would be answered by them. This I wished because I was persuaded it would express their approbation of your conduct, and afford you that intimate knowledge of their sentiments, which the delicacy of your situation renders particularly important. They have, however, judged it proper to refer the letter to me. I shall endeavor to preserve the advantages I have mentioned to you, by reporting this answer.

Acquainted with the expectations of Congress, and the grounds on which they formed them, you will easily believe, that they are equally surprised and concerned at the little attention hitherto shown by Spain to their respectful solicitations. They had learned from every quarter that

---

[1] See note to Livingston's letter of that date, *ante.*

his Catholic Majesty, among the princely virtues he possesses, was particularly distinguished for his candor, and
that open dignity of character, which is the result of having
no views that he found any reluctance in disclosing ; and
that the Ministers in whom he confided, breathing the spirit
of the Prince, were above those artifices, which form the
politics of inferior powers.   They knew the insults which
Spain had received from Great Britain, and they could conceive no reason why she should conceal or refuse to return
them by supporting openly the people, whom Britain un-
justly endeavored to oppress.   These principles, confirmed
by the frequent recommendations of those whom they
believed to be acquainted with the sentiment of the Court
of Madrid, induced them to send a Minister to solicit the
favorable attention of his Catholic Majesty to a people who
were struggling with oppression, and whose success or miscarriage could not but be important to a sovereign, who
held extensive dominions in their vicinity.   Give me leave
to add, Sir, that in the choice of the person, they were not
inattentive to the dignity of the Court ; or to the candor
and integrity by which they were supposed to be influenced.
I would not have you infer from what I have said, that the
favorable sentiments, which the United States have hitherto
entertained of the Court of Madrid, have undergone the
least alteration.   They are satisfied that nothing would be
more injurious to both nations, than to permit the seeds of
distrust or jealousy to be sown among them.

But though those who are well informed feel no abatement of respect or esteem for the virtue and magnanimity
of his Majesty, and do full justice to the integrity and abilities of his Ministers, accepting the apolgies you mention,
and attributing to their true causes the delays and neglects
you have unhappily experienced, yet they are in the utmost
pain, lest they should work some change in the sentiments
of the people at large, in whom with us the sovereignty

resides, and from thence diffuse themselves into the government, and be productive of measures ruinous to that friendly intercourse, that spirit of amity, which it is the wish of those who are acquainted with the true interests of both countries to promote.

After the war was declared by Spain, those among us who had formed the highest ideas of her magnanimity, persuaded themselves that she would act advisedly for us when she found us in distress. They grounded their belief upon the avowed spirit of the nation, and the policy of adopting measures to re-animate us and damp the ardor of the enemy, and to make such impressions upon our hearts, as to give them in future a considerable influence on our councils. Our disappointment in this expectation, though perhaps to be accounted for upon very natural principles, has been greatly aggravated by the sedulous endeavors of the enemies of both countries to create distrust and jealousies. They artfully insinuate, that Spain seeks only to draw advantages from our wants, without so far interfering in our affairs as to involve herself, if we should be unsuccessful. These insinuations are gaining ground, and it becomes daily more necessary for Congress to be furnished with reasons to justify to their constituents the concessions they have proposed to make, or to withdraw those concessions when they are found ineffectual. Yet they find much reluctance in discovering the least want of confidence in the Court of Madrid; and though their present situation might fully justify them in not parting with the important rights you are empowered to concede, without stipulating some very valuable equivalent, yet they cannot be induced to make any alteration in your instructions on this subject, till you shall have reason to conclude, that nothing can be done towards forming the alliance they have so much at heart; not only because of the influence it will immediately have in accelerating the peace, but because of the advantages, which Spain and

America may reciprocally promise each other in future, from the lasting connexion which will be erected thereon.

Though the delays you have met with afford room to suspect, that Spain wishes to defer a particular treaty with us till a general peace, yet I see so many political reasons against such a measure, that I can hardly presume they will adopt it.

At the close of a successful war, a great and powerful nation, to whom a character for justice and moderation is of the last importance, can in no case demand more than a compensation for the injuries received. This compensation will, indeed, be measured in part by their success. But still it has bounds, beyond which a nation cannot go with dignity. Spain has insisted upon the cession of Gibraltar as a preliminary to a peace. This is, of itself, a considerable compensation for any damage she may have sustained. Should she carry her demands further, and agreeably to the ideas of the Spanish Ministers, expect to have any exclusive right to the Gulf of Mexico, and the river Mississippi, she must not only demand East and West Florida of the British, but she must support the claims of Great Britain against those of America, the claims of an enemy against the rights of a friend, in order that she may make still further demands.

Will it consist with the dignity of his Catholic Majesty to ask, for the short space in which he has been engaged in the war, not only Gibraltar, but the two Floridas, the Mississippi, the exclusion of Great Britain from the trade to the Bay of Honduras; while the other branch of the House of Bourbon, who engaged early in the controversy, confines her demands to the narrowest limits? Will he expose himself to the imputation of despoiling an ally, (for such we are in fact, though we want the name) at the instant that he is obtaining the greatest advantages from the distress, which that ally has, at least in part, contributed to bring upon his enemy? And this too, without the least necessity, when he may, by accepting and purchasing our title, appear to have contended for the rights of the United States. This will then make no part of the satisfaction to which he is entitled from Great Britain; he may justly extend his demands to other objects; or exalt his character for moderation, by limiting them to narrower bounds. This mode of reasoning will come with more weight, when we display our rights before impartial mediators, and show that recent conquests have been added to our ancient title, for it cannot be doubted, that we shall at the close of the war make the most of those rights, which we obtain no equivalent for, while it continues.

I persuade myself, therefore, that Spain will not risk the loss of so important an object as the exclusive navigation of the Mississippi, by postponing the treaty to a general peace, more particularly as a treaty with us will secure our concurrence in their views at a general Congress, as well as save them the necessity of making demands inconsistent with that character for moderation, which their great power renders important to them.

Congress flatter themselves, that the surmises on this subject are groundless, and that before this reaches you, the treaty will be far advanced. Should they be mistaken, you will take measures to know from Spain, whether she accepts your concession as the price of our alliance, and upon what terms. If they are such as you cannot close with, and the treaty must break off, be persuaded, that any steps you have taken or shall take, not inconsistent with the respect due to his Catholic Majesty, to prevent the cessions you are empowered to make from militating against our rights, will be approved by Congress.[1]

---

[1] This statement taken in connection with Livingston's remark in his letter of the 28th to the effect that Congress meant to clog Jay with as few instructions as possible, directs attention to certain resolutions touching the proposed

Congress presume you will find no difficulty in knowing the intentions of his Majesty on this subject, since they wish you to treat his Ministers with that unreserved confidence, which becomes the representative of a nation, which has no views that it does not avow, and which asks no favor which it does not hope to return, and, as in the present happy state of his Majesty's affairs, they can conceive no reason for disguising his designs, they are satisfied, that your frankness will meet from his Ministers with the confidence it merits.

I make no observations on the hint the Count de Florida Blanca gave you, with respect to the restitution of such sums as Spain might be pleased to advance to us : because,

cession of Mississippi rights to Spain. The instructions from Congress to Jay of October 4, 1780, emphasize the American claim to the free navigation of the river. By new instructions, February 15, 1781, Jay was authorized to recede from that claim if Spain "unalterably insisted" upon it. This change of base is fully explained by Madison in his letter to the editor of Niles' *Register*, dated January 8, 1822 (*Madison Papers*, vol. i., App. xix.), in which the delegates from Georgia and South Carolina are represented to have become alarmed at the progress of the enemy in the South and the contingency that a peace might be sprung upon Congress on the basis of *uti possidetis*, and to have proposed, as a necessity of the situation, to tempt Spain to an immediate alliance with America, by offering her the exclusive navigation of the Mississippi below the thirty-first degree of latitude. The State which would be especially concerned with such a proposal was Virginia with her immense western territory. Her two delegates in Congress, Madison and Bland, disagreed as to the propriety of the cession, and they jointly deferred to their State Legislature for instructions in the case. That body, showing neither haste nor alarm in its action, considered the matter in connection with the cession of its own northwestern lands to Congress and disposed of it in the same resolutions, as follows, passed January 2, 1781 :

"Virginia having thus, for the sake of the general good, proposed to cede a great extent of valuable territory to the Continent, it is expected in return, that every other State in the Union, under similar circumstances as to vacant territory, will make similar cession of the same to the United States for the general emolument.

"*Resolved*, That the navigation of the River Mississippi ought to be claimed by Virginia only as co-extensive with our territory, and that our delegates in Congress be instructed to procure for the other States in the Union the free whatever claims we might set up to a subsidy from the share we take in the burthen of the war, and the utility of our exertions in the common cause, we are far from wishing to lay ourselves under any pecuniary obligations for a longer time than is absolutely necessary. A few years of peace will enable us to repay with interest any sums, which our present necessities compel us to borrow.

I cannot close this letter without expressing the grateful sense, that Congress entertain of the disinterested conduct of Spain, in rejecting the proffers of Great Britain, which must undoubtedly have been considerable, if they bore that proportion to the importance of his Catholic Majesty in the great system of politics, which those that have been fre-

---

navigation of that river as extensively as the territorial possessions of the said States reach respectively. And that every further or other demand of the said navigation be ceded, if insisting on the same is deemed an impediment to a treaty with Spain.

" *Provided*, That the said delegates use their endeavors to obtain, on behalf of this State, or others States having territory on said river, a free port or ports below the territory of such States respectively."

On the strength of this action, Bland of Virginia moved the alteration in Jay's instructions as adopted by Congress on February 15, 1781. Madison proceeds to state that " the instant the menacing crisis was over " Virginia revoked her instructions and " Congress seized the first moment, also, for revoking theirs to Jay." A misleading impression, however, is conveyed here, for Congress made no definitive revocation of its instructions to Jay respecting the Mississippi until a year and a half later, and then not because the situation had ceased to be menacing, but because of Spain's conspicuously dilatory course and unfriendly attitude to American interests. Jay's report of October, 1781, thoroughly impressed Congress with this, and gave Madison the opportunity to offer the following resolution, adopted April 30, 1782 :

" *Resolved*, That the Minister Plenipotentiary of the United States at the Court of Madrid be informed, that Congress entirely approve of his conduct as detailed in his letter of the 3d of October last ; that the limitation affixed by him to the proposed surrender of the navigation of the Mississippi in particular corresponds with the views of Congress ; that they observe, not without surprise and concern, that a proposition so liberal in itself, and which removed the only avowed obstacle to a connexion between the United States and his Catholick Majesty, should not have produced greater effects on the counsels of the latter ; that the surrender of the navigation of the Mississippi was meant as the price of the advantages promised by an early and intimate alliance with the Spanish quently thrown out to lead the United States to a violation of their engagements, have done to their comparatively small weight in the general scale. But as America never found the least inclination to close with the insidious proposals of Great Britain, so she finds no difficulty in believing, that the wisdom and magnanimity of his Catholic Majesty will effectually guard him against every attempt of his natural enemy, to detach him from those, who are daily shedding their blood to avenge his injuries in common with their own.

I have the honor to be, &c.

ROBERT R. LIVINGSTON.

monarchy ; and that if this alliance is to be procrastinated till the conclusion of the war, the reason of the sacrifice will no longer exist ; that as every day which the proposed treaty is delayed detracts from the obligation and inducement of the United States to adhere to their overture, it is the instruction of Congress that he urge upon the Ministers of his Catholick Majesty the obligation it imposes on Spain to make the treaty the more liberal on her part, and that in particular he use his endeavours to obtain, in consideration of such delay, either an enlargement of her pecuniary aids to the United States, a facilitating of the use of the Mississippi to the citizens thereof, or some peculiar indulgences in the commerce of the Spanish colonies in America."—*Secret Journals of Congress*, vol. iii., p. 98.

Jay's letter of April 28, 1782, following that of October 3d, convinced Congress that nothing could be expected from Spain, and that not only the offer of the cession to her of the navigation of the Mississippi, but all other proffers, should be withdrawn. Accordingly, on August 7, 1782, it was

"*Resolved*, That the American Minister at Madrid be instructed to forbear making any overtures to that Court or entering into any stipulations in consequence of overtures which he has made ; and in case any propositions be made to him by the said Court for a treaty with the United States, to decline acceding to the same until he shall have transmitted them to Congress for approbation."—*Thompson Papers*, N. Y. Historical Society Publications, 1878, p. 92.

By the time these instructions reached Jay he was absorbed with Franklin in the greater work of the final peace, when the negotiation with Spain had ceased to be of interest or material consequence. It is to be observed that, in adopting the course as outlined above, both Jay and Congress retired from the atmosphere of the Spanish Court with greater dignity and self-respect than would have been possible had that body changed its policy and professions with the changes in the military situation. The acceptance of the Mississippi cession had been left open to Spain full eight months after the Yorktown success.

ROBERT R. LIVINGSTON TO JAY.

PHILADELPHIA, April 28th, 1782.

DEAR SIR :

You will receive with this a letter dated yesterday. You will judge how far it may be expedient to ground demands on the right we have to a compensation for our share of the burden and expense of the war, if the issue should be as favorable as we have reason to expect. Our strength is so much underrated in Europe, that you will find it proper to represent it as it really is. Our regular army, including the French troops, will consist of about   men. They are well disciplined, clothed, and fed ; and having for the most part seen seven years' hard service, I believe they may be counted equal to any troops in the world. Our militia are in excellent order, and chiefly disciplined by officers who have left the regular service. While the army lies in the middle States, it can in ten or fifteen days receive a reinforcement of   men for any particular service. Facts, that you can easily call to mind, will evince that any deficiency in the regular troops is amply made up by this supply. These are loose hints by no means directory to you. Congress mean as little as possible to clog you with instructions. They rely upon your judgment and address to reconcile whatever differences may appear to be between the views of Spain, and the interests of these States.

I have the honor to enclose an important resolution, which I fear to put in cypher, both because you seem to be at a loss about your cypher, and because it would be of little use, considering the accident which you say has happened to it.

I have the honor to be, &c.

ROBERT R. LIVINGSTON.

JAY TO ROBERT R. LIVINGSTON.[1]

MADRID, April 28, 1782.

DEAR SIR:

My letter to his Excellency, the President of Congress, of the 3d of October last, of which a copy has also been since sent, contained a full and accurate account of their affairs here. Many minute and not very interesting details of little difficulties were omitted, and among others, those which arose from my having no funds for the bills payable in October and November, etc., etc. The experience I had gained of the disposition of this Court, and the delays which attend all their decisions and operations, induced me to consider my obtaining timely supplies from hence as very uncertain. I therefore wished to have an occasional credit from Dr. Franklin, to be made use of as necessity might require, and, for that purpose, wrote him the following letter on the 10th of September, viz. :

TO DR. BENJAMIN FRANKLIN.

ST. ILDEFONSO, September 10, 1781.

DEAR SIR:

My last to you was of the 20th day of August last, by Dupin, the French Ambassador's courier. Major Franks, with despatches from Congress, and from Mr. Robert Morris, is now with me, and will proceed to Passy as soon as I shall be enabled to write to him.

---

[1] This was Jay's fourth report on Spanish affairs. See note to his communication of October 3, 1781, p. 75.

He will bring you a copy of Mr. Morris' letter to me, from which you will see the present state of American finances, and the measures he is prosecuting to ameliorate them. My former letters mentioned my apprehensions, that many more bills had been drawn upon me, than those for which the sum you authorized me to draw upon you for would satisfy. Near seventy thousand dollars will be wanted to pay those which have since arrived, and although I cannot think it improbable that provision may here be made for at least a part of that sum, yet the delays which usually attend operations of this kind render it highly necessary that occasional resources be elsewhere had.

This consideration, so far as it applies to the payments to be made in the two succeeding months, obliges me again to recur to you.

The sanguine expectations entertained by our country from the appointment of Mr. Morris, his known abilities, integrity, and industry, the useful reformations he has begun, and the judicious measures he is pursuing abroad, as well as at home, afford reason to hope that, under his direction, American credit will be re-established, and the evils which have long threatened us on that head avoided.

It will be useless, therefore, to remark how important it is to prevent our credit from receiving a deep additional wound at the very moment when so much is doing to recover it. The protest of any of our public bills for want of payment would at this period be more injurious than heretofore, and unless again saved by you, that cruel necessity must take place with respect to those on me. Besides, as the singular policy of drawing bills without previous funds will now be relinquished, we have reason to flatter ourselves that we shall in future have no embarrassments of this kind to struggle with. I am well persuaded that Mr. Morris will not pursue such hazardous and unprecedented measures, and therefore, as in all human probability the present difficulties will be all that we shall have to surmount, I hope you will think with me, that the utmost exertions should be made for the purpose, and that after having done so much to save the credit of American bills you will still be disposed to do every thing in your power to put it out of danger.

When it will be in my power to replace the sums drawn from you, is hard to divine. All I can say or do is to assure you that nothing but want of ability shall delay or prevent it.

When I consider how much might have been saved had my bills on you been sold to those who would have taken them on the best terms, I cannot forbear thinking it would be advisable to give me only general authority to draw for such sums as I may want, not exceeding the one you may limit.

The sum wanted for October is twelve thousand five hundred and sixty-seven dollars, and for November three thousand and six hundred.

I particularize only the payments due in these two months, because before the first of December I hope my expectations from other quarters will at least be ascertained.

I am, dear sir, with great and sincere regard and esteem, your obliged and obedient servant,

JOHN JAY.

P. S.—The Marquis d'Aranda has received a letter from Mr. Grand, informing him that no more bills are to be drawn upon you by me without further order. I am a little at a loss to determine whether this restriction is intended to extend to the balance which remains of the twenty-five thousand dollars allotted for the payment of the bills at two months' sight, and for which I was only to draw as occasion might require.

Lest my having refused to accept some bills drawn upon me by Congress should give rise to reports prejudicial to their credit, I transmit herewith enclosed a state of that case. You will be pleased to make such use of it as circumstances may render necessary. I gave a copy of it to the gentleman who presented the bills, and desired that it might be recited at large in the protest.

J. J.

It was not till after several of the bills due in October had become payable that I received the Doctor's friendly answer of the 29th of September, in which he permited me to draw for the sum requested, so that had not M. Cabarrus, my banker, consented to make the necessary advances, I should have been extremely embarrassed, for, as I before apprehended, my reliance for immediate though small supplies from this Court would have proved delusive.

This credit from Dr. Franklin enabled me to see our bills duly paid for two months, and I had some faint hopes that before the month of December should arrive with further bills, the intention of this Court on the subject of supplies might be ascertained.

I will now proceed to resume the narrative of our affairs here from the date of my above-mentioned letter to the President, of the 3d of October last, confining myself to such matters as appear to me necessary to enable you to form a just and clear idea of my negotiations.

My letter of the 3d of October mentions my having been then lately promised that a person should be appointed to confer with me, as well on the subject of my propositions for a treaty as on that of my application for aids, and that his instructions should be completed before the Court should remove from St. Ildefonso to the Escurial, which was soon to take place.

This communication was made to me on the 27th of September, and, lest pretext for delay might arise from my absence, I determined to remain at St. Ildefonso until the Court should be on the point of leaving it.

On the 5th of October I found that no further progress in our affairs was to be made before the Court should be settled at the Escurial, to which they were then preparing to go. I therefore concluded to return to Madrid, and, with the approbation of the Ambassador of France, I wrote the following note to the Minister, viz. :

" Mr. Jay presents his compliments to his Excellency, the Count de Florida Blanca, and has the honour of informing him that he purposes to return to Madrid to-morrow, and will with pleasure attend his Excellency's orders at the Escurial as soon as it may be convenient to his Excellency to render his presence there necessary.

"St. Ildefonso, October 5, 1781."

To this I received the following answer:

[Translation.]

" The Count de Florida Blanca presents his compliments to Mr. Jay, and wishes him a pleasant journey. He will write to him as soon as he can say any thing positive on the subject of his last note.

"October 5, 1781."

Four days afterwards the Count sent me a complaint against Commodore Gillon, of the *South Carolina* frigate, then lying at Corunna, and I insert copies of the papers which passed between us on that occasion, not only because I ought to give an account of all interesting public transactions, but also that my conduct on this occasion may stand contrasted with that of the Minister on some other similar ones.

Recital of a Complaint Exhibited by the Count De Florida Blanca Against Commodore Gillon.

[Translation.]

"An American vessel of war has arrived at Corunna, having on board two soldiers, deserters from the Irish regiment of infantry. The commander of the Province having claimed them, the captain refuses to deliver them up on any pretext whatever, pretending, among other reasons, that all his equipage belongs to his Most Christian Majesty. This is not at all probable, for if the officers and crew were subjects of France, it would have been improper to pass off the vessel for a frigate of the United States, under the American flag. Besides, these deserters having fled to a French vessel of war, to the demand of their surrender by the Spanish commander it was replied on the word of honour of the captain, that they were not on board; so that, supposing the frigate to be a French ship, there is reason to suppose that they would have been surrendered.

" The Count de Florida Blanca has thought it necessary to inform Mr. Jay of these facts, in the full persuasion that he will have the goodness to write by the first post to the captain, in such terms as to induce him to surrender the deserters; it shall be understood, that they shall not be punished, and shall finish their engagements in their own corps, or in some other better paid.

" Mr. Jay is too reasonable not to grant that it would be unjust for a vessel to appear in a port, solely to require and receive all sorts of attentions and marks of respect (without any previous claim or engagement), and at the same time to refuse to deliver up any subjects, which it should have on board, of the sovereign of the country in whose name all these tokens of respect have been rendered.

" October 8, 1781."

ANSWER TO THE ABOVE.

MADRID, October 9, 1781.

SIR :

The letter which your Excellency did me the honour to write on the 8th instant arrived this morning. I consider myself much obliged by the communication of the facts mentioned in it, especially as it affords me an opportunity of manifesting to his Majesty and to Congress my attention to his rights and to their orders.

I perfectly agree in sentiment with your Excellency respecting the impropriety of detaining on board the American frigate at Corunna, the two men claimed by the commandant there, as deserters from one of his Majesty's regiments.

Your Excellency's remarks on this subject are no less delicate than just ; and your assurance that these men shall not be punished renders a compliance with the requisition to deliver them up no less consistent with humanity than with justice.

It gives me pleasure to confess, that the hospitable reception given to American vessels in the ports of Spain gives his Majesty a double right to expect, that their conduct should at least be inoffensive. In the present case (as stated in your Excellency's letter), I am fully convinced of the justice of this demand, that I should not hesitate to comply with it, even though made on a similar occasion by the Court of Portugal, from whose affected neutrality we suffer more evils than we should experience from any open hospitality she is capable of executing.

Agreeably to your Excellency's desire, I have written a letter (of which the enclosed is a copy) to the commanding officer of the frigate in question ; and as the manner in which your Excellency's letter to me treats this subject cannot fail making agreeable impressions on Americans, I shall take the liberty of sending a copy of it to Congress, as well as to the above-mentioned officer.

I cannot omit this opportunity of expressing my acknowledgments for your Excellency's promise to write to me from the Escurial, as soon as you shall be in a capacity to speak positively on the subject of my late letter. Permit me only to remark that the season wears away fast, and that Congress must be extremely anxious so hear that the delays which have so long kept them in a disagreeable state of suspense are finally and happily terminated.

I have the honour to be, etc.,

JOHN JAY.

The letter written to the commanding officer of the frigate, a copy of which was furnished to the Count de Florida Blanca, is as follows :

TO COMMODORE GILLON.

MADRID, October 9, 1781.

SIR :

The paper herewith enclosed is a copy of a letter which I received this morning from his Excellency, the Count de Florida Blanca, his Catholic Majesty's Principal Secretary of State and Minister for Foreign Affairs.

You will perceive from it that two men on board your frigate are claimed by his government as deserters from one of his Majesty's Irish regiments of infantry ; and that you are said to have refused to deliver them up, because, among other reasons, your crew are the subjects of his Most Christian Majesty.

If the men in question are citizens of one or other of the United States of North America, and admitted to be such, refusing to deliver them up, as deserters from the service of Spain, may be proper, because, while their own country is at war, they cannot without her consent enter into the service of any other power.

If they are Spaniards, then they are the subjects of his Catholic Majesty, and ought not to be withheld from him.

If they are foreigners, in that case whatever right they might have to enter into the American service, they certainly had an equal one to enter into that of Spain ; and if they had previously engaged with the latter, their subsequent enlistments with you were void, and Spain being in friendship with us has a just right to reclaim them.

If they deny their having enlisted in the Spanish service, still like all other foreigners who come into this kingdom they ought to submit to the justice of the country, and you ought not to screen them from it, especially as it cannot be presumed that the charge made against them is destitute of probability.

As to the circumstance of your crew's being subjects of the King of France, I cannot think that any argument to justify your detaining them can be drawn from it. For admitting them to be French subjects, yet as it may be lawful for them (Spain and France being allies) to enter into the service of Spain, the right of Spain to enlist must necessarily involve a right to compel obedience, and also to retake and punish deserters. Besides, as any questions about the legality of such enlistments concern only those two crowns, Americans cannot with propriety interfere.

In whatever light I view this affair, I cannot perceive the least right that you have to detain these men, after having been thus formally and regularly demanded by proper authority, as deserters from the service of his Catholic Majesty.

You may observe that I treat this subject merely as a question of justice, arising from that general law which subsists and ought to be observed between friendly nations.

I forbear making any remarks on the impolicy of your persisting to detain these men. I hope never to see America do what is right merely because it may be convenient. I flatter myself that her conduct will uniformly be actuated by higher and more generous principles, and that her national character will daily become more and more distinguished by disinterested justice and heroic magnanimity.

I shall take the earliest opportunity of transmitting a particular state of this affair to Congress, and I cannot doubt but that your conduct will merit their approbation, by being perfectly consistent with a just regard to the dignity and rights of a sovereign who has acted not only justly but generously towards our country.

If your reluctance to deliver up those men should have arisen from an apprehension of their suffering the punishment which on conviction would be due to their offences, that reluctance ought now to cease, because his Excellency, the Minister, has been pleased to assure me, that they shall not be punished, but only obliged to fulfil those engagements which they ought to have honestly performed instead of deserting.

In short, sir, although, on the one hand, I will never advise or encourage you to violate the rights of the meanest man in the world, in order to answer political purposes; yet, on the other, I shall always think it my duty to advise and encourage both you and others to render unto Cæsar whatever may belong unto Cæsar. I am, etc.,

JOHN JAY.

In answer to this letter, the Commodore wrote me one, which, according to the state of facts mentioned in it, showed that the charge against him was precipitate, and, as he in that letter predicted, I have never since heard any thing further from the Minister on the subject.

You may recollect that copies of certain letters from Colonel Searle and Mr. Gillon, which I had just received, were subjoined to my letter of the 3d of October last. These letters were soon followed by several others. Colonel Searle's representations against the Commodore's conduct were very strong, and tended to create an opinion that the ship and public stores on board of her were in danger. He desired me to send some person to Corunna, with proper instructions on the subject, and as an additional inducement offered to transmit to me through him some important information, which had been confidentially communicated to him in Holland by Mr. Adams, and which he did not choose to hazard by a common conveyance.

Considering the nature of these representations, and the limits and objects of my commission and instructions, it became a difficult question how far I ought, and in what manner I could interfere. I finally judged it would not be improper to send Mr. Carmichael down with instructions to make a full inquiry into the facts alleged against the Commodore, and to use my influence with this government to stop the vessel for the present, in case on such inquiry there should arise a very strong presumption that such a step would be necessary to preserve her. Mr. Carmichael did not think that a business of this kind was within the duty of his appointment, and he doubted his being able to ride post so far. This was a delicate business, and the management of it could with propriety be only committed to one in whose prudence and circumspection much confidence might be reposed. It would have been improper for me to have undertaken it, because I could not justify exposing by my absence our negotiations for aids and a treaty to unseasonable delays.

Soon afterwards I received a very long exculpatory letter from the Commodore. This letter placed his transactions in a different point of view, and inclined me to think that the proposed interposition on my part would have been unnecessary.

I forbear burdening these despatches with copies of the various letters I have received and written on this subject, as well because, as they relate to transactions in Holland and France with the public agents and Ministers in those countries, they are not properly within my province, as because they contain nothing of sufficient importance to make it necessary for me again to send further copies.

You will be pleased to observe that my last letter to the Minister was dated the 9th of October, and that there is a paragraph in it soliciting his speedy attention to the affairs on which he had promised to write me. I received no answer. Some weeks elapsed and the same silence continued.

I consulted the Ambassador of France, as to the propriety of my going to the Escurial, and endeavouring to prevail upon the Minister to proceed in our affairs, observing that the measures of Spain with respect to us might be important, if not to this, yet to the next, campaign, and that the sooner they were decided, the better enabled Congress would be to regulate their future operations. He was of opinion that, as the Minister had promised to give me notice of the time when he would be able to transact these affairs with me, it would be most prudent to wait with patience somewhat longer, and not, by an appearance of too great solicitude, to give him uneasy sensations. All things considered, this advice appeared to me discreet, and I followed it.

Thus the month of October produced nothing but expectation, suspense, and disappointment.

About this time M. Gardoqui mentioned to me a singular ordinance which occasioned, and is explained in, the following letter from me to the Minister, viz. :

JAY TO FLORIDA BLANCA.

MADRID, October 28, 1781.

SIR :

M. Gardoqui informs me that his Majesty was pleased in the month of March last to order " that when a prize taken by a French or Dutch vessel should arrive in a port of Spain, the Marine Judge of the District should reduce to writing the evidence of the capture, and deliver it to the French or Dutch consul (as the case might be), to be by him transmitted to the Admiralty, from whence the commission of the captors issued, in order that the legality of the capture might there be tried ; and further, that the sentence which might there be passed should, on being duly certified to the aforesaid judge, be executed under his direction." I am also informed that on the 12th instant his Majesty was pleased to extend the above-mentioned order to prizes taken by American vessels of war and sent into any of the ports of Spain.

So far as this order affects the United States of America, I take the liberty of representing to your Excellency, that the execution of it will necessarily be attended with the following inconveniences :

1st. The distance of America from Spain is so great, and the intercourse between the two countries rendered so precarious by the war, that many months must unavoidably elapse before the sentence of an

American Court of Admiralty can be obtained and executed here.

2dly. That by these delays all cargoes, or parts of cargoes, which may be of a perishable nature, will be lost, and the value of the vessel and rigging greatly diminished.

3dly. That as his Majesty has not as yet been pleased to grant the United States the privilege of having consuls in his ports, it is not in their power to provide for the transmission of the evidence of captures in the manner specified in the above-mentioned order.

4thly. That in case the prize should be claimed as a neutral vessel, the claimants must either prosecute their claim in America, or the sentence given there could not be influenced by it ; and yet it is more probable that those claimants would endeavour to avoid that expense and trouble, by applying here for an order to suspend the execution of the sentence, as well as for a trial of the merits of their claim by a Spanish tribunal. In which case the same cause would become subject to two jurisdictions, and tried by two different independent courts, in two different countries.

This order not being published, it is possible that my information respecting it may not be right in all its parts ; though I have reason to believe from the usual accuracy of M. Gardoqui, (from whom I received this information) that I am not mistaken.

There is at present an American prize at Bilboa, and all judicial proceedings respecting it are now at a stand.

The importance of this subject to the United States, and in some measure to the common cause, will I hope apologize for my troubling your Excellency with these remarks, and for requesting that the embarrassments in question may be removed in such a manner as may be most agreeable to his Majesty.

I have the honor to be, etc.

JOHN JAY.

To this letter I never received any answer whatever. After waiting six or eight days, I asked M. Gardoqui, who almost daily applied to me on the subject, what could be the reason of so much delay in a case that admitted of so little doubt. He said he could only account for it by supposing that the Minister had sent for the original order to prevent mistakes. I asked whether these royal orders were not regularly recorded at the time they were issued. He told me they were not.

For my own part, I rather suspect that this order treated us as an independent nation, and that the Minister found it difficult to establish any general regulations respecting our prizes or commerce without meeting with that obstacle. M. Gardoqui informed me that one of the judges permitted him to read it, but would not let him take a copy of it, and that it only contained an extension to American prizes of the regulations before ordained for Dutch and French ones.

As to the prize at Bilboa, a particular order was issued in that case for selling the ship and cargo, on the captors giving security to produce, within a year, an exemplification of a sentence of an American Court of Admiralty to justify it.

On the 5th of November, M. Gardoqui communicated to me certain letters and papers, from which it appeared that the *Cicero*, Captain Hill, had been stopped at Bilboa, by an order of the Minister, on a charge of improper conduct towards one of the King's cutters. Upon this subject I wrote the following letter to the Count de Florida Blanca, viz. :

JAY TO FLORIDA BLANCA.

SIR : MADRID, November 6, 1781.

It gives me much concern to be informed that the conduct of Captain Hill of the *Cicero*, an American private ship of war, towards one of his Catholic Majesty's cutters, has been so represented to your Excellency as to have given occasion to an order for detaining him at Bilboa.

This unfortunate affair is represented to me as follows, viz. :

That Captain Hill in the *Cicero* with a prize he had taken was going from Corunna to Bilboa ; that in the night of the 26th of October last he discovered an armed vessel approaching the prize. Captain Hill, suspecting it to be a Jersey privateer, hailed her, and ordered her to send her boat on board. They answered in *English* that their boat was out of repair. This circumstance increased his suspicions that she was an enemy, and induced him to insist on their sending a boat on board, which not being complied with he was persuaded it was an enemy, and accordingly gave them a broadside. Upon this they sent a boat to the *Cicero*, and convinced Captain Hill that the vessel was a Spanish cutter.

If this is really a true state of the fact, and I have good reason to believe it is, I am persuaded that your Excellency will not think Captain Hill's conduct was unjustifiable or contrary to the common usage in such cases. Having a valuable prize under his care, it was his duty to protect it, and as it was impossible for him at night to discover an enemy from a friend in another manner than the one he used, the captain of the cutter certainly appears to have been remiss in not sending out his boat at first as well as at last.

Both the *Cicero* and her prize now lie at Bilboa laden with valuable cargoes and expected to sail from thence for North America on the 16th instant. The privateer alone has one hundred and forty men on board, and should they not be permitted to sail at the time appointed, a very considerable expense must inevitably be incurred, because they would be obliged to wait for the next spring tides.

As no American vessel can have the least temptation to violate the rights of Spain, but as on the contrary it is the well-known interest as well as disposition of the United States to cultivate the friendship of his Catholic Majesty, I am convinced that there was not in this case the least intention of disrespect to the Spanish flag. Permit me therefore to hope that your Excellency will be pleased either to permit the departure of these vessels by a general order, or on Captain Hill's giving security for the payment of such damages as he may become chargeable with on the issue of a judicial inquiry into this transaction.

I assure your Excellency that no citizen of America will be countenanced by the United States in any improper conduct toward his Catholic Majesty, or any of his subjects ; and if I had the least reason to think that Captain Hill was in this predicament, it would give me much more pleasure to hear of his being punished than released.

I have the honour to be, with great consideration and respect, Your Excellency's

Most obedient and humble servant,

JOHN JAY.

THE COUNT'S ANSWER.

[Translation.]

" The Count de Florida Blanca has the honor to present his compliments to Mr. Jay, and to assure him that the information he has received relative to the affair of the *Cicero* privateer, as set forth in his letter of the 6th instant, is not correct, the Count having received from persons of respectability and entirely worthy of credit very accurate statements. It is therefore necessary that some suitable satisfaction should be given, in order to serve as an example to restrain the captains of the American privateers within proper bounds. This is the more necessary, as it is not the first time that we have had reason to complain of their conduct, and to demand reparation.

"ST. LORENZO, November 8, 1781."

JAY'S REPLY TO THE ABOVE.

SIR :   MADRID, November 12, 1781.

I have received the letter, which your Excellency did me the honour to write on the 8th instant.

It gives me pain to hear that the conduct of an American vessel of war should be so reprehensible as that of the *Cicero* has been represented to be. It is proper that I should inform your Excellency that the captains of all American private ships of war give bond with sureties, to fulfil the instructions they receive with their commissions ; and that these instructions enjoin them to behave in a proper manner towards friendly nations.

As the honour and interest of the United States render it highly necessary that their officers and citizens should, upon all occasions, pay the most scrupulous regard to the rights of other nations, I must request the favour of your Excellency to communicate to me a state of the facts charged against Captain Hill, that by being transmitted immediately to America, Congress may be enabled to take such measures relative to him as to deter others from the commission of the like offences.

Your Excellency would also oblige me by informing me how the satisfaction demanded of Captain Hill is to be ascertained, and to whom it is to be paid. As his remaining much longer in his present situation would be a great loss to his owners, I wish, for their sakes, that he may be released as soon as possible ; and, I am persuaded, that your Excellency will not think it necessary to detain him longer than until the satisfaction in question can be ascertained and paid.

I greatly regret that other American privateers have also given occasion to complaints. I assure your Excellency that nothing on my part shall be wanting to prevent the like in future, and I am sure that Congress would consider themselves obliged by your Excellency's putting it in my power to convey to them exact details of any complaints against their officers. I have the honour to be, etc.

JOHN JAY.

Much reason has been given me to believe that the hard proceedings against Captain Hill were not justifiable, and the Minister's declining to furnish me with a state of the facts supposed to be alleged against him speaks the same language. What intelligence the Count may have respecting this misconduct of any other of our armed vessels, I know not, nor have I heard any other insinuations of that kind, except what are contained in his note.

The Count omitted to take any notice of my last letter on this subject, and it was not before the 26th of November that the matter was determined by the order alluded to in the following polite letter:

[Translation].

MY DEAR SIR:

From respect to your Excellency and to the American Congress, the King has determined that Captain Hill, on satisfying, or giving security to satisfy, the damage he has done to one of our vessels, on account of which he is detained, shall be at liberty to return to his country when he pleases. For this purpose I communicate the enclosed order to the Corregidor of Bilboa, and repeating myself to be at the service of your Excellency, I pray God to preserve you many years.

COUNT DE FLORIDA BLANCA.

The next day I sent the Count some American papers, which had just come to hand, and enclosed them with a card, in which there was this paragraph:

" Mr. Jay has received the letter, which his Excellency did him the honour to write yesterday by M. Gardoqui, and is greatly obliged by the permission granted to Captain Hill to depart, as well as by the polite terms in which that circumstance is communicated to Mr. Jay."

As further remonstrance on this subject would have been useless, I thought it best to appear satisfied, and not, by any expressions of discontent, to hazard new obstacles to the attainment of our more important objects.

I must now return to the old subject. Although the Count had been some weeks at the Escurial, and I had in vain waited with great patience for the letter which the Minister had promised to write to me on leaving St. Ildefonso, yet as many bills would become payable in December, and I was unprovided with funds, I thought it high time to remind the Minister of my situation.

I therefore wrote him the following letter :

JAY TO FLORIDA BLANCA.

Sir: MADRID, November 16, 1781.

I find myself constrained to beseech your Excellency to think a little of my situation. Congress flatter themselves that the offers they have made would certainly induce his Majesty at least to assist them with some supplies. The residue of the bills drawn upon me remain to be provided for. Those payable in the next month amount to thirty-one thousand eight hundred and nine dollars. Would it be too inconvenient for your Excellency to lend us this sum? Before January, when further bills would become payable, your Excellency may probably find leisure to give me an answer respecting our propositions. The time presses; I entreat your Excellency's answer. I can only add that I am, with great consideration and respect, etc.   JOHN JAY.

To this letter I never received any answer, and it is remarkable that the Count's subsequent letter of the 26th of November, announcing the permission given to Captain Hill to depart, does not take the least notice of it. Whatever might be the Minister's real intentions as to furnishing me with the funds necessary to pay the bills to become due in December, it appeared to me imprudent to neglect any means in my power to provide for the worst. I therefore apprised Dr. Franklin (to whom I am under great obligations, and have given much trouble) of my hazardous situation by the following letter:

JAY TO BENJAMIN FRANKLIN.

MADRID, November 21, 1781.

DEAR SIR:

It seems as if my chief business here was to fatigue you and our good allies with incessant solicitations on the subject of the ill-timed bills drawn upon me by Congress. It is happy for me that you are a philosopher, and for our country that our allies are indeed our friends—*amicus certus in re incerta cernitur.*

This Court continues to observe the most profound silence respecting our propositions.

I cannot as yet obtain any answer to any of my applications for aid ; heretofore the Minister was too sick or too busy. At present his Secretary is much indisposed. I have requested that he would lend us for the present only as much as would satisfy the bills of December, viz., thirty-one thousand eight hundred and nine dollars ; no answer. What is to be done ? I must again try and borrow a little, and, as usual, recur to you. Thank God, no new bills arrive. If they did I should refuse to accept them ; only a few straggling old ones appear. Would not the Court of France, on your representing this matter to them, enable you to put an end to this unhappy business. Thirty thousand pounds sterling would do it. I am sure the evils we should experience from the protest of these bills would cost even France a vast deal more. You see my situation. I am sure I need not press you to deliver me from it if in your power. I cannot yet believe that all the assurances of this Court will vanish into air. I still flatter myself that they will afford us some supplies, though not in season. I think we might very safely offer to repay the French Court the proposed sum in America, for surely Congress would not hesitate to prefer that to the loss of their credit.

I enclose a newspaper which gives us reason to indulge the most pleasing expectations. God grant they may be realized. I have a letter from Mr. Gerry, dated at Marblehead, the 9th October. He was then in daily expectation of hearing that Lord Cornwallis and his army were our prisoners. He describes the last harvest as very abundant, and the general state of our affairs as very promising—much more so indeed than ever they have been.

I am, dear sir, with sincere regard and attachments,

Your obliged obedient servant,

JOHN JAY.

This letter was conveyed by a courier of the French Ambassador. I did not choose, by putting it in the post-office, to give this Court an opportunity of knowing that I was endeavouring to obtain a credit for the sum in question, lest that circumstance might become an additional motive with them to withhold their assistance.

In short, sir, the whole month of November wore away without my being able to advance a single step. M. Del Campo's illness afforded a tolerable good excuse for delay during the latter part of November, and the first three weeks in December.

On the 1st of December I found myself without any answer from Dr. Franklin, with many bills to pay, and not a farthing in bank. M. Cabarrus, fortunately for me, was willing as well as able to make further advances, and to him I am indebted for being relieved from the necessity I should otherwise have been under, of protesting the bills due in that month.

The Court removed from the Escurial to Madrid without having bestowed the least attention either on the propositions or different memorials on commercial matters which I had submitted to the Minister.

It was natural to expect that our successes in Virginia would have made a very grateful impression on this Court; but I am far from being persuaded that they considered these events as favorable to their views. Of this, some judgment may be formed from their subsequent conduct.

On the 6th of December I sent the Minister the following card, and a memorial from Mr. Harrison at Cadiz, the nature of which will be best explained by a recital of it :

" Mr. Jay presents his compliments to the Count de Florida Blanca, and has the honour of requesting his attention to the enclosed memorial.

" Mr. Jay had the honour of calling at his Excellency's on Tuesday evening last, but had the misfortune of not finding him at home. As Mr. Jay wishes to regulate his visits by his Excellency's convenience, he begs the favour of his Excellency to inform him when it would be agreeable that Mr. Jay should wait on his Excellency, and have an opportunity of conversing with him on the object of Mr. Jay's mission."

The answer I received to the letter, which accompanied this memorial, is as follows :

[Translation.]

" The Count de Florida Blanca will receive Mr. John Jay whenever he may please to come, in the evening at half-past seven or later, in his Secretary's office in the palace, except on Saturday evening next, when he will be engaged."

This note was not dated, but I received it the 7th of December. On the same day I received a letter from General Washington, dated the 22d of October, and enclosing copies of the articles of capitulation of Yorktown and returns of prisoners, etc.

This letter was brought to France by the frigate which carried there the first intelligence of that important event, and yet it is remarkable that it did not reach me until after these articles had been published in the Paris and Madrid gazettes. I nevertheless immediately sent copies to the Minister.

As to Mr. Harrison's memorial, no answer has been given it to this day. Nor indeed have any of the representations I have hitherto made to the Ministers relative to commercial grievances procured the least redress. Even the hard case of the Dover cutter still remains unfinished, notwithstanding my repeated and pressing applications on behalf of the poor captors. It is now more than a year since the Minister promised me that the cutter should be immediately appraised, and the value paid to the captors, one of whom afterwards came here, and after waiting two or three months returned to Cadiz, without having received any other money than what I gave him to purchase his daily bread.

As the Minister could not see me on Saturday evening, it was not till Monday evening the 10th of December that I had an opportunity to converse with him.

He began the conversation by observing that I had been very unfortunate, and had much reason to complain of delays, but that they had been unavoidable. That M. Del Campo had been appointed near three months ago to treat and confer with me; that shortly after the Court removed from St. Ildefonso that gentleman's health began to decline; and that his indisposition had hitherto prevented his attending to that or any other business, but that he hoped by the time the Court should return from Aranjues (to which the King was then about to make a little excursion) he would be able to proceed on it, and that he should have the necessary instructions for the purpose.

I told the Count that these delays had given me great concern, and that I was very solicitous to be enabled to give Congress some positive and explicit information on the business alluded to. He replied that I must now confer on those subjects with M. Del Campo, for that for his part his time and attention were so constantly engaged by other matters, that he could not possibly attend to this, especially while at Madrid, when he always enjoyed much less leisure than at the Sitios. He then proceeded to congratulate me on our late successes in Virginia; he assured me that the King rejoiced sincerely in those events, and that he himself was happy to see our affairs assume so promising an aspect. I was about to descend to particulars, and to remind the Count of the various memorials, etc., which still remained to be considered and despatched, when he mentioned he was engaged for the rest of the evening in pressing affairs. This intimation put an end to the conference.

It is somewhat singular that M. Del Campo should have been appointed near three months past to treat and confer with me, and yet I should be left all that time without any information of it. It shows that the King is ready to do what may depend upon him, but that his Ministers find it convenient to interpose delays without necessity, and without even the appearance of it.

After the King's return from Aranjues, I took an opportunity of asking M. Del Campo when I might promise myself the pleasure of commencing our conferences. He replied that his health was not as yet sufficiently re-established to permit him to do business. The fact, however, was otherwise.

On the 27th of December, I again waited on him for the same purpose. He told me it was very uncertain when our conferences could commence, and that he must first converse with the Count on the subject. I asked him whether he had not received his instructions. He answered that he had not, for that they were not as yet completed, nor indeed, as he believed, as yet begun.

In this state things remained during the whole time the Court continued at Madrid. Above a month since the date of my letter to Dr. Franklin about our bills had elapsed without an answer, nor had any prospect of obtaining aids here opened. I therefore wrote him the following letter :

JAY TO DR. BENJAMIN FRANKLIN.

My Dear Sir : MADRID, December 31, 1781.

I learn from the Marquis d'Aranda, that my letter of the 21st ultimo has reached you. The want of a good opportunity has for some time past prevented my writing to you so particularly as I could have wished.

Things remain here exactly in *statu quo*, except that your aid daily becomes more necessary, and will soon be indispensable. These are matters that require no explanation. I have received two letters, dated the 22d and 26th of November, from Mr. Adams, on the subject of certain instructions, passed the 16th of August, which he had lately received, and of which I was ignorant until the arrival of these letters. I think them wise. A courier from France arrived here two days ago; by his return I hope to write you particularly, etc.

I am, etc.

JOHN JAY.

On the 11th of January I wrote the following letter to the Doctor, by the Ambassador's courier:

JAY TO DR. BENJAMIN FRANKLIN.

MADRID, January 11, 1782.

DEAR SIR:

The last letter I had the pleasure of writing to you was dated the 31st ultimo, and referred to a former one of the 21st of November last, in which I stated my difficulties on account of the bills, the improbability of my obtaining any relief here, and consequently the necessity I was under of recurring to your inter-position to save them from protest.

I have not as yet been favoured with your answer. I can readily conceive that this affair has added not a little to your embarrassments, and therefore I lament, not complain of the delay. I borrowed from M. Cabarrus about thirty thousand dollars. He is not perfectly easy, and I have no prospect of borrowing more from him or others, at least without assurances of speedy repayment, which I am not in capacity to give. The Court indeed owes me, on their old promise of one hundred and fifty thousand dollars, a balance of about twenty-five thousand six hundred and fifteen dollars, but I have no reason to rely on receiving it soon, if at all.

I also begin severely to feel the want of my back salary. It is in vain for me to expect it from America, and unless you can supply it, it will be necessary for me immediately to disencumber myself of most of my expenses, and confine myself to mere necessaries, until a change may take place for the better. This circumstance conspires with those of a more public nature, to make me very solicitous to know what you can or cannot do for me.

As to the affairs of the negotiation, they have not advanced since Major Franks left me. The Minister is too sick, or too busy, to attend to American affairs. He refers me to M. Del Campo, who has been named for the purpose, and when I apply to him he tells me that his instructions are not yet completed, and that he cannot tell when they will be.

I am, etc. JOHN JAY.

I must, however, do the Minister the justice to say that for some little time then past, and during the whole month of January, I have good reason to believe that he was greatly and constantly engaged in pressing business, for on speaking several times during that period to the Ambassador of France, about the delays I experienced, and the propriety of pressing the Minister to pay some attention to our affairs, he repeatedly told me that he knew the Minister to be then extremely hurried, and advised me not to make any application to him for the present.

On the 26th of January, 1782, agreeably to a previous appointment, I had a long conference with the Ambassador of France. I entered into a detail of the various pretexts and delays which the Minister had used to avoid coming to any decision on our affairs, and made some remarks on their keeping me suspended at present, between the Count's incapacity to do business and M. Del Campo's want of instructions.

I reminded the Ambassador that the fate of the bills drawn upon me was a serious subject, and if protested might eventually prove injurious to France and Spain, as well as America, and that though France had already done much for us, yet that it still remained a question of policy whether it would not be more expedient for her to advance about thirty thousand pounds sterling to save these bills, than risk the expensive evils which the loss of our credit might occasion even to her. The Ambassador seemed to admit this, but was apprehensive that the great and pressing demands for money, caused by the great armaments which France was preparing to send to different parts of the world, would render such an advance very inconvenient, if not impracticable.

I recapitulated in the course of the conference the

various ill consequences which might result from protesting these bills. Among others, I hinted at the necessity I should be under of assigning to the world in those protests the true reasons which had occasioned them, viz., that I had placed too great confidence in the assurances of his Catholic Majesty. The Ambassador objected to this as highly imprudent, and as naturally tending to embroil the two countries, which was by all means to be avoided, even though I could make good the assertion. I then enumerated the various assurances I had at different times received from the Minister, adding, that whatever might be the consequence, I should think it my duty to pay a higher regard to the honor of the United States than to the feelings of a Court by whose *finesse* that honor had been drawn into question.

There was also another circumstance to which I desired him to turn his attention, viz., that as our independence had not been acknowledged here, the holders of the bills might commence actions against me on them, and that it was easy to foresee the embarrassments which would result to all parties from such a measure. The Ambassador saw this matter in the same point of view.

It appeared to me useful to take a general view of the conduct of Spain towards us ever since my arrival, and to observe the natural tendency it had to encourage our enemies, impress doubts on the minds of our friends, and abate the desire of Congress to form intimate connections with Spain, and that this latter consequence might become interesting also to

France by reason of the strict alliance subsisting between the two kingdoms.

I begged the favour of him to give me his candid advice what would be most proper for me to do. He confessed that he was perplexed, and at a loss what to advise me to ; he hoped that the Dutch loan would enable Dr. Franklin to make the advances in question, and that though he could not promise any thing from his Court, yet that he would write and do his best. He advised me to give the Doctor a full statement of our affairs here, but that I had already done by giving him the perusal of my letters to Congress of the 3d of October, etc.

He said he had written to the Count de Vergennes about the delays and embarrassments I had met with, and that he had received for answer, " that Spain knew her own business and interest, and that France had no right to press her on such points."

The Ambassador advised me by all means to continue patient and moderate, and to cherish the appearance of our being well with this Court. I observed to him that one protested bill would dissipate all these appearances. He said that was very true ; that he saw difficulties on every side, and that he really pitied my situation, for that these various perplexities must keep me constantly in a kind of purgatory. I told him if he would say mass for me in good earnest I should soon be relieved from it ; he renewed his promise to write, and we parted.

The next day, viz., 27th of January, I received the following letter from Dr. Franklin :

BENJAMIN FRANKLIN TO JAY.

DEAR SIR :   PASSY, January 15th, 1782.

Mr. Grand tells me, that he hears from Madrid, you are
uneasy at my long silence. I have had much vexation and
perplexity lately with the affair of the goods in Holland, and
I have so many urgent correspondences to keep up, that
some of them at times necessarily suffer. I purpose writing
fully to you next post. In the meantime I send the enclosed for your meditation. The ill-timed bills, as you justly
term them, do us infinite prejudice ; but we must not be
discouraged.

I am ever, with the greatest esteem, &c.

B. FRANKLIN.

The paper above-mentioned to be enclosed is in
these words :

COUNT DE VERGENNES TO B. FRANKLIN.

[Translation.]

SIR :   VERSAILLES, December 31st, 1781.

I have received the letter you did me the honor to write
me the 27th instant. I shall not enter into an examination
of the successive variations and augmentations of your
demands on me for funds to meet your payments. I shall
merely remark, that whenever you shall consider yourself
fully authorised to dispose of the proceeds of the Dutch
loan, on behalf of Congress, I will propose to M. de Fleury
to supply you with the million required, as soon as it shall
have been paid into the royal treasury. But I think it my
duty, Sir, to inform you, that if Mr. Morris issues drafts on
this same million, I shall not be able to provide for the payment of them, and shall leave them to be protested. I ought
also to inform you, that there will be nothing more supplied than the million abovementioned, and if the drafts,

which you have already accepted, exceed that sum, it must
be for you to contrive the means of meeting them. I shall
make an exception only in favor of those of Mr. Morris,
provided they shall not exceed the remainder of the Dutch
loan, after deducting the million, which shall be placed at
your disposal, and the expenses of the loan.

I have the honor to be, &c.

DE VERGENNES.

P. S.—I remit to you herewith the letter of Mr. Grand.

Although this letter of Dr. Franklin does not in
express terms promise me the aid I had desired, yet
the general tenor of it, together with the grant of the
million mentioned by the Count de Vergennes, led me
to suppose that on the receipt of it he would be able
to make me the necessary advances. Under this idea
I returned the following answer to the Doctor's letter :

JAY TO BENJAMIN FRANKLIN.

My Dear Sir : MADRID, January 28, 1782.

I had yesterday the satisfaction of receiving your
favor of the 15th instant. You will find by a letter,
which I wrote you on the 11th instant, that I imputed
your silence to its true cause, being well persuaded,
that the same attention you have always paid to the
public affairs in general would not be withheld from
those which call for it in this kingdom.

I am happy to find, that you have a prospect of
terminating the difficulties which the bills drawn
upon me have occasioned, and though I cannot but
observe that Count de Vergennes' letter is peculiarly
explicit and precise, yet I must confess I should not

have been surprised if it had been conceived in terms still less soft. Would it not be well to transmit a copy of it to Congress? France has done and is still doing so much for us, that gratitude, as well as policy, demands from us the utmost moderation and delicacy in our applications for aids; and considering the very singular plan of drawing bills at a venture, I think we have no less reason to admire the patience, than to be satisfied with the liberality, of our good and generous allies.

M. de Neufville had given me a hint of the embarrassments occasioned by the affair of our goods in Holland.

It seems as if trouble finds its way to you from every quarter. Our credit in Holland leans upon you on the one hand, and in Spain on the other. Thus you continue, like the keystone of an arch, pressed by both sides, and yet sustaining each. How grateful ought we to be to France for enabling you to do it.

Mr. Joshua Johnson, in a letter dated the 18th instant, mentions the arrival at Nantes of the brig *Betsey* from Philadelphia, that she brought letters for me, and that the captain put them in the post-office. None of them have as yet reached me.

I have received too many unequivocal proofs of your kind attention, to render a punctilious return of line for line necessary to convince me of it. Let such ideas, therefore, be banished, and be assured that matters of ceremony and etiquette can never affect the esteem and affectionate regard with which I am, etc., etc.

JOHN JAY.

Not having heard any thing further from M. Del Campo respecting his instructions, I wrote him on that subject as follows :

"MADRID, February 1, 1782.

"Mr. Jay presents his compliments to M. Del Campo, and requests to be informed whether he has as yet received the instructions necessary to enable him to execute his appointment relative to the affairs of the United States at this Court.

"Mr. Jay begs leave again to mention his being ready and anxious to enter, with M. Del Campo, into the discussion of these affairs at any time and place that may be agreeable to him."

On the 5th of February, I received the following answer.

[Translation.]

" M. Del Campo has the honor to address his compliments to Mr. Jay, and to transmit him several bundles of letters, which he has just received. He regrets that he is obliged to inform Mr. Jay, that the Count, by reason of the delicate state of his health, and other difficulties, has not yet been able to arrange the instructions under consideration."

" THE PARDO, February 3d, 1782."

The packets mentioned in the above note were the first public letters I have had the honour of receiving from you.

I afterwards found that these despatches were brought to Cadiz from Philadelphia by the brig *Hope*. How they came into M. Del Campo's hands I am not informed. On the same day (February 5, 1782) I received a letter from Dr. Franklin, which almost entirely dissipated my hopes of aid from him. The following extract from it contains every part of it except a few paragraphs that have no relation to our affairs here :

BENJAMIN FRANKLIN TO JAY.

DEAR SIR :   PASSY, January 19th, 1782.

In mine of the 15th, I mentioned my intention of writing fully to you by this day's post. But understanding since, that a courier will soon go from Versailles, I rather choose that conveyance.

I received duly your letter of November 21st, but it found me in a very perplexed situation. I had great payments to make for the extravagant and very inconvenient purchase in Holland, together with large acceptances by Mr. Adams, of bills drawn on Mr. Laurens and himself, and I had no certainty of providing the money. I had also a quarrel upon my hands with Messrs de Neufville and others, owners of two vessels hired by Gillon to carry the goods he had contracted to carry in his own ship. I had worried this friendly and generous Court with often repeated after-clap demands, occasioned by these unadvised, (as well as ill-advised) and, therefore, unexpected drafts, and was ashamed to show my face to the Minister. In these circumstances, I knew not what answer to make you. I could not encourage you to expect the relief desired, and, having still some secret hope, I was unwilling to discourage you, and thereby occasion a protest of bills, which possibly I might find means of enabling you to pay. Thus I delayed writing perhaps too long.

But to this moment, I have obtained no assurance of having it in my power to aid you, though no endeavors on my part have been wanting. We have been assisted with near twenty millions since the beginning of last year, besides a fleet and army ; and yet I am obliged to worry them with my solicitations for more, which makes us appear insatiable.

This letter will not go before Tuesday. Perhaps by that time I may be able to say explicity yes or no.

I am very sensible of your unhappy situation, and I believe you feel as much for me.

You mention my proposing to repay the sum you want in America. I tried that last year. I drew a bill on Congress for a considerable sum to be advanced me here, and paid there in provisions for the French troops. My bill was not honored.

I was in hopes the loan in Holland, if it succeeded, being for ten millions, would have made us all easy. It was long uncertain. It is now completed. But, unfortunately, it has most of it been eaten up by advances here. You see by the letter of which I sent you a copy, upon what terms I obtained another million of it. That (if I get it) will enable me to pay the thirty thousand dollars you have borrowed, for we must not let your friend suffer. What I am to do afterwards God knows.

I am much surprised at the dilatory and reserved conduct of your Court. I know not to what amount you have obtained aids from it, but if they are not considerable, it were to be wished you had never been sent there, as the slight they have put upon our offered friendship is very disreputable to us, and, of course, hurtful to our affairs elsewhere. I think they are short-sighted, and do not look very far into futurity, or they would seize with avidity so excellent an opportunity of securing a neighbor's friendship, which may hereafter be of great consequence to their American affairs.

If I were in Congress I should advise your being instructed to thank them for past favors, and take your leave. As I am situated, I do not presume to give you such advice, nor could you take it if I should. But I conceive there would be nothing amiss in your mentioning in a short memoir, the length of time elapsed since the date of the secret article, and since your arrival, to urge their determination upon it, and pressing them to give you an explicit, definitive, immediate answer, whether they would enter into treaty with us or not, and in case of refusal, solicit your recall, that you may not continue from year to year at a great expense, in a constant state of uncertainty with regard to so important a matter. I do not see how they can decently refuse such an answer. But their silence, after the demand made, should in my opinion be understood as a refusal, and we should act accordingly. I think I see a very good use that might be made of it, which I will not venture to explain in this letter.

I know not how the account of your salary stands, but I would have you draw upon me for a quarter at present, which shall be paid, and it will be a great pleasure to me if I shall be able to pay up all your arrears.

Mr. Laurens being now at liberty perhaps may soon come here, and be ready to join us if there should be any negotiations for peace. In England they are mad for a separate one with us, that they may more effectually take revenge on France and Spain. I have had several overtures hinted to me lately from different quarters, but I am deaf. The thing is impossible. We can never agree to desert our first and our faithful friend on any consideration whatever. We should become infamous by such abominable baseness.

With great and sincere esteem, I am ever, &c.

B. FRANKLIN.

You will easily perceive, sir, that my situation now became very unpleasant; largely indebted to M. Cabarrus, and without funds, as well as almost without the hopes of speedily procuring any, either to satisfy him or pay the swarm of bills that would be payable the next month.

M. Cabarrus had offered to advance, or rather to supply me with any sum of money, that the Minister would authorize him to furnish, on the same terms on which he procured money for the government. The answer I received to this proposition was, that the government had occasion for all the money that M. Cabarrus could possibly collect. He also repeatedly offered to advance the money wanted for the month of March, if the Minister or the Ambassador of France would become responsible for the repayment of it, with interest, within a reasonable time, sometimes mentioning seven months, and at others extending it to ten or twelve. The Ambassador did not conceive himself authorized to enter into any such engagement, and the Minister remained silent; M. Cabarrus began to grow uneasy, and a day was appointed between us to confer on this subject. Some intervening business, however, prevented his attendance, and on the 10th of February he wrote me the following letter:

M. CABARRUS TO JAY.

[Translation.]

SIR: MADRID, February 10th, 1782.

I was summoned yesterday to the Pardo, which prevented me from paying you my respects as I had intended. Not knowing whether I shall be able to do it before Tuesday, I write to inform you, that it will be necessary for me to know on what I am to depend in regard to the reimbursement you were to make me by drafts on Paris. You are aware, that I have actually advanced seven hundred and fifty thousand reals vellon. Independently of this sum, on the 14th of March, which we are now approaching, nearly thirty-five thousand dollars of your bills will become due.

I will not conceal from you, that although this double advance is neither beyond my means nor my disposition, yet the former is entirely absorbed by the necessities of the government, so that I shall be the more desirous, that you would enable me to meet these engagements, as I shall always find a difficulty in disposing of your paper. I speak to you frankly, since I shall always endeavor, as I have heretofore done, to serve you in the same spirit.

I have the honor to be, &c.

CABARRUS.

By way of answer to this letter, I instructed Mr. Carmichael to inform M. Cabarrus of the exact state I was in, with respect to my expectations of aid both here and from France, for I did not choose to commit a matter of this kind in writing to M. Cabarrus' discretion. I could not give him positive assurances of being speedily repaid, either by a credit on Dr. Franklin, or by money to be obtained here, but I submitted to his consideration the improbability that this or the French Court would permit these bills to be protested, and assured him that Dr. Franklin was using his best endeavours in our favour, and had so far succeeded as to encourage me to expect that he would soon be able at least to replace the sum which M. Cabarrus had already advanced to me.

The next day, viz., the 11th of February, I waited upon the Ambassador of France. I represented to him in the strongest terms the critical situation of our credit, and communicated to him the contents both of Dr. Franklin's and M. Cabarrus' letters.

I requested him to speak seriously and pressingly to the Minister on the subject, and to remind him that M. Cabarrus' offer was of such a nature as to remove any objection that could arise from the low state of the public funds. The Ambassador was just then setting out for the Pardo. He promised to speak to the Minister accordingly, and that his Secretary, the Chevalier de Bourgoing (who has been very friendly, and given himself much trouble on this occasion) should inform me of the result in the evening.

I received in the evening the following letter from the Chevalier de Bourgoing, viz. :

[Translation.]

SIR:

The dreadful weather to-day prevents me from coming to inform you orally, what M. de Montmorin has to communicate to you in pursuance of his interview of this morning. I give you the result briefly.

The Minister being informed of your embarrassment feels for you sincerely, and would be glad to remedy it. He will make every effort, but as the actual necessities of the government are pressing, he cannot answer for his success. He assures Mr. Jay, that if the misfortune he apprehends should take place, Mr. Jay may be perfectly easy in regard to personal consequences, as the Minister will take care that no inconvenience shall follow it.

I have thought that these few lines would serve to calm your apprehensions, until M. de Montmorin shall have an opportunity to give you further information.

I have the honor to be, &c.

DE BOURGOING.

I returned by the bearer of the above letter the following answer :

JAY TO CHEVALIER DE BOURGOING.

" Mr. Jay presents his compliments to the Chevalier de Bourgoing. The Minister's answer to the Ambassador is polite and cautious, and, if sincere (which time can only ascertain), will demand Mr. Jay's thanks and acknowledgments.

" The Minister is mistaken if he supposes that Mr. Jay views personal consequences as of any other importance than as they may affect the political interests of the two countries; and, when considered in that light, they merit a degree of attention to which mere personal considerations could not entitle them.

" Mr. Jay requests the favour of the Chevalier to present his cordial acknowledgments to the Ambassador for his friendly interposition on this occasion, and to assure him that Mr. Jay will never cease to be influenced by the gratitude which every American owes to the first friend and steadfast ally of the United States.

" MADRID, February 11, 1782."

, I also wrote this evening to Dr. Franklin, and I insert the following extracts from the letter, because they contain matters proper for you to know :

JAY TO BENJAMIN FRANKLIN.

MADRID, February 11, 1782.

DEAR SIR :

I have been so engaged these two days as not to have had time to reply fully to yours of the 19th ult.

I flattered myself that the loan in Holland would have afforded funds for all our bills and present demands, and am sorry to hear that this is not the case. Could not that loan be extended to a further sum?

The conduct of this Court bears few marks of wisdom. The fact is, they have little money, less credit, and very moderate talents.

My ideas correspond exactly with yours respecting the propriety of presenting such a memoir as you propose. The Ambassador of France, however, is decided against it, and it appears to me imprudent to disregard his opposition.

I have not as yet received a single letter by or from the Marquis de Lafayette.

I am, etc.,

JOHN JAY.

On the 15th of February the first advices of the surrender of Fort St. Philip arrived, and the Ambassador of France having been informed at the Pardo that M. del Campo's instructions would be completed by the end of the week, I thought both these circumstances rendered it proper that I should pay the Minister a visit. I accordingly went to the Pardo the next evening. The Minister was too much indisposed (as was said) to see company. He sent me an apology, and a request that I would speak to M. del Campo, who was then in the Secretary's office. I did so.

I found M. del Campo surrounded by suitors. He received me with great and unusual civility, and carried me into his private apartment. I told him that, as he was evidently very busy, I could not think of sitting down, and wished only to detain him a few minutes. He said that he was indeed much engaged, but that we might, nevertheless, take a cup of chocolate together. I mentioned to him, in a summary way, the amount of the bills which remained to be paid, and the promises made by the Minister to the Ambassador on that subject, desiring that he would be so obliging as to give that business all the despatch in his power. He replied that the urgent demands of government rendered advances of money very inconvenient; that the Minister had not mentioned to him any thing on that head, but that he would speak to him about it. I told him that, as the greater part of these bills would be payable in March, I was anxious to see the arrangements for paying them speedily made; that my hopes were chiefly confined to this Court, for that France having this year supplied us with near twenty millions, besides a fleet and army, it would be unreasonable to ask for more. To this he remarked that France received from us with one hand (in the way of commerce) what she paid out with the other, whereas Spain was called upon for supplies without enjoying any such advantage. I told him if he had been more at leisure it would have given me pleasure to have entered with him into the discussion of that point. I nevertheless observed that Spain was indebted to the American war for the recovery of West Florida, and the possession of Minorca, and that the time would come and was approaching when

Spain would derive essential benefit from our trade and independence; that he overrated the value of our commerce to France, which at present did not compensate for the expenses she sustained on our account.

I mentioned to him M. Cabarrus' offer in very precise terms, and told him I was glad to hear from the Ambassador that his instructions were nearly completed. He avoided saying whether they were or not, but answered, generally, that he hoped things would soon be settled to the satisfaction of all parties; that it would always give him pleasure to treat with me; that he was much my friend; that he esteemed my private character, and many such like compliments improper as well as unnecessary for me to commit to paper. He promised to speak to the Minister, and to write me his answer. I desired him to present my congratulations to the Count, and to inform him how much I regretted the indisposition which prevented his seeing company that evening.

All this looked very fair, but experience had taught me that professions were sometimes insincere. On the 18th of February I communicated the substance of this conference to the Ambassador of France, requesting him to remind the Minister of his promise, and to press the importance of his performing it. The Ambassador promised to take every proper opportunity of doing it. On the 24th of February your letter by the Marquis de Lafayette arrived safe.

On the 25th of February I received the following letter from M. Cabarrus, viz. :

M. CABARRUS TO JAY.

[Translation.]

SIR: MADRID, February 25th, 1782.

I have the honor to remit you herewith three accounts, relative to the payments made for you, viz:

One of the 4th of October last, signed by the former house of Cabarrus and Aguirre, for payment of which I have credited you 46,447 reals vellon. A second, signed by me the 7th of November following, settled by 135,715–10 reals vellon, carried to your credit. A third, signed also by me, dated the 19th inst, and balanced by 667,170–17 reals vellon, which I have credited you with. In support of these accounts, I transmit you the original vouchers, and beg you to proceed to the verification of both, to assure me of their reception and correctness. I flatter myself that you will take measures for my speedy reimbursement, and I ask it with the more urgency, as I have a pressing necessity for this sum, on the payment of which I have relied. I have the honor to be, &c.

CABARRUS.

This letter needs no comments; it breathes the fears and precautions of a creditor, striving to make the most of a failing debtor, and therefore I considered this letter as inauspicious. I returned a verbal answer, that an examination of these accounts must precede a settlement of them, and that as to a speedy payment of the balance due to him he knew my exact situation.

A day or two before the date of this letter, M. Cabarrus had a conference with the Minister on these subjects, and, according to M. Cabarrus' representations, the Minister then declared that he would pay the balance due on the one hundred and fifty thousand dollars, and no more; that the King was dissatisfied at America's having made no returns to his good offices, either in ships or flour, etc., etc. ; that he had mentioned to me a year ago his desire of having the men-of-war building in New England, but had not yet received an answer, etc.

It appeared to me very extraordinary that the Minister should promise the Ambassador to do his best, and yet tell M. Cabarrus that he would do nothing, and yet so I believe were the facts.

The next morning, viz., the 26th of February, I paid the Ambassador an early visit, and mentioned these circumstances to him minutely. I expressed my apprehensions that the pretended discontents of the King belonged to the same system of delays and pretexts with which we had been so long amused ; and which in this instance were probably dictated by a desire of avoiding inconvenient advances.

I reminded him that Dr. Franklin had given me expectations of his being able to replace the money I had borrowed of M. Cabarrus, and that this sum, added to the balance to be paid by the Court, would reduce the remainder of the money wanted to less than twenty thousand pounds sterling ; and that it would appear a little surprising in the eyes of Europe, as well as America, that our credit should be permitted either by France or Spain to suffer essential injury for the want of such a sum. I requested him to advise me what to do. He said that he knew not what advice to give me ; that he saw no resources anywhere ; that he should dismiss a courier on Sat-

urday next, and that he would again write to the
Count de Vergennes on the subject. I observed to
him that the answer, if favourable, would probably
come too late, as a great number of the bills would
become payable about the 14th of March. He replied that, if the Court should resolve to supply the
money, he should soon be informed of it.

We had some conversation about the Marquis de
Lafayette. The Ambassador spoke well of him, and
as a proof of the confidence of Congress in the attachment of that nobleman, I mentioned my having
received orders to correspond with him.

I then drew the conversation to our affairs in
Holland, and the prospects of an alliance with the
Dutch. He said those prospects were less fair than
ever ; for that though Mr. Wentworth had been sent
there by England on pretence of settling a cartel, yet
that his real business was to negotiate a separate
peace. I observed that, in my opinion, England
would be the first nation to acknowledge our independence (for there are many reasons that induce
me to think that France does not in fact wish to see
us treated as independent by other nations until after
a peace, lest we should become less manageable in
proportion as our dependence upon her shall diminish). I threw out this opinion to see how it would
strike him. He made a short pause, and then asked
me if I had heard that Lord Germaine had resigned.
I told him I had, and as he chose to waive the subject
I did not resume it, lest he should from my pressing it
suspect that I meant more than a casual remark. The

conversation then turned upon our affairs here. I re-marked that the friends of Spain in America must greatly diminish, that the manner we were treated by this Court was far from conciliatory, and that it would perhaps have been better, as things have turned out, if America had not sent a Minister here. He gave in to this opinion, but added we must be contented here now during the war ; that Spain was necessary ; that she was to be treated like a mistress. He also said that if I had been landed in France, instead of Spain, I should not probably have come to Madrid so soon as I did, and was going to explain himself, when the entry of his servants with breakfast interrupted us.

Having made it a rule to give Dr. Franklin frequent and minute information of my situation, I wrote him the following letter by the Ambassador's courier :

JAY TO BENJAMIN FRANKLIN.

MADRID, March 1, 1782.

MY DEAR SIR :

I have lately received a very friendly letter from the Marquis de Lafayette, covering some despatches from Mr. Livingston. I find that the objects of his voyage are interesting to us, and that it is the desire of Congress that we should correspond with him. My answer to his letter is herewith enclosed. Peruse and dispose of it.

I have given him a summary account of my situa-tion here ; he will doubtless be willing, and perhaps able, to afford you assistance relative to the difficul-ties it imposes upon you.

The Minister has ordered the balance due (about twenty-six thousand dollars) on the one hundred and fifty thousand dollars to be paid to M. Cabarrus on my account, and has through him informed me that no more is to be expected.

M. Cabarrus is exceedingly anxious about the money we owe him, and which the twenty-six thousand dollars he is to receive will not pay.

He declines making further advances. The Ambassador of France can afford me no resources. M. Cabarrus is ready to supply what we may want, on the promise of either France or Spain to repay him in ten or twelve months.

The Ambassador will write (by a courier to France, who sets out to-morrow) on these subjects to the Court. All that remains in my power is to endeavor to keep the public creditors quiet until his or your final answer shall arrive. That this Court should permit our credit to be ruined for the want of about twenty-five thousand pounds sterling does not greatly surprise me ; but I should be astonished if the Minister of France should act the same part, for I have a high opinion of his wisdom.

I am, etc.,

JOHN JAY.

I forbear inserting my letter to the Marquis, because this and my former letters render it unnecessary. I solicited his immediate attention to the state of our bills, etc.

As there could be no doubt but that the Minister

mentioned to M. Cabarrus the King's discontents, by way of apology for not granting further supplies, and with design that they should be represented to me in that light, I thought it prudent to write to the Minister on the subject, although in other circumstances it might have been more proper for me to have omitted taking notice of such an indirect communication. I wrote him as follows : [1]

This letter, if I may use the expression, might have been higher mounted, and the strange conduct of this Court would have justified my writing in a different style, but I feared that offence might have been taken, though, perhaps, for no other purpose than to cover a refusal to aid us with a plausible pretext.

Although I had little confidence in M. Del Campo's late professions of friendship, yet, as the present occasion afforded an opportunity of trying their sincerity, and as men ill-disposed towards us are sometimes pushed into acts of friendship, merely by an opinion of their being thought friendly, I enclosed the above letter in the following note to him :

"Madrid, March 2, 1782.

"Mr. Jay presents his compliments to M. Del Campo, and takes the liberty of enclosing a letter to his Excellency, the Count de Florida Blanca, which he requests the favor of him to deliver.

"M. Del Campo may not, perhaps, in future have an opportunity of rendering a more welcome and inter-

---

[1] This letter of March 2, 1782, appears on p. 182.

esting proof of his friendship for America than at present ; and Mr. Jay will esteem his country and himself greatly obliged by M. Del Campo's friendly attention and interposition on this occasion."

A week elapsed without my receiving any answer either from the Minister or M. Del Campo. The time when our bills would be due was drawing very nigh. My expectations of aid from France were at best uncertain, and every consideration urged me not to leave any thing in my power undone here, to avoid the catastrophe I had so much reason to apprehend. I therefore concluded to wait on the Minister, and in a plain and pointed manner enter into a detail of the reasons given us to expect supplies from this Court, and the impolicy of withholding them.

For this purpose I went to the Pardo on the 9th of March.

The Minister received me with great cordiality ; he was in uncommon good spirits. He entered largely into the nature of his indisposition ; the effect of the weather upon his nerves, and how much he found himself the better for the last three fine days ; and after we had conversed awhile about the conquest of Minorca, and the importance of it, he said he supposed that I wished also to speak to him on the subject of our affairs.

I told him that was really the case, for that the bills which remained to be paid, and the want of funds for the purpose, gave me great uneasiness. He interrupted me by remarking that he had ordered the balance due on the one hundred and fifty thousand dollars to be paid. That the public exigencies had even rendered this payment inconvenient, but that he was an honest man, a man of his word, and, therefore, as he had promised me that sum, he was determined that I should not be disappointed. That as to further aids he could promise nothing *positively* that he would *do his best*, and shrugging his shoulders, intimated that he was not Minister of Finance.

I observed, that the sum now wanted was not very considerable, and that M. Cabarrus' offer rendered the advancing of it very easy. He was in a very good humor ; and after a few hesitations, he told me cheerfully and smilingly that when I found myself very hard pressed I should desire M. Cabarrus to wait upon him.

This I considered as an implied consent to comply with M. Cabarrus' offer, in case such a step should become absolutely necessary to save our bills ; and I imagined he chose to delay it as long as possible, in hopes that the French Ambassador might in the meantime interpose his credit, as he had before done on a similar occasion. I was content that the matter should rest there, and would not hazard losing what I thought I had gained by requiring more at present.

I thanked him for this mark of favour, and then turned the conversation to Major Franks' arrival, and my anxiety to communicate some certain intelligence to Congress relative to the proposed treaty, and what they might expect on that head.

The Count went into a detail of excuses for the delays which had ensued since our leaving St. Ildefonso. His indisposition, and that of M. Del Campo, his forgetting to give M. Del Campo the papers, and M. Del Campo's neglecting to ask for them, were the chief topics from which these excuses were drawn. He said the Ambassador of France had talked to him about the matter eight days ago ; and he promised me that the conferences should begin at Aranjues, to which place the Court would soon remove. He authorized me to communicate this to Congress, adding, that pressing business obliged him to postpone it till then, though I might now begin to speak on the subject to M. Del Campo if I pleased.

I remarked that I had so often disappointed Congress by giving them reason soon to expect M. Gardoqui, that I wished to be enabled to give them accurate information on that point. He replied that a variety of particular circumstances had intervened to prevent his departure, but that he *certainly* should go unless he made personal objections to it, and that *I might tell Congress so.*

I rose to take my leave. *He repeated what he had before said respecting my sending M. Cabarrus to him,* and assured me of his disposition to do what he could for us. I again thanked him, and we parted in great good humour.

It is remarkable that during the course of this conference, which was free and diffusive, the Minister did not mention a syllable of the King's discontents, nor hint the least dissatisfaction at the conduct of Congress towards this Court. I cautiously avoiding making any harsh strictures on the delays I constantly met with, and though the Minister's excuses for them were frivolous and merely ostensible, yet it could have answered no good purpose to have declared that opinion of them, especially at so delicate a period of our affairs.

As many bills to a considerable amount would be payable on the 14th of March, I thought it high time that the Minister should declare his intentions at least a day or two before, and therefore I desired M. Cabarrus to wait upon the Minister and confer with him on the subject. M. Cabarrus accordingly went to the Pardo on the evening of the 11th of March. He saw the Minister and mentioned the purpose of his visit. The Minister said I must have misunderstood him ; that it was not until the last extremity that I was to send him, and he desired M. Cabarrus to inform him when that should arrive. M. Cabarrus repeated to me his former offers, and assured me that nothing on his part should be wanting.

The *Madrid Gazette* of the 12th of March contained a paragraph, of which you ought not to be ignorant. I shall therefore copy it *verbatim*, and add a translation as literal as I can make it :

" By a letter from the Commandant General of the army of operations at the Havanna, and Governor of Louisiana, his Majesty has advices, that a detachment of sixty-five militiamen and sixty Indians of the nations Otaguos, Sotu, and Putuami, under the command of Don Eugenio Purre, a captain of militia, accompanied by Don Carlos Tayon, a sub-lieutenant of militia, by Don Luis Chevalier, a man well versed in the language of the Indians, and by their great chiefs Eleturno and Naquigen, who marched the 2d of January, 1781, from the town of St. Luis of the Illinois, had possessed themselves of the Post of St. Joseph, which the English occupied at two hundred and twenty leagues' distance from the above-mentioned St. Luis, having suffered in so extensive a march and so rigorous a season the greatest inconveniences from cold and hunger, exposed to continual risk from the country being possessed by savage nations, and having to pass over parts covered with snow, and each one being obliged to carry provisions for his own subsistence, and various merchandises, which were necessary to content, in case of need, the barbarous nations through whom they were obliged to cross. The commander, by seasonable negotiations and precautions, prevented a considerable body of Indians, who were at the devotion of the English, from opposing this expedition ; for it would otherwise have been difficult to have accomplished the taking of the said post. They made prisoners of the few English they found in it, the others having perhaps retired in consequence of some prior notice. Don Eugenio Purre took possession in the name of the King of that place and its dependencies, and of the river of the Illinois ; in consequence whereof the standard of his Majesty was there displayed during the whole time. He took the English one, and delivered it on his arrival at St. Luis to Don Francisco Cruyat, the commandant of that post.

" The destruction of the magazine of provisions and goods which the English had there (the greater part of which was divided among our Indians and those who lived at St. Joseph, as had been offered them in case they did not oppose our troops) was not the only advantage resulting from the success of this expedition, for thereby it become impossible for the English to execute their plan of attacking the fort of St. Luis of the Illinois ; and it also served to intimidate these savage nations and oblige them to promise to remain neuter, which they do at present."

When you consider the ostensible object of this expedition, the distance of it, the formalities with which the place, the country, and the river were taken possession of in the name of his Catholic Majesty, I am persuaded it will not be necessary for me to swell this letter with remarks that would occur to a reader of far less penetration than yourself.

I will therefore return to our bills.

The 14th of March arrived, the bills then due were presented, and I prevailed upon the holders of them to wait till the next day at noon for my answer. As the last extremity in the most literal sense had now arrived, I presumed that the Minister would not think me too hasty in requesting his determination. I wrote him the following letter, and sent it by the post, which passes every evening between Madrid and the Court :

JAY TO FLORIDA BLANCA.

MADRID, March 14, 1782.

SIR :

Bills to a considerable amount have been presented to me this afternoon for payment. The holders of them consent to wait till to-morrow noon for my positive and final answer.

Your Excellency is too well apprized of every thing that can be said on this subject, to render it necessary for me to multiply observations upon it.

I have no reason to expect aid from France, and I request the favour of your Excellency to inform me explicitly whether I may flatter myself with any and what relief from the friendly interposition of his Majesty.

I have the honour to be, etc.

JOHN JAY.

I thought it advisable to send a copy of the above letter to the Ambassador of France with the following note :

" Mr. Jay presents his compliments to his Excellency, the Ambassador of France, and has the honour of transmitting herewith enclosed a copy of a letter he has written this evening to the Count de Florida Blanca.

" The Ambassador will perceive from this letter in what a critical situation Mr. Jay finds himself. He requests the favour of the Ambassador's advice, and will do himself the honour of waiting upon him in the morning to receive it.

" MADRID, Thursday evening; March 14, 1782."

On this day, being Thursday, on which day in every week M. Cabarrus had for some time past kept an open table, M. Del Campo was unexpectedly one of the guests, having visited M. Cabarrus but once before on those days. Mr. Carmichael was present. Some earnest and private conversation passed between M. Del Campo and M. Cabarrus. In the afternoon Mr. Carmichael, by my desire, pressed M. Cabarrus to write to the Minister that on the morrow our bills must be either paid or protested. M. Cabarrus replied that he had already given that information to M. Del Campo, and that he would not risk that gentleman's displeasure by repeating it to the Minister, for it would look as if he doubted M. Del Campo's attention to it. Mr. Carmichael informed me at the same time that M. Cabarrus' manner appeared changed and somewhat embarrassed.

On the morning of the 15th of March I waited on the Ambassador. He promised to speak to the

Minister that morning to obtain his final answer, and if possible to render it favourable. On his return from the Pardo he wrote me the following letter :

COUNT MONTMORIN TO JAY.

[Translation.]

March 15th, 1782.

SIR :

I have just come from the Pardo. The Count de Florida Blanca had not received your letter of yesterday, but I supplied the deficiency by explaining to him your critical and difficult situation. He told me that you might accept the drafts to the amount of fifty thousand dollars, provided M. Cabarrus remains in the same disposition he has displayed hitherto, relative to the time he would wait for the reimbursement of the sums he has advanced for this purpose. You can, therefore, make an arrangement with M. Cabarrus for the acceptance of the bills to the amount of forty or fifty thousand dollars, and show him this note as his security.

I hope that this sum will relieve you from your present embarrassment, and give you time to adopt measures meeting the bills, which shall hereafter become due.

Although this information is not so fully satisfactory as I could wish, I take pleasure in communicating it to you, with assurances of my sincere and inviolable attachment.

THE COUNT DE MONTMORIN.

You will doubtless think with me it was very extraordinary that the Minister should not have received my letter sent him yesterday by the Court courier. Why and by whose means it was kept back can only be conjectured. Had not the Ambassador's application supplied the want of it, a pretext for the

Minister's silence would thence have arisen. The letter did not in fact miscarry, for the Minister afterwards received it. The Minister's caution in making his becoming engaged for the advances in question to depend on M. Cabarrus' persisting in the same dispositions he had lately declared, relative to the time he would be content to wait for a reimbursement, is somewhat singular, considering that his offers on that head had been repeatedly and explicitly communicated to the Minister, and to the Ambassador of France, both by him and by me. Immediately on receiving the Ambassador's letter, I gave it to Mr. Carmichael, with instructions to show it to M. Cabarrus, and bring me back his answer without delay, for I was then expecting the notary and others with bills.

Mr. Carmichael returned and informed me that he had communicated the letter to M. Cabarrus, and that instead of abiding by his former offer, to be content with the Minister's engaging to see him repaid in ten or twelve months, he insisted on being repaid in four months, in four equal monthly payments, and those payments secured by orders on the rents of the general post-office, and that M. Cabarrus promised either to write or speak to the Minister about it.

A new application to the Minister became necessary, and consequently further time and indulgence from the holders of the bills was to be solicited.

I told the notary that I was in treaty with M. Cabarrus for the supplies I wanted, and that one or two articles remained to be adjusted, which could not be done till the next day.

I therefore requested him to suspend the protest for twenty-four hours more, and to apply to the holders of the bills for permission, adding that near twenty of them belonged to M. Cabarrus, and that from the friendly conduct of several of the others I had reason to flatter myself that they would readily consent. He seemed surprised at what I said respecting my expectations from M. Cabarrus, and with a degree of indignation told me that M. Cabarrus was more pressing than any of the others, and had already sent him two messages to conclude the matter with me without delay, that he had received one of the messages the day before, and the other that morning. He nevertheless cheerfully undertook to obtain permission from the holders of the bills to wait till the next afternoon, and succeeded in it.

The next morning, viz., the 16th of March, I waited upon the Ambassador. I mentioned to him these several facts, and told him that my hopes from M. Cabarrus were at an end, for that exclusive of other circumstances it was not probable that, considering his lucrative connections with government, he would risk treating the promise of the Minister, made in consequence of his own offer, with so little respect as to demand such formal and unusual securities for the performance of it, unless there had been some previous concert, or indirect management, in the case. The Ambassador declined assenting to this opinion. He promised to see the Minister, with whom he was that day to dine, and to send me his positive and final answer by four o'clock in the afternoon.

Having prepared the draft of a protest, I thought it would not be amiss to show it to the Ambassador. He returned it to me without making any other remark, than that it was rather pointed.

From the Ambassador's I went to M. Cabarrus'; he had not been at the Pardo, and was then at a meeting of merchants, to whose consideration his plan of a bank had been referred.

The Ambassador went to the Pardo and mentioned the matter to the Minister, who replied briefly, "that affair is already with M. Cabarrus," but the Chevalier de Bourgoing, having been desired to bring back a decided answer, applied to M. Del Campo on the subject, who told him, "that they could not possibly comply with M. Cabarrus' terms; that he had written so that morning to M. Cabarrus by a private courier, and that in the evening the Minister would repeat it to him officially." On the Chevalier's mentioning this to the Ambassador, he was clearly of opinion that I had not any resource left, and, therefore, that the bills must be protested, and that the Chevalier should tell me so. I showed the protest, as translated into Spanish by M. Gardoqui, to the Chevalier. The original in English is as follows:

" Mr. Jay says, that when he accepted the bills hereunto annexed, he had good reason to expect to be supplied with the funds necessary to pay them. That he has been disappointed in the expectations he was encouraged to entertain on this subject, and that his endeavors to obtain moneys for the purpose both here and elsewhere have been unsuccessful, although the bills which remain to be paid by him, together with all his other engagements, do not exceed twenty-five thousand pounds sterling. That these disappointments being unexpected, he cannot, for want of time, have recourse to Congress, and, therefore, finds himself reduced to the mortifying necessity of permitting them to be protested."

The Chevalier approved of the protest, but the notary on reading it observed that the sum was really so trifling, that he thought it would do better to strike it out. The Chevalier was struck with this remark, and advised me with some earnestness to make no mention of the sum, for, said he, "it will appear very extraordinary, that you should be obliged to protest the bills of Congress for the want of such a sum, and people will naturally turn their eyes towards France, and ask how it happened that your good allies did not assist you ; it will look as if we had deserted you."

I replied that, since the bills must be protested, I was content that my true situation should be known. I admitted his inferences to be just, and naturally flowing from the facts, adding that as France knew my situation and had withheld relief, she had so far deserted us ; but that I was, nevertheless, mindful of the many proofs we had received of her friendship, and should not cease to be grateful for the ninety-nine acts of friendship she had done us, merely because she had refused to do the hundredth.

In short, I directed the notary to recite this protest *verbatim.*

This protest was drawn at my leisure, and with much consideration. It operated as I expected, and I am persuaded you will see the reason of each sentence in it without the aid of my comments. I will only remark that I was at first induced to insert, and afterwards to refuse striking out, the sum, lest from leaving it uncertain the public might have had room to conjecture, or individuals to insinuate, that I had imprudently run into such rash and expensive engagements as to render it improper for Spain or France to afford me the necessary supplies.

Nor did it appear to me that both of them should have reason to be ashamed of permitting our credit to be impeached and injured for such an unimportant sum. Both Courts were blamed, and we not only acquitted, but pitied by the public.

I ought to inform you that the sum which I really wanted did not amount to twenty-five thousand pounds, but as some straggling bills frequently made their appearance, and it could not be foreseen how much those which might still be behind would amount to, I thought it advisable to make a considerable allowance on that score ; for in case I should have asked for less than might afterwards have proved indispensable, I should, doubtless, have been put to great difficulties in obtaining a supply for the deficiency.

In justice to the bankers who held the protested bills, I must say that they in general appeared disposed to show me every reasonable indulgence. The house of Joyce & Sons, though considered as anti-American, were particularly civil. They offered to take such of the bills as had been remitted to them on themselves, provided I would only pass my word for the payment of them within a few weeks; but as I had no assurance of funds, I could not risk it. Besides, unless all the bills due could have been suspended on the like terms, it could have answered no purpose, because the difference of protesting a few bills more or less was unimportant. The conduct of Don Ignacias Salaia, the notary, was so particularly and singularly generous, that I cannot forbear mentioning it. Though without expectations, and uninfluenced by promises from me, he behaved as if the case had been his own, and proved the sincerity of his professions by doing every thing in his power to serve me. On perceiving how much he was engaged in my favour, I did not choose to lessen the appearance of its being disinterested by promises of rewards. But after the bills were protested, and he could be of no further use, I sent him a gold piece of sixteen dollars, as an acknowledgment for the trouble I had given him. He returned it with an assurance that he wished to serve me from other motives, and the next day waited upon me to thank me for that mark of attention, and again to assure me that his best services were always at my command.

When the bills were protested, and M. Cabarrus' conduct mentioned in his presence, the poor fellow literally shed tears. I was much affected by the warmth and generosity of this man's heart, and should not have readily pardoned myself, had I neglected to bear this testimony to the goodness of it.

During the whole time that this matter was in agitation, that is from the 11th to the 16th of March, and for some time afterwards, M. Cabarrus did not come near me.

On the 18th I wrote a letter to Dr. Franklin, informing him of the protest, and reciting the reasons assigned for it. I also hinted the propriety of taking up the bills at Paris, if possible.

The national pride of the Ambassador of France was hurt by this event ; I am sure he regretted it as disreputable and impolitic. I remarked to him that most of our cross accidents had proved useful to us, and that this might save us the Mississippi. For I thought it more prudent to appear a little incensed than dispirited on the occasion. I suspect that there has been an interesting conversation between the two Courts about us. He told me, this winter, that he believed Spain wished to modify our independence, and to keep herself in a situation to mediate between us and England at the general peace. He did not explain himself further. As great successes on our part must operate against such designs, the Spanish Minister can neither rejoice in nor be disposed to promote them ; and this may help both to account for the little impression made by the capitulation of York, and for their conduct as to our bills and propositions, etc. I am sure that they fear us too, and the more, perhaps, as they have misbehaved towards us.

Not many days elapsed before a special courier from Paris brought advices to this Court that the British Parliament had resolved to advise the King to cease all offensive operations against us, etc. This, and the subsequent debates and resolutions of Parliament relative to the American war, made a deeper impression here in our favour than any event which has happened since my arrival. New ideas seemed to pervade the whole Court and people, and much consultation as well as surprise was occasioned by it.

On the 26th of March I received the following letter from Dr. Franklin, from the hands of M. Cabarrus, to whom I behaved, on that occasion, with reserved and cold politeness:

BENJAMIN FRANKLIN TO JAY.

PASSY, March 16, 1782.

DEAR SIR:

I have received your several favors of January 30th, February 11th and March 1st, and propose to write fully to you by the next post. In the meantime this line may serve to acquaint you, that I paid duly all your former bills drawn in favor of M. Cabarrus, and that having obtained a promise of six millions for this year, to be paid me quarterly, I now see that I shall be able to pay your drafts for discharging the sums you may be obliged to borrow for paying those upon you, in which however I wish you to give me as much time as you can, dividing them so that they may not come upon me at once. Interest should be allowed your friends who advance for you. Please to send me a complete list of all the bills you have accepted, their numbers and dates, marking which are paid, and what are still to pay.

I congratulate you upon the change of sentiments in the British nation. It has been intimated to me from thence that they are willing to make a separate peace with us exclusive of France, Spain, and Holland, which so far as relates to France is impossible; and I believe they will be content that we leave them the other two; but Holland is stepping towards us, and I am not without hopes of a second loan there. And since Spain does not think our friendship worth cultivating, I wish you would inform me of the whole sum we owe her, that we may think of some means of paying it off speedily.

With sincerest regard, I am, &c. &c.

B. FRANKLIN.

P. S. The Marquis de Lafayette has your letter.

I answered this letter as follows, by a French courier:

JAY TO BENJAMIN FRANKLIN.

MADRID, March 29, 1782.

DEAR SIR:

On the 18th instant I informed you of my having been reduced, by M. Cabarrus' want of good faith, to the mortifying necessity of protesting a number of bills which were then payable.

Your favour of the 16th instant reached me three days ago. It made me very happy, and enabled me to retrieve the credit we had lost here by those protests. I consider your letter as giving me sufficient authority to take the necessary arrangements with the Marquis d'Yranda for paying the residue of my debts here, as well as such of the protested bills as may be returned for that purpose.

The account you request of all the bills I have accepted is making out, and when finished shall be transmitted by the first good opportunity that may offer. You may rely on my best endeavours to render my drafts as little inconvenient to you as possible.

The British Parliament, it seems, begin to entertain less erroneous ideas of us, and their resolutions afford a useful hint to the other powers in Europe. If the Dutch are wise, they will profit by it. As to this Court, their system (if their conduct deserves that appellation) with respect to us has been so opposite to the obvious dictates of sound policy, that it is hard to divine whether any thing but experience can undeceive them. For my part, I really think that a treaty with them daily becomes less important to us.

That Britain should be desirous of a separate peace with us is very natural, but as such a proposal implies an impeachment of our integrity, I think it ought to be rejected in such a manner as to show that we are not ignorant of the respect due to our feelings on that head. As long as France continues faithful to us, I am clear that we ought to continue hand in hand to prosecute the war until all their, as well as all our, reasonable objects can be obtained by a peace, for I would rather see America ruined than dishonoured. As to Spain and Holland, we have as yet no engagements with them, and therefore are not obliged to consult either their interest or their inclinations, further than may be convenient to ourselves, or than the respect due to our good allies may render proper.

France, in granting you six millions, has acted with dignity as well as generosity. Such gifts, so given, command both gratitude and esteem, and I think our country possesses sufficient magnanimity to receive and remember such marks of friendship with a proper degree of sensibility. I am pleased with your idea of paying whatever we owe to Spain. Their pride, perhaps, might forbid them to receive the money. But our pride has been so hurt by the littleness of their conduct, that I would in that case be for leaving it at the gate of the palace, and quit the country. At present such a step would not be expedient, though the time will come when prudence, instead of restraining, will urge us to hold no other language or conduct to this Court than that of a just, a free, and a brave people, who have nothing to fear from, nor to request of, them.

I am, etc., etc.,   JOHN JAY.

On receiving Dr. Franklin's letter I sent for my good friend the notary, and desired him to make it known among the bankers, that I had received supplies equal to all my occasions, and was ready to pay to every one his due. He received the commission with as much pleasure as I had the letter. He executed it immediately, and our credit here was re-established.

M. Cabarrus became displeased with himself, and took pains to bring about a reconciliation by the means of third persons, to whom I answered that as a Christian I forgave him, but as a prudent man, could not again employ him. As this gentleman has suddenly risen into wealth and importance, and is still advancing to greater degrees of both, I shall insert a letter which I wrote in reply to one from him on the subject:

JAY TO M. CABARRUS.

MADRID, April 2, 1782.

SIR :

I have received the letter you did me the honour to write on the 29th of March last.

As soon as the examination of your accounts shall be completed, I shall be ready to pay the balance that may be due to you, either here or by bills on Paris.

I should also be no less ready to subscribe a general approbation of your conduct, if the latter part of it had been equally fair and friendly with the first.

Although it always affords me pleasure to recollect and acknowledge acts of friendship, yet, sir, I can consider only one of the five instances you enumerate as entitled to that appellation. I shall review them in their order. You remind me :

1st. *That you risked the making me considerable advances, at a time when I could only give you hopes, and not formal assurances, of repayment.*

I acknowledge freely and with gratitude that (exclusive of the commissions due to you for paying out the various sums I had placed in your hands) you did advance me between twenty and thirty thousand dollars ; but as the United States of America were bound to repay it, and I had reason to expect supplies to a far greater amount, I conceived, and the event has shown, that you did not run any great risk, although the uncertainty of the time when these supplies would be afforded, prevented my giving you positive and formal assurances of the time and manner of repayment.

2dly. *That you augmented these advances to quiet the demands of the Marquis d' Yranda.*

Permit me to remind you that this circumstance might have been more accurately stated. The fact was as follows : I had received about fifty thousand dollars, which, by a prior contract, I had agreed to pay the Marquis on account of a greater sum borrowed from him in paper. The sum in question was in specie. You and others offered to exchange it for paper at the then current difference. The preference was given to you. Under that confidence, and for that express purpose, the specie was sent to your house, and you did exchange it accordingly. With what propriety, sir, can you consider this transaction in the light of making advances, or lending me money to quiet the Marquis d'Yranda ? It is true that by sending the money to your house I put it in your power, by retaining part of it, to repay yourself what you had before advanced. But, sir, such a proceeding would have been a flagrant breach of trust ; and I cannot think any gentleman ought to give himself, or expect to receive, credit for merely forbearing to do a dishonourable action.

3dly. *That you gave me, on my signature, the money for which I applied to you for my personal use, without detaining any part of it on account of the balance then due to you.*

The transaction you allude to was as follows. I had authority to draw from his Excellency, Dr. Franklin, on account of my salary. It happened to be convenient to me to draw for a quarter. You agreed to purchase my bill on him, and to pay me in specie at the current exchange. As it was post-day, I signed and sent you the bill before I had received the money. These are the facts, and it seems two favours are to be argued from them. First, that you did not scruple my signature, or, in other words, that you took my bill. To this I answer that you had no reason to doubt its being honoured. All my former ones had been duly paid. Nor could you or others produce a single instance in which my signature had not justified the confidence reposed in it. Secondly, that by sending you the bill before you had sent me the money for it I gave you an opportunity of keeping the money, and giving my public account credit for it, and that in not taking this advantage you did me a favour.

After having agreed to purchase this bill, and pay me the money for it, you could have no right to detain it. And surely, sir, you need not be informed that there is a wide distinction between acts of common justice and acts of friendship. I remember that there was then but little demand for bills on Paris, and so far as you may have been induced to take this one, from regard to my convenience, I am obliged to you.

4thly. *That by your agency you accelerated the payment of the twenty-six thousand dollars.*

I really believe, sir, that you did accelerate it, and you would have received my thanks for it, if the unusual and very particular manner in which the order for that payment was expressed had not been less consistent with delicacy, than with those improper fears and apprehensions which the confidence due to my private as well as public character ought to have excluded from your imagination. All the preceding orders, which had been given on similar occasions, directed the money to be paid to me. But in this instance, as I owed you a considerable balance, care was taken that the twenty-six thousand dollars should not, as formerly, be paid to me, but to you on my account.

5thly. *That you offered to make me further advances, if either the Ambassador of France or the Minister of State would give you a positive order for the purpose, which you say they constantly refused.*

It is true, sir, that you offered to supply me with money to pay my acceptances for the month of March, provided the Minister of State or the Ambassador of France would engage to see you repaid with interest, within a certain number of months, sometimes saying that you would be content to be repaid within seven months, and at others within ten or twelve months, and you repeated this offer to me in these precise terms on the 11th of March last.

This offer was friendly. I accepted it with gratitude, and in full confidence that you would punctually perform what you had thus freely promised. I accordingly made this offer known to the Minister, and solicited his consent. On the 15th day of March he authorized the Ambassador of France to inform me that you might advance me from forty to fifty thousand current dollars on those terms. The Ambassador signified this to me by letter, and that letter was immediately laid before you. Then, sir, for the first time did you insist on being repaid in four months, and that in four equal monthly payments, secured by orders on the rents of the post-office, or on the general treasury, etc., etc. These terms and conditions were all new, and never hinted to me in the most distant manner until after the Minister had agreed to your first offer, and until the very moment when the holders of the bills were demanding their money, and insisting that the bills should either be paid or protested.

The Minister rejected these new conditions, and you refused to abide by the former ones. The bills were then due. I had no time even to look out for other resources, and thereby was reduced to the necessity of protesting them.

Such conduct, sir, can have no pretensions to gratitude, and affords a much more proper subject for apology than for approbation. I confess that I was no less surprised than disappointed, and still remain incapable of reconciling these deviations from the rules of fair dealing, with that open and manly temper which you appear to possess, and which I thought would insure good faith to all who relied on your word.

How far your means might have failed, how far you might have been ill-advised, or ill-informed, or unduly influenced, are questions which, though not uninteresting to you, are now of little importance to me.

I acknowledge with pleasure that, until these late singular transactions, I had reason to believe you were well attached to the interests of my country, and I present you my thanks for having on several former occasions endeavoured to promote it.

I am, etc., etc.,

JOHN JAY.

As M. Cabarrus was concerned in contracts with government for money, and was the projector of several of their ways and means for supplying the Royal Treasury, it appeared to me expedient that he should wish us well, and be our banker. Some advantages have arisen from it, and they would probably have been greater, if not opposed by the great and unfriendly influence of M. Del Campo. At the same time that I blame M. Cabarrus, I cannot but pity him, for there is much reason to consider him in the light of the *scape-goat.*

I have now employed Messrs. Drouilhet to do our business; that house is one of the most considerable here in the banking way.

I showed Dr. Franklin's letter to the Ambassador of France, and made him my acknowledgments for the generous supply afforded by his Court to ours. He seemed very happy on the occasion, and regretted it had not been done a little sooner.

His secretary remarked to me that Spain would suspect that this subsidy had been granted in consequence of the protest of our bills, and that this Court would make it the cause of complaint against France.

The Court left the Pardo, and passed the Easter holidays at Madrid. I denied myself the honour of waiting on the Minister on that occasion, nor have I seen him since the protest of our bills. My judgment, as well as my feelings, approved of this omission. The Court are now at Aranjues, where I have taken a house, and purpose to go soon after these despatches shall be completed.

On the 30th of March I was surprised by the following note, being the first of the kind which I have received from the Minister since my arrival:

[Translation.]

" The Count de Florida Blanca has been to take the orders of V. S.[1] for Aranjues, where he hopes to have the honour of the company of V. S. at his table every Saturday after the 11th of May next ensuing."

This invitation is imputable to the late news from England, and the grant of six millions by France was probably accelerated by it. Both Courts are watching and jealous of us. We are at peace with Spain, and she neither will nor indeed can grant us a present subsidy. Why then should we be anxious for a treaty with her, or make sacrifices to purchase it? We cannot now treat with her on terms of equality, why therefore not postpone it? It would not perhaps be wise to break with her; but delay is in our power, and resentment ought to have no influence.

Time would secure advantages to us, which we should now be obliged to yield. Time is more friendly to young than to old nations, and the day will come when our strength will insure our rights.

---

[1] Vuestra Senoria, *Your Lordship*, or *Your Excellency.*

Justice may hold the balance and decide, but if un-armed will for the most part be treated like a blind woman.   There is no doubt that Spain requires more cessions than England, unless extremely hum-bled, can consent to.   France knows and fears this. France is ready for a peace, but not Spain.   The King's eyes are fixed on Gibraltar.   The Spanish finances indeed are extremely mismanaged, and I may say pillaged.   If England should offer us peace on the terms of our treaty with France, the French Court would be very much embarrassed by their alliance with Spain, and as yet we are under no obligations to persist in the war to gratify this Court. It is not certain what England will do, nor ought we to rely on the present promising appearances there ; but can it be wise to instruct your Commissioners to speak only as the French Ministers shall give them utterance?   Let whatever I write about the French and their Ambassador here be by all means kept secret.   Marbois gleans and details every scrap of news.   His letters are very minute, and detail names and characters.

Sweden is leaning towards us, and it will not be long before the Dutch become our allies.   Under such circumstances, Spain ought not to expect such a price as the Mississippi for acknowledging our independence.

As it is uncertain when I shall again have so good an opportunity of conveying a letter to you as the present, I have been very particular in this.   The facts might perhaps have been more methodically arranged, but I thought it best to state them as they arose; and though some of them separately considered do not appear very important, yet when viewed in connection with others they will not be found wholly uninteresting.

You will readily perceive, on reading this letter, that parts of it relate to Mr. Morris' department. I hope he will excuse my not repeating them in a particular letter to him, especially as he will readily believe that the length of this, and the ciphers used in it, have fatigued me a good deal.

All the ciphers in this letter are those in which I correspond with Mr. Morris, and the only ones I have received from him. They were brought by Major Franks, and marked No. 1. Several of my former letters to Mr. Thomson and you mentioned that his cipher was not to be depended upon. The copy of it, brought by Mr. Barclay, which is the only copy I have received of the original by Major Franks, having passed through the post-office, came to my hands with marks of inspection on the cover.

I received, the 12th of April, a packet of newspapers, which I believe was from your office. It was brought to Bilboa by Mr. Stockholm; but not a single line or letter from America accompanied it.

On the back of the packet there was this endorsement: " Bilboa, April 3d, 1782, brought and forwarded by your Excellency's very humble servant, Andrew Stockholm." Notwithstanding this, it was marked *Paris* by the post-office, and charged with postage accordingly, viz., one hundred and six reals of vellon. I sent the cover to the director of the post-office, but he declined correcting the mistake. Thus are all things managed here.

The *Courier de l'Europe* informs us that the English Ministry are totally changed, and gives us a list of those who form the new one. I think it difficult to predict how this change may eventually operate with respect to us. I hope we shall persevere vigorously in our military operations, and thereby not only quiet the fears and suspicions of those who apprehend some secret understanding between us and this Ministry, but also regain the possession of those places which might otherwise counterbalance other demands at a peace.

Great preparations are making here for a serious attack on Gibraltar. The Duc de Crillon will doubtless command it. His good fortune has been very great.

It is natural as well as just, that Congress should be dissatisfied with the conduct of this Court; they certainly have much reason; and yet a distinction may be made between the Ministry and the nation, the latter being more to be pitied than blamed.

I must now resume a subject which I did not expect to have had occasion to renew in this letter.

You may observe from the copy of the Count de Florida Blanca's note, containing an invitation to his table at Aranjues, and left at my house by his servant, that it was not expressly directed to me. This omission raised some doubt in my mind of its being intended for me, but on inquiry I found that the other

Ministers had in the same manner received similar ones, and not directed to them by name. I mentioned my having received it to the Ambassador of France. He told me the Count had not mentioned a syllable of it to him. I desired him to take an opportunity of discovering from the Count, whether or no there was any mistake in the case, and to inform me of the result, which he promised to do.

On the 23d of April instant, the Ambassador being then in town, I paid him a visit. He told me that on mentioning the matter to the Count, he said it must have happened by mistake, for that he intended only to ask my orders for Aranjues, but that he was nevertheless glad the mistake had happened, as it would give him an opportunity, by mentioning it to the King, to obtain his permission for the purpose, and to that end desired the Ambassador to write him a note stating the fact. The Ambassador did so, and the Count afterwards informed him that he had communicated it to the King, who, with many expressions of regard for our country, had permitted him to invite me as a private gentleman of distinction belonging to it. He authorized the Ambassador to communicate this invitation to me, and also to inform me that I might bring Mr. Carmichael with me.

Much conversation ensued between the Ambassador and myself, consisting of my objections to accepting this invitation, and his answers to them. But as we continued to differ in sentiment, and he was going out, I agreed to think further of the matter before I gave my final answer.

For my part I doubt there having been any mistake. I think it more probable that the Minister, afterwards reflecting on the use that might be made of this note, wished to render it harmless by imputing it to mistake, and substituting a more cautious invitation. For it can hardly be supposed, either that his servant would, for the first time in two years, leave such a note at my house unless ordered, or that he himself would for the first time in his life, and that in writing, inform me of his having called to take my orders for Aranjues, without taking care that his amanuensis wrote as he dictated. He was probably warmed by the news from England and Holland, and, in the perturbation of spirits occasioned by it, was more civil than on cool reflection he thought was expedient, especially on further considering, that the Ambassador might not be well pleased at not having been privy to it.

A few days afterwards I wrote the Ambassador the following letter on the subject.[1]

Reasons similar to those assigned for this refusal have induced me ever since my arrival to decline going to Court, where I might also have been presented as a stranger of distinction, but as Mr. Carmichael had been presented in that character previous to my coming to Madrid, I never objected to his making subsequent visits.

I am, dear sir, with great regard and esteem, your most obedient and very humble servant,

JOHN JAY.

---

[1] This letter appears on p. 199—Jay to Montmorin, April 27, 1782,

TO MRS. JAY FROM HER MOTHER.

ELIZABETH-TOWN, April the 21, 1782.

MY DEAR SALLY,

I hope you don't harbour a thought that my not writing to you proceeds from any abatement of my affection for you, but rather impute it to the true reason, which is the attention of your sisters, by which means you have every information concerning our family and likewise everything interesting out of it. My dear child of my heart, I love you most tenderly and have often attempted to write to you, but was too much affected to finish a letter. I have felt more for you than I chose to discover. I long and pray for the happy period that shall bring you to my embraces. It is my daily prayer that you may be preserved in health and safety to your native Country; your absence is one of the afflictions of my life. I feel distrest at the thought of Brockholst's leaving you lest it make it more lonesom for you; otherwise I shall be very happy to see him if a kind Providence permit me that blessing.

Your dear little son is a great comfort to me; he is amiable and has the love and esteem of all that know him. He is not yet returned from a visit to his grand pappa Jay, where he went last August accompany'd by his Aunt Susan. . . . I heard from him a few days ago by Dr. Latham who lives somewhere up the river. He says that the old gentleman, Mr. Jay, is declining fast; he don't get out of his bed; the rest of the family embrace health and that Peter and Susan would have returned with him if they had known it sooner.

Sir James Jay has been one of my family since the first of February. I often told him that he was in a very unsafe place, and that my house was indanger'd by him to be plundered (I was told so), and that they were only waiting an opportunity. Last Monday morning he left us with an intent to be back again in two days, but unfortunately he was taken off from Mr. Scylars [Arent Schuyler's] and carried into the king's lines, where he is at present. His clothing is here at my house. Your pappa keeps a constant correspondence with his little grandson; he prints all his letters so that my dear little Peter can read them for himself.

This is such a scroll that I am ashamed to send it. Susan is my pen maker when at home. I expect Kitty to spend the summer with us at home. Give my love to Mr. Jay and B[rockholst] if with you.

MRS. MARGARET LIVINGSTON [1] TO JAY.

CLAREMONT, 21 April, 1782.

MY DEAR SIR,

I hope you'l not think me capable of neglecting to acknowledge the honor and pleasure your Letter gave me in [reply to] mine wrote sixteen months agoe and sent to the Committee at Philadelphia to transmit to you.—Sorry I am to have occasion to condole with you upon the Death of your honoured Parent. Your long separation from him, his advanced Age together with his infeebled state for some time past, must have lessened the shock which you doubtless felt on the melancholy occasion; this at least we hope for your peace.—This must be your consolation that he is safe in the Haven of bliss. . . . Will you permit a friend who loves and honours you to beg of you not to let your Immortal soul starve under the weight of cares and business, altho' that must necessarily take up much of your time and thoughts, but not your whole time I hope. Your God has blest you with many talents; those I trust you improve for his Glory and the good of your country. Wisdom is the gift of God, and he has promised additions to it

---

[1] Mother of Chancellor R. R. Livingston and Edward Livingston, subsequently United States Senator from Louisiana, jurist, etc., both of whom are mentioned in the letter. See Jay's answer, August 26, 1782.

to those that ask it, for he giveth liberally and like himself.
You are ingaged in a just and virtuous cause; you know
an Holy God befriends it, so that you may come boldly
with affiance to the throne of Grace for every requisite to
enable you for the dutys of your exalted station. I am persuaded that you believe these truths, nor will the repetition
be irksom altho' known and practiced by you.

I have the happyness to inform you that my Robert has
paid me a visit a few weeks since, and that he is in perfect
health. His little Bess you would be delighted with was
you to see her; you can't think what a little cherub she is
—her temper the finest you can imagine. But I think I
hear his Excellency tell his sweet Lady setting near him—
'Set an old woman a writing or talking about a favourite
grandchild and she will be so profuse, &c.'

My Edward has always been honored with your particular attention, and I must say something of him. He passed
through his College Education last fall, and except a little
jaunt with me to Boston last winter, he has applied himself
to learning the French language under Mr. Tetard who,
with a German refugee minister, I took in the house to
teach him German. He is master of the French and reads
and understands the other. You may form an opinion of
him from this anecdote: He was three days at Albany on
a visit to his sister Lewis. He refused going to a dance
with the young patron saying he did n't know the company.
He is now going to study law under Benson. I long much
to know how my Cousin, your Lady, does.

Last week a noted partizan was taken near Albany with
letters wrote in cypher from Canada to New York. I hear
three more are taken. I sigh for the evacuation of our
Capital. When shall we meet? You can have no idea of
the sufferings of many who from affluence are reduced to
the most abject poverty, and others who die in obscurity.
But I forget that it is impolite to make too long a visit to

a statesman ; but as I have had no opportunity of a little conversation with you since I had the pleasure of receiving your Letter, you will forgive my Rusticity. Please to present my love to my Cousin and compliments to my friend Brockholst, and believe me to be, my Dear Sir,

With the most perfect esteem,

Yours sincerely,

MARGARET LIVINGSTON.

P. S. I must thank you for the melon seed you sent. The seeds were distributed but nobody had the luck to raise any melons but myself by ye meer dint of watching every morning to kill the buggs. I shall be much obliged by a new supply next year. Will you indulge me with some flower seed in a Letter, or shrub seed. I forgot to tell you that your Son grows a very fine boy.

JAY TO COUNT DE MONTMORIN.

SIR :   MADRID, 1st May, 1782.

The letter brought for me by your Excellency's courier was from Dr. Franklin, pressing me to go to Paris. As the Count de Florida Blanca has assured me that our conferences for a treaty shall commence at Aranjues in earnest, I doubt the propriety of going to France at present, especially as serious negotiations for peace will not probably take place before the end of the campaign.

I submit to your discretion the mentioning this to the Count de Florida Blanca. If this Court really means to treat of an alliance with us, would it not be advisable to postpone my journey to Paris ? But if, on the other hand, I am to expect further delays, it would be unnecessary for me to remain here.

Permit me to request the favour of your friendly advice on this subject, and to assure you of the esteem and attachment with which I have the honour to be Your Excellency's most obedient

and very humble servant,

JOHN JAY.

JAY TO BENJAMIN FRANKLIN.

MADRID, 8th May, 1782.

DEAR SIR :

I have received your favours of the 22d and 23d ult. They have determined me to set out for Paris. I shall leave this place the latter end of next week. Mrs. Jay and my nephew go with me. Be pleased to take lodgings for me and to inform me of them by a line to Mr. Delap (?) or Mr. Bondfield at Bordeaux.

The Embassador of France does not dislike this step,[1] and the Count de Florida Blanca will refer the instructions intended for M. Del Campo, to the Count d'Aranda at Paris.

I am, dear sir, with great regard and esteem, your obliged and obedient servant,   JOHN JAY.

[1] The " Embassador," Montmorin, had written three days earlier to Vergennes at Paris as follows : " I suppose that you will very soon see Mr. Jay at Paris ; at least Mr. Franklin urges him to go. Mr. Jay has asked my advice. I thought I ought to mention the matter to Count de Florida Blanca, who assures me that it would not be at all inconvenient, and that instructions would be sent to M. d'Aranda so that that Minister could treat with him. Besides Mr. Carmichael would remain here, and as he has the same powers that Mr. Jay has, they could confer as well with him. I intend giving this reply to Mr. Jay, who doubtless has determined to leave this Court which so greatly annoys him, and which in fact cannot have been agreeable to him during the two years of his residence here. At the same time if he is called upon to negotiate with M. d'Aranda I am not confident of their coming to an understanding with each other as they are neither of them inclined to be conciliatory."

ROBERT R. LIVINGSTON TO JAY.

PHILADELPHIA, May 9th, 1782.

DEAR SIR:

Your letter of the 6th of February, with a duplicate of August last, directed to the President, has been received and read in Congress. I am extremely surprised to find from that and yours to me, that so few of my letters have reached you, since no vessel has sailed from this, or, indeed, from any of the neighboring ports, without carrying letters or duplicates of letters from me. The whole number directed to you, including the duplicates from October to this time, amounts to twenty-four; so that they must certainly be suppressed in many instances. But what astonishes me more, is to find that you cannot read my letter, No. 3, and the duplicate of No. 2; when, upon examining my letter book, I find it is written in the very cypher, which you acknowledge to have received, and in which your letter of the 20th of September is written; so that if it is not intelligible, it must have undergone some alteration since it left my hands, which I am the more inclined to think, because you speak of a cypher said to be enclosed, of which my letters make no mention, and only notes a slight alteration in Mr. Thompson's cypher. My first letter was in our private cypher; this you had not received. My second, by the Marquis de Lafayette, in cypher, delivered to me by mistake by Mr. Thompson, and lost with Mr. Palfrey. My third, in the cypher sent by Major Franks, a duplicate of which was sent by Mr. Barclay; and that enclosed a copy of my letter, No. 2. I had then discovered the mistake, so that I can in no way account for your being unable to decypher it.

Since my last, of the 28th of April, we have been informed of the change in the British administration. We have seen the act for enabling the King to make peace, and the new plan has begun to open itself here under the direction of Sir Guy Carleton. You, who know your country-men, will feel little anxiety on this subject. It is proper, however, that you should be enabled to calm the appre-hensions, which those who know us less and are interested in our measures may entertain. I have the pleasure of assuring you, that it has not produced the slightest altera-tion in our sentiments; that we view a change of men and measures with the utmost philosophic indifference. We believe that God has hardened the heart of Pharaoh, so that he cannot let the people go, till the first born of his land are destroyed; till the hosts are overthrown in the midst of the sea; and till poverty and distress, like the vermin of Egypt, shall have covered the land. The general sentiment here seems to be that new endeavors will be so used to detach us from our ally, that the best answer to such attempts to disgrace us will be a speedy and spirited preparation for the ensuing campaign.

When Sir Guy Carleton arrived at New York, he found them in violent convulsions about the demand that General Washington had made of the persons who perpetrated the murder upon an officer of the Jersey levies, one Captain Huddy, whom they made prisoner, carried to New York, and afterwards taking him out of jail hung him in the county of Monmouth. I enclose the General's letter, and the other letters that have passed on that occasion. The affair has not yet ended; the British officers insist upon his [*i. e.* Lippincott, who hung Huddy] being given up. The refugees support him. A court martial is now sitting for his trial. In the extracts sent out by General Robertson are contained the cases of all the persons, that have been tried and convicted of robbery, horse stealing, &c., in the Jerseys since the war, as they have protected every species of villany. They wish us to consider every felon we hang, as a part of their regular corps.

Your last despatches by Colonel Livingston did not come

to hand. The vessel in which he sailed was taken and carried into New York. He destroyed his letters. He was immediately committed to the Provost, where he met with your brother, who had been sometime confined there. On the arrival of General Carleton, which was a few days after, both were liberated on their *paroles*, so that Mr. Livingston can give us no intelligence of any kind. Carleton spoke to him in the most frank and unreserved manner, wished to see the war carried on, if it must be carried on, upon more generous principles than it has hitherto been; I told him he meant to send his secretary to Congress with despatches, and asked whether the Colonel would take a seat in his carriage. Mr. Livingston told him, that his secretary would certainly be stopped at the first post; upon which he expressed surprise, and inquired whether Mr. Livingston would himself be the bearer of them, which he declined, unless they contained an explicit acknowledgment of our independence, and a resolution to withdraw the British troops. He replied, he was not empowered to make any such proposition, and that his letter was merely complimentary. The next day he wrote to the General the letter, a copy of which, No. 1, is enclosed. The General sent the answer, No. 2; these letters being laid before Congress, they came to the resolution No. 3. You will judge from these circumstances, whether it is probable, that Britain will easily seduce us into a violation of the faith we have pledged to our allies.

I am particular in giving you every information on this head, because I am persuaded, that means will be used by our enemies to induce a belief that this country pines after peace and its ancient connexion with England. It is strictly true, that they are very desirous of peace. But it is also true, that the calamities of war press lighter upon them every day, from the use they are in to bear them, and from the declining strength of the enemy. They consider themselves as bound, both in honor and interest, to support the alliance, which they formed in the hour of distress; and I am satisfied, that no man would be found in any public assembly in America sufficiently hardy, to hint at a peace upon any terms, which should destroy our connexion with France.

I yesterday took the sense of Congress upon the propriety of giving you leave of absence. They have declined giving any answer to that part of your letter, from which you are to conclude that they do not conceive it advisable at present. I enclose the resolution I proposed, which they thought it proper to postpone.

In all our transactions in Spain we are to consider the delicate situation in which they stand with France, the propensity of the former to peace, and the need that the latter has of their assistance. I should conceive it necessary, therefore, rather to submit with patience to their repeated delays than give a handle to the British party at Court. For this reason I conceive that no advantage could result from demanding a categorical answer, and that it might involve us in disagreeable circumstances. The resolution enclosed in my last will either serve as a stimulus to the politics of Spain, or leave us a latitude on the negotiation for a peace, which will be of equal advantage to us with any of those slight aids, which Spain seems willing or able to give us. Congress have found so little advantage from sending embassies to Courts, who have shown no disposition to aid them, that they have passed the enclosed resolution, No. 4. Every saving is an object of importance with them, and they feel very heavily the expense of their foreign embassies, which are in some particulars unnecessarily expensive.

The complaints, which have justly been made of the mode in which our Ministers are paid, have induced Congress to direct the financier to fall upon some other mode. The one adopted will be very advantageous to our Ministers. He proposes to make his payments here quarterly. I shall, as your agent, receive the amount, make out the account, and vest it in bills at the current rate, and remit them to Dr. Franklin, and send you advice when I do it; or, when opportunity offers, send them directly to you. I shall follow your directions if you have any other to give, with respect to the money due to you, and consider myself liable in my private capacity for all the money I receive on your account, till you appoint another agent. This will simplify Mr. Morris's account, he only opening one with the department of Foreign Affairs.

Your present account will commence the 1st of January. I wish you to transmit a state of your account prior to that date, and I will procure and remit you the balance.

We have nothing new but what you may collect from the papers enclosed. The Count de Montmorin will see with pleasure, that the birth of a Dauphin has been received here at this critical time in such a manner as to evidence our attachment to the King, his father, and the French nation.

I am embarrassed beyond expression at the misfortune that happened to Mr. Thompson's cypher. I shall enclose another with this, and send them both to Mr. Harrison, with special directions to send them safely to you.

It must have been long since you heard from me. Our ports have been totally shut up for some time, and no less than three vessels with despatches from me to you have been taken and carried into New York within two months.

As you seem to suppose my appointment has not been sufficiently notified to you, to authorize your directing your letters to me, I enclose the resolution for my appointment, together with that for the organization of the office.

I have the honor to be, &c.
ROBERT R. LIVINGSTON.

JAY TO ROBERT R. LIVINGSTON.

MADRID, May 14, 1782.

DEAR SIR :

A letter from Dr. Franklin calls me to Paris. I set off in about five days. He has doubtless written to you on this subject. Major Franks is on the way to you with despatches from me. Be pleased to send your future letters for me under cover to Dr. Franklin. No inconveniences will be caused by my absence. The instructions intended for M. Del Campo are to be sent to the Count d'Aranda. I congratulate you on the recognition of our independence by the Dutch. The French have lost a ship of the line, and, they say, thirteen transports bound to the Indies.

I hope my future letters will be less unfortunate than many of my former ones. Rely upon it, that I shall continue to write particularly and frequently to you.

With great regard and esteem,

JOHN JAY.

ROBERT R. LIVINGSTON TO JAY.

PHILADELPHIA, 22d May, 1782.

DEAR JOHN :

The express who is to carry my public letter waits while I hastily write this. More vessels having private and public letters for you have been carried into New York tho' as I believe the letters were destroyed. I heard of this opportunity so late that I can not send you duplicates of the latter. I most sincerely condole with you on the death of your father, an event which you must too long have expected not to be prepared for it. But with all your preparation and your conviction that a greater blessing could not have happened to him considering the state in which he has been for a long time past, I am satisfied you will feel no small degree of pain on this event. It would be impertinent and ill timed to offer you consolation; let me change the subject.

Sir James, as I informed you in my last, having been carried to New York and confined to the provost till the arrival of Genl. Carleton, was enlarged but not permitted to leave the City. It is since said that he is gone to England but whether as a prisoner or of his own accord I cannot say tho' I presume, if the account is true, that it must be as a state prisoner.

I informed you in my public letter that I would remit bills for one quarter's salary; it has been found impossible to get the amounts posted to procure the bills on this short notice. I shall send them by the next conveyance.

I am, dear Sir,

Yours affectionately,

R. R. LIVINGSTON.

WILLIAM TEMPLE FRANKLIN TO JAY.

PASSY, 5 June, 1782.

DEAR SIR:

I have by my Grandfather's directions been looking out for an apartment for you and Mrs. Jay. I have, tho' with some difficulty, found one which I believe will suit. It is situated on the Palais Royale, *à l'hotel de la Chine, Rue Neuve des petits Champs, vis a vis la Compagnie des Indes.* The price per month is twenty-five Louis.

Please to make my respectful Compliments to Mrs. Jay, and believe me to be with sincere esteem and respect,

Your Excellency's most

obedient and obliged humble servant,

W. T. FRANKLIN.

JAY TO ROBERT R. LIVINGSTON.

BORDEAUX, 14 June, 1782.

DEAR ROBERT :

My letter of the 11th May mentioned my being called to Paris by a letter from Dr. Franklin. Our journey thus far has afforded much variety, and, excepting some bad roads, fleas, and bugs, was not unpleasant. Both Spanish and French Biscay contain a number of romantic, pretty scenes, and I assure you we found ourselves perfectly disposed to enjoy the beauties of the charming season.

Our health has been greatly improved, or I may say restored, in the journey. The rheumatism has left me, and the only disagreeable circumstance which at present attends us is the indisposition of our little girl, who has the whooping-cough, and is cutting her teeth. We have taken the liberty of naming you for her godfather.

We have received many attentions and civilities both here and at Bayonne. Mr. Bondfield has been particularly obliging. The inhabitants of this city are preparing to present their King with a ship-of-the-line. Commerce flourishes here some say more than before the war. Bayonne, I hear, is soon to be declared a free port. Remember us to Mrs. Livingston and such others of your family as may be with you, and also to Mr. and Mrs. Morris, Mr. and Mrs. Meredith, and my friend, Gouverneur Morris. Adieu.

I am, dear Robert, your friend,

JOHN JAY.

ROBERT R. LIVINGSTON TO JAY.

DEAR SIR: PHILADELPHIA, June 23d, 1782.

The only letter I have received from you, since that of the 6th of February last, was a few lines, which covered an account of the surrender of Fort St. Philip. This success is important, as it not only weakens an enemy, and operates against their future resources, but as it gives reputation to the arms of a nation, that have our sincerest wishes for their prosperity, notwithstanding the little attention we have received from them. This letter goes by too hazardous a conveyance to admit of my entering into many of those causes of complaint, which daily administer food to distrusts and jealousies between Spain and the people of this country. The Havana trade, notwithstanding the important advantages it affords to Spain, meets with the most unjustifiable interruptions. Vessels have been detained for months together, in order to carry on the expeditions which Spain has formed, no adequate satisfaction being allowed for them, and then sent away without convoy; by which means many of them have fallen into the hands of the enemy, and where they did not, the expense and disappointment occasioned by their detention have thrown the greatest discouragements on the trade. The Bahama Islands having surrendered to the arms of Spain, if the copy of the capitulation, published by Rivington, may be depended upon, it is a counterpart to that of Pensacola, and the troops will probably be sent to strengthen the garrisons of New York and Charleston. These transactions, together with the delays and slights you meet with, cannot but have a mischievous effect upon that harmony and confidence, which it is the mutual interests of Spain and America to cultivate with each other. It seems a little singular to this country, that the United Provinces, which never gave us the least reason to suppose that they were well inclined towards us, should precede Spain in acknowledging our rights. But we are a plain people; Courts value themselves upon refinements, which are unknown to us. When a sovereign calls us friends, we are simple enough to expect unequivocal proofs of his friendship.

Military operations have not yet commenced, so that the field affords us no intelligence, and the Cabinet seems to be closed, by the determination of Congress not to permit Mr. Morgan to wait upon them with General Carleton's compliments.

General Leslie, in consequence of the late alteration in the British system (together with the scarcity of provisions in Charleston) proposed to General Greene a cessation of hostilities. I need hardly tell you, that the proposal met with the contempt it deserved. Those, who are unacquainted with our dispositions, would be surprised to hear that our attachment to an alliance with France has gathered strength from their misfortune in the West Indies, and from the attempts of the enemy to detach us from it. Every legislative body, which has met since, has unanimously declared its resolution to listen to no terms of accommodation, which contravenes its principles.

Congress have it in contemplation to make some alteration in their foreign arrangements, in order to lessen their expenses, but as nothing is yet determined on, I do not think it worth while to trouble you with a plan, which may not be carried into effect. I have the honor to be, &c.,

ROBERT R. LIVINGSTON.

EXTRACTS FROM JAY'S DIARY.[1]

1782, 23d June.—Arrived at Paris about noon. Spent the afternoon at Passy with Dr. Franklin. He informed me of the state of the negotiation, and that he kept an exact journal of it.

[1] As given in "Life of Jay," vol. i., p. 136. Further extracts appear under dates of October 21st and December 22d.

24th.—Waited upon M. Vergennes with the Dr. The Count read to us his answer to the British Minister.

25th.—Wrote to Count Aranda. Wrote to the Secretary for Foreign Affairs.

26th.—After breakfast with the Dr. met with Mr. Grenville.

JAY TO ROBERT R. LIVINGSTON.

PARIS, June 25, 1782.

DEAR SIR :

My letters from Madrid, and afterwards a few lines from Bordeaux, informed you of my being called to this place by a pressing letter from Dr. Franklin.

The slow manner of travelling in a carriage through Spain, Mrs. Jay's being taken with a fever and ague the day we left Bordeaux, and the post-horses at the different stages having been engaged for the Count du Nord, who had left Paris with a great retinue, prevented my arriving here until the day before yesterday.

After placing my family in a hotel, I immediately went out to Passy, and spent the remainder of the afternoon in conversing with Dr. Franklin on the subjects which had induced him to write to me. I found that he had then more reason to think my presence necessary than it seems to be at present.

Yesterday we paid a visit to Count de Vergennes. He gave me a very friendly reception, and entered pretty fully with us into the state of the negotiation. His answer to the British Minister appeared to me ably drawn. It breathes great moderation, and yet is so general as to leave room for such demands as circumstances, at the time of the treaty, may render convenient.

There is reason to believe that Mr. Fox and Lord Shelburne are not perfectly united, and that Rodney's success will repress the ardour of our enemies for an immediate peace. On leaving the Count, he informed us that he was preparing despatches for America, and that our letters, if sent to him to-morrow morning, might go by the same opportunity. This short notice, together with the interruptions I meet with every moment, obliges me to be less particular than I could wish ; but as Dr. Franklin also writes by this conveyance, you will doubtless receive from him full intelligence on these subjects.

My last letters also informed you that the Court of Spain had commissioned the Count d'Aranda, their Ambassador here, to continue with me the negotiation for a treaty with our country. I have not yet seen him, and Dr. Franklin concurs with me in opinion that it is more expedient to open this business by a letter than by a visit.

Mr. Adams cannot leave Amsterdam at present, and I hear that Mr. Laurens thinks of returning soon to America, so that I apprehend Dr. Franklin and myself will be left to manage at least the skirmishing business, if I may so call it, of our commission, without the benefit of their counsel and assistance. You know what I think and feel on this subject, and I wish things were so circumstanced as to admit of my being indulged.

You may rely on my writing often, very often.

My letters will now have fairer play, and you will find that I have not ceased to consider amusement and rest as secondary objects to those of business.

I shall endeavour to get lodgings as near to Dr. Franklin as I can. He is in perfect good health, and his mind appears more vigorous than that of any man of his age I have known. He certainly is a valuable Minister, and an agreeable companion.

The Count d'Artois and Duc de Bourbon are soon to set out for Gibraltar. The siege of that place will be honoured with the presence of several princes, and therefore the issue of it (according to the prevailing modes of thinking) becomes in a more particular manner interesting. The Duc de Crillon is sanguine; he told me that, in his opinion, Gibraltar was far more pregnable than Mahon. It is possible that fortune may again smile upon him.

I am, dear sir, etc.,

JOHN JAY.

JAY TO COUNT DE MONTMORIN.

DEAR SIR :   PARIS, 26th June, 1782.

I devote this first leisure moment which has occurred since my arrival to the pleasure of writing a few lines to you.

Our journey was pursued, without any avoidable intermission, to Bayonne, where it became advisable to rest a few days, and where we received many kind attentions from Mons. Formalaguer, to whom, it seems, you had been so obliging as to make friendly mention of us. That city is turning its attention to the American trade, and its situation, in certain respects, is favourable to that design.

Your friend, Mons. Risleau, at Bordeaux, pleased me much ; there is a frankness in his manner, and a warmth about his heart, that is very engaging. I made some agreeable acquaintances in that city, and wish I could have stayed longer with them. Commerce appears to flourish there ; and if their trade with America could be properly protected there is reason to think that it would soon become an object of great importance.

On leaving Bordeaux, Mrs. Jay caught an intermitting fever, which, with the great demand made for post-horses by the Prince du Nord, delayed us greatly.

I went with Dr. Franklin to Versailles the day after our arrival. The Minister spoke of you in terms very friendly and very just, and my next visit would have been to the Countess de Montmorin ; but as we learned that a mail was to be dismissed for Philadelphia to-day, we returned immediately to prepare our despatches, so that I have been obliged to deny myself the honour of paying my respects to a lady whose character and connection with you render me particularly desirous of seeing. To-morrow we are promised a visit from the Marquis de Lafayette and his lady, after which I shall take the first opportunity *me poner a los pies de la Condesa De Montmorin.* I am not sure that this is good Spanish ; if not, I wish the inspectors of the post-office may be so obliging as to correct it.

I had written thus far when a variety of interruptions prevented my proceeding for several days, and then I became violently attacked with the influenza, from which I am now just beginning to recover. It has been very severe on all my family. Mrs. Jay has been obliged to struggle with that and the intermittent fever together, and this is the first day she has been out of the house since our arrival.

I am very much mortified at not having yet seen the Countess de Montmorin. The day before I was taken sick I did myself the honour of calling at her house, but she was from home. As soon as the doctor sets me at liberty, the first use I will make of it will be to renew my visit.

What I have seen in France pleases me exceedingly. Dr Franklin has received some late noble proofs of the King's liberality, in the liquidation of his accounts, and the terms and manner of paying the balance due on them. No people understand doing civil things so well as the French. The aids they have afforded us received additional value from the generous and gracious manner in which they were supplied ; and that circumstance will have a proportionable degree of influence in cementing the connection formed between the two countries.

I think the late resolutions and conduct of America, respecting Mr. Carlton's proposed correspondence with Congress must have given you pleasure. As Mons. de Clonard passed through Spain he doubtless brought you copies. Some letters and instructions I have received by the same vessel contain strong evidence of the determination of Congress to consult the interest and wishes of France upon all occasions.

I have seen and dined with the Count d'Aranda; his conversation leads me to suspect that his Court is, at last, in earnest. This, however, is a question which facts, and not words, must determine. It is hard to judge of men, especially of old politicians; at present I like the Count, for he appears frank and candid, as well as sagacious. They say he is a little obstinate, but, for my part, I prefer plain-dealing, obstinate men, to those unstable ones who, like the moon, change once a fortnight, and are mere dispensers of borrowed light.

I cannot forbear mentioning that I am particularly indebted to the polite attention of your friend, Count d'Estaing. He is at Passy, enjoying *otium cum dignitate*. There is a singular taste displayed in the ornaments of his house. The very walls (like Portius in Addison's "Cato") are ambitiously sententious, and show that they do not belong to an ordinary man.

I am, dear sir, with great esteem and affection,

    Your most obedient and very humble servant,

                JOHN JAY.

JAY TO ROBERT R. LIVINGSTON.

                    PARIS, June 28, 1782.

DEAR SIR:

I had the pleasure of writing to you on the 25th instant. As the express, which is to carry that letter, will not depart till to-morrow morning, I have a good opportunity of making this addition to my despatches.

Agreeably to the desire of Congress, as well as my own wishes, I have had the satisfaction of conferring with the Marquis de Lafayette on several interesting subjects. He is as active in serving us in the cabinet as he has been in the field, and (there being great reason to believe that his talents could be more advantageously employed here than an inactive campaign in America would admit of there) Dr. Franklin and myself think it advisable that he should postpone his return for the present. The Marquis inclines to the same opinion, and, though anxious to join the army, will remain here a little longer.

The intentions of the British Ministry with respect to us are by no means clear. They are divided upon the subject. It is said that Mr. Fox and his friends incline to meet us on the terms of independence, but that Lord Shelburne and his adherents entertain an idea of making a compact with us, similar to that between Britain and Ireland, and there is room to apprehend that efforts will be made to open a negotiation on these subjects at Philadelphia. When it is considered that the articles of a general peace cannot be discussed in America, and that propositions for a separate one ought not to be listened to, it is evident to me that their sending out commissions can be calculated for no other purpose than that of intrigue.

I should enlarge on this topic, were I not persuaded that you will see this matter in the same point of view, and that any proposition which they may offer will be referred to the American Commissioners in Europe. How far it may be prudent to permit any

British agents to come into our country, on such an ostensible errand, is an easy question, for where an unnecessary measure may be dangerous it should be avoided. They may write from New York whatever they may have to propose, and may receive answers in the same manner.

If one may judge from appearances, the Ministry are very desirous of getting some of their emissaries into our country, either in an avowed or in a private character, and, all things considered, I should think it most safe not to admit any Englishman in either character within our lines at this very critical juncture. A mild and yet firm resolution, on the impropriety and inexpediency of any negotiation for peace in America, would give great satisfaction to our friends and confirm their confidence in us. We, indeed, who know our country, would apprehend no danger from any thing that British agents might say or do to deceive or divide us ; but the opinions of strangers, who must judge by appearances, merit attention ; and it is doubtless best not only to be steadfast to our engagements, but also to avoid giving occasion to the slightest suspicions of a contrary disposition. An opinion does prevail here, that in the mass of our people there is a considerable number who, though resolved on independence, would nevertheless prefer an alliance with England to one with France, and this opinion will continue to have a certain degree of influence during the war. This circumstance renders much circumspection necessary.

I am, with great esteem and regard, etc.,

JOHN JAY.

RALPH IZARD TO MRS JAY.

[Paris] Tuesday, 2ᵈ· July, 1782.

Dear Madam:

When I came home last evening I found a letter from a friend of mine in London, which confirms the information I saw in the Newspapers with regard to your brother, and to Sir James Jay, and adds farther, that Sir James was arrived in London, and that he came over in the last Packet from New York.

My letter also mentions the duel between Mʳ· Delany and Mʳ· Allen. Mʳ· Delany has fallen a sacrifice, and has left a young and pretty Widow without friends or fortune. I am glad to hear that it is not Mʳ· Allen of Philadelphia, who was the cause of this misfortune. It is one from Maryland.

I am very angry with myself for being so negligent as not to offer you my services with regard to Mantua makers, Milleners, &c. I was going to do it several times yesterday, but was as often prevented by other conversation. I beg you will believe that I shall be extremely glad to be useful to you, in any way that you wish to employ me. This day will I hope convince you that your fever has entirely taken leave of you. I am, Dear Madam,

Your obedt· Servt·,

R. Izard.

Best Compliments to Mʳ· Jay.

JAY TO COUNT D'ESTAING.

Mr. Jay is greatly mortified that his being abroad has deprived him of the honour of receiving the Count D'Estaing, to whom private esteem and public obligations have long excited the warmest attachment. He did not receive the Count's polite card, nor hear of his having been here, till this moment ; and had it not been too late in the evening, he would have immediately expressed his acknowledgments in person for these repeated marks of attention.   Mr. Jay will do himself the honour of dining with his Excellency to-morrow, agreeable to his polite invitation.

2d July, 1782,
  9 o'clock.

ROBERT R. LIVINGSTON TO JAY.

PHILADELPHIA, July 6th, 1782.

DEAR SIR:

Since my letter of the 23d ultimo, Congress have passed the enclosed resolution.   My letter had already anticipated it, so that it will only serve to show, that I was warranted in the observations I had made, and am sorry to add, that my prediction, that the troops taken by Spain would be sent to serve against us, seems to be confirmed by an account received from Charleston of a number of soldiers, taken in Pensacola, having been sent there.   Could I suppose the Court of Spain entirely regardless of our interests, I should presume, that an attention to their own would keep them from affording such reinforcements to the British here, as will enable them to detach to Jamaica, or any other of their islands, which Spain may have it in contemplation to reduce.

I am, therefore, fully persuaded, that every measure of this kind must originate merely in the inattention of the officer, and, that if mentioned to his Majesty's Ministers, it will be prevented in future.   You will therefore take the earliest opportunity to state it to them, and to show them the pernicious influence it will have, not only upon our measures, but upon those sentiments of friendship and affection, which Congress wish the people of these States to entertain for a nation, that is engaged in the same cause with them, and with whom a variety of considerations will lead them to maintain in future the most intimate connexion.

I have remitted to Dr Franklin the amount of one quarter's salary due to you, which I have invested in bills at six and three pence this money for five livres, which yields a profit to you of about five and a half per cent, and will be more than sufficient to pay the expense of commissions, that this new mode of paying your salaries will subject you to. I have directed an account to be opened with you, and will receive your directions, unless you shall think it proper to appoint some other agent. My Secretary, Mr. Morris, will enclose a particular state of your account, exclusive of contingencies, an account of which I wish you to remit me, that I may get it discharged for you. The second quarter being now due, I shall get the accounts passed and the bills remitted by the next opportunity. You will be pleased to pay particular attention to the enclosed paper in cyphers, as it relates to a private transaction of some importance to both of us.

Let me hear from you on this subject as soon as possible.

I have the honor to be, &c.,

ROBERT R. LIVINGSTON.

JOHN ADAMS TO JAY.

THE HAGUE, July 8, 1782.

SIR :

The Duke de la Vauguyon has this moment kindly given me notice that he is to send off a courier this evening at eleven, and that the Dutch fleet sailed from the Texel this morning.

I shall take advantage of the courier simply to congratulate you on your arrival at Paris, and to wish you and Mrs. Jay much pleasure in your residence there. Health, the blessing which is sought in vain among these meadows and canals, you can scarcely fail of enjoying in France.

I shall beg the favor of you to write me from time to time the progress of the negotiations for peace. . . . I hope in God that your Spanish negotiation has not wrecked your constitution as my Dutch one has mine. I would not undergo again what I have suffered in body and mind for the fee simple of all their Spice Islands. I love them, however, because with all their faults and under all their disadvantages they have at bottom a strong spirit of Liberty, a sincere affection for America and a kind of religious veneration for her cause.

There are intrigues going on here which originate in Petersburg and Copenhagen which surprize me. They succeed very ill, but they are curious. Have you discerned any coming from the same sources at Madrid or Versailles? Whether the object of them is to stir up a party in favor of England to take a part in the war or only to favor her in obtaining moderate terms of peace, or whether it is simply to share some of her guineas by an amusement of this kind, like a game of cards, is a problem.

As to peace, no party in England seems to have influence enough to dare to make one real advance towards it. The present Ministers are really to be pitied. They have not power to do any thing. I am surprized they don't all re sign; if they dissolve Parliament I don't believe they would get a better one. Is Mr. Carmichael at Paris with you, or does he continue at Madrid?

With great esteem I have the honour to be, Sir, your most obedient servant,

J. ADAMS.

JAY TO JOHN ADAMS.

PARIS, 2d August, 1782.

SIR :

Your friendly letter of the 8th ult. should not have remained so long unanswered had I not been obliged by sickness, which lasted several weeks, to postpone writing to any of my correspondents. Mrs. Jay has also been much indisposed ; indeed neither of us has been blessed with much health since we left America.

Your negotiations in Holland have been honourable to yourself as well as useful to your country. I rejoice in both, and regret that your health has been so severely taxed by the business of your employers. I have also had my share of perplexities, and some that I ought not to have met with. I congratulate you on the prospect of your loan succeeding, and hope that your expectations on that subject may be realized. I commend your prudence, however, in not relying on appearances. They deceive us sometimes in all countries.

My negotiations have not been discontinued by my leaving Madrid. The Count d'Aranda is authorized to treat with me, and the disposition of that Court to an alliance with us seems daily to grow warmer. I wish we could have a few hours' conversation on this subject, and others connected with it. As we have no cipher, I must be reserved. I had flattered myself with the expectation of seeing you here, and still hope that when your business at the Hague will admit of a few weeks' absence you may prevail upon yourself to pay us a visit. I really think that a free conference between us might be useful as well as agreeable, especially as we should thereby have an opportunity of making many communications to each other that must not be communicated on paper.

As to negotiations for peace, they have been retarded by the late changes in the British Ministry. Mr. Oswald is here, and I hear that Mr. Fitzherbert is to succeed Mr. Grenville. Lord Shelburne continues to profess a desire for peace, but his professions, unless supported by acts, can have little credit with us. He says that our independence shall be acknowledged, but it is not done, and therefore his sincerity remains questionable. War must make peace for us, and we shall always find well appointed armies to be our ablest negotiators.

The intrigues you allude to I think may be also traced at Madrid, but I believe have very little influence anywhere, except perhaps at London. Petersburg and Copenhagen, in my opinion, wish well to England, but are less desirous to share in the war than in the profits of it. Perhaps, indeed, further accessions to the power of the House of Bourbon may excite jealousy, especially as America as well as Holland is supposed to be very much under the direction of France.

Did you receive my letters of 18th March and 15th April? Think a little of coming this way.

I am, dear sir, with great esteem and regard,

Your most obedient and very humble servant,

JOHN JAY.

DR. JOHN BARD TO JAY.

BELL VALE [N. Y.], Aug. 6th, 1782.

DEAR SIR :

Since I had the pleasure of your favour, I have moved my Family to Bell Vale. Interest, rather than pleasure has occasioned this remove—The mellons you obliged me with are now advanced to their Second Generation. Remember Sir you are to taste them in the Third, and under my roof I hope. Mr. Schemahorn calls upon me from Pough-keepsy, which he left yesterday, and acquaints me your Family were well, and gives me this oppertunity of paying you my respects. The Algaroba Seeds you was so kind to send me have not produced the kind of tree you described. Mr. Johnston and myself planted them with great care, and they came up and grew Vigorously, but produced only a kind of Vine, which died on the approaching frost. We think there has been some mistake in the Seeds. The Mellons are higher flavoured than any I have ever before tasted. Perhaps the Algaroba Seeds given to you, have not been (by some mistake) the real Algaroba Seeds. That tree as you describe it, would be a Valluable Acquisition and exceeding usfull in this country.

Mr. Johnston and my self think our selves much obliged to you for so kindly remembering us, amidst the important conserns you are ingaged in which I acknowledged in a Former letter. I shall always have great pleasure in hearing of your prosperity and wellfare and sincerely hope the time is not far distant when I shall again have the happiness of a Social hour with my honorable friend in America.

I am with real esteem

your most obliged and

most Humble Servt.,

JOHN BARD.

PETER VAN SCHAACK TO JAY.

LONDON, 11th August, 1782
(Rathbone-place) No. 20 Charlotte Street.

DEAR SIR:

Though I have taken up my pen to write to you, I own I hardly know what to say; embarrassed as I am by a consideration of the strange predicament we stand in to each other, compared with our connexion in earlier life. I write, therefore, without any precise object, trusting to what chance (if any thing it should) may produce from it. One thing, however, I must premise, which is, that I have no design of making this introductory to any improper request. Pride, or whatever it may be called, will restrain me from any application that might expose me to the mortification of a refusal; and I am not so weak as to *attempt* to prevail in any matter inconsistent with your *duty*, and in *your* sense of it. The impressions of my youth are not easily effaced; and the new scenes I have passed through have not altered my old notions of right and wrong. *Cœlum, non animum.* Whether what has passed has altered your opinion of me as *a man*, I own, is a question I could wish to have resolved. The artificial relations, introduced by a state of society, may vary or be dissolved by events and external circumstances; but there are others which nothing but deviation from moral rectitude can, I think, annihilate.

I congratulate you on the increase of your family, and sincerely wish you and Mrs. Jay every domestic happiness.

I am, dear sir,

Your most obedient servant,

PETER VAN SCHAACK,

JOHN ADAMS TO JAY.

THE HAGUE, 13 August, 1782.

DEAR SIR:

The public papers announce Fitzherbert's commission to be to treat with "the four powers at war with Great Britain." But whether they mean Hyder Ali or the Mahrattas, is uncertain.

. . . .

For my own part I am not the minister of any " fourth State " at war with Great Britain, nor of any " American Colonies," and therefore I should think it out of character for us to have any thing to say with Fitzherbert, or in the Congress at Vienna, until more decently and consistently called to it. It is my duty to be explicit with you, and to tell you sincerely my sentiments. I think we ought not to treat at all until we see a minister authorized to treat with " the United States of America," or with their ministers.[1] Our country will feel the miserable consequence of a different conduct if we are betrayed into negotiations, in or out of a congress, before this point is settled ; if gold and diamonds, and every insidious intrigue and wicked falsehood can induce anybody to embarrass us, and betray us into truces and bad conditions, we may depend upon having them played off against us. We are and have been no match for them at this game. We shall have nothing to negotiate with, but integrity, perspicuity and firmness. There is but one way to negotiate with Englishmen,—that is, clearly and decidedly ; their fears only govern them. If we entertain an idea of their generosity or benevolence towards us, we are undone. The pride and vanity of that nation is a disease, it is a delirium, it has been flattered and

---

[1] Adams had written to Jay, three days earlier, in the same vein : " I think I ought not to go to Paris while there is any messenger there from England unless he has full powers to treat with Ministers of the United States of America. If the three American ministers should appear at Paris at the same time with a real or pretended minister from London, all the world would instantly conclude a peace certain, and would fill at once another year's loan for the English. In Lord Shelburne's sincerity I have not the smallest confidence, *and I think we ought to take up Fox's idea and insist upon full powers to treat with us in character, before we have a word more to say on the subject.* They are only amusing us."

inflamed so long by themselves and by others that it perverts everything. The moment you depart one iota from your character and the distinct line of sovereignty, they interpret it to spring from fear or love of them, and from a desire to go back.

Fox saw we were aware of this, and calculated his system accordingly. We must finally come to that idea and so must Britain. The latter will soon come to it if we do not flinch. If we discover the least weakness or wavering, the blood and treasures of our countrymen will suffer for it in a great degree. Firmness! firmness and patience for a few months will carry us triumphantly to that point where it is the interest of our allies, of neutral nations, nay, even of our enemies, that we should arrive. I mean a sovereignty universally acknowledged by all the world; whereas, the least oscillation will, in my opinion, leave us to dispute with the world, and with one another, these fifty years.

With great respect, &c.

JOHN ADAMS.

JAY TO EGBERT BENSON.

My Good Old Friend: PARIS, 26th August, 1782.

. . . . . .

From your account of the Vermont business[1] it appears to me that *obsta principiis*, though an old and wise maxim, was neglected; but, as Putnam used to say, "it is not worth while to cry about spilt milk." The calves have kicked over the pail, and there is an end of the matter. You have some other lines still to settle, and the sooner it is done the better. Every good American will zealously endeavour to remove

---

[1] See Benson to Jay, Nov. 27, 1781.

all ground of future dissension between the States. Our power, respectability, and happiness will forever depend on our union. Many foreign nations would rejoice to see us split to pieces, because we should then cease to be formidable, and such an event would afford a fine field for their intrigues. Let us keep peace among ourselves, for whenever the members quarrel the whole body must suffer.

My last letter from Frederick is dated December 1, 1781; it arrived here the 18th ult., and makes the fourth letter I have received from him since we parted. Tell me something of Peter and Nancy. Assure them of my fixed resolution to return and spend the remainder of my days with them. They are never out of my mind and heart. I hope they keep up their spirits and are careful of their health, which I am very anxious about on my own account as well as theirs. Some happy, tranquil years with them forms one of the most pleasing of the prospects I have left. I have desired R. Livingston to pay (through you) to them and to Fady one hundred and fifty pounds York money, viz., fifty pounds to each. He is also to place fifty pounds in your hands for the occasional relief of such of our old servants as may from time to time have need of it; it may not, perhaps, prove necessary; if not, say nothing of the matter.

Inform me of the time and manner of my father's death. I feel too much to enlarge on this subject. Sir James is in England, but I know not in what capacity. I have not a line from him since I left

Philadelphia. Present my best compliments to your mother and brothers. Tell Dr. Van Wyck I remember him with gratitude. Your Governor owes me some letters; he has my esteem and regard. I have written two or three letters to Chas. De Witt, but none from him have ever reached me. We have all (except my nephew) been very sick, but are now, thank God, better. God bless and preserve you.

JOHN JAY.

JAY TO MRS. MARGARET LIVINGSTON.

PARIS, 26th August, 1782.

DEAR MADAM:

Your favor of the 21st April reached me the 18th July last, and is the only letter I have as yet been honoured with from you, the one you allude to having miscarried. I regret its loss, for I am persuaded it was a friendly one.

The first and only intelligence I have received of my father's death is contained in your and Robert's letters. That event was not unexpected, but my long absence greatly increased the bitterness of it. From the day I left him I never ceased to regret that it was not in my power to soften his troubles by those soothing attentions and returns of gratitude which he had a right to expect, and which always make the most pleasing impressions on those by whom we have been the most highly obliged. His affection for me was unbounded, and he knew how sensible I was of it. He has had severe trials, but they are over. I have lost in him an honest friend and a kind father, who never denied me any thing, but from my youth was ever studious to anticipate my very wishes. Thank God, there is another world in which we may meet and be happy! His being there is a new motive to my following his footsteps. I assure you I know the value of Christian resignation; it has been friendly to me on several occasions, which may perhaps one day furnish me with matter for conversation. I thank you most sincerely for reminding me of the great business purpose of my life. Such admonitions, so given, are never unseasonable and always kind. I am persuaded that many who have no regard for their own souls will seldom have much for the happiness or interest of others, and I have learned to expect no sincere attachment from those whose principles of action are created by occasional convenience. These reflections afford a test for professions, and that test tells me to believe yours to be real, and to rely upon it accordingly. The regard and good opinion of the good yield rational pleasure, and I value this ground of satisfaction too highly to omit any opportunity of cultivating it.

I rejoice in Robert's good health, and in that of his daughter. I believe every syllable you say of her temper and disposition, for unless by supposing some perverse cross it would be difficult to account for her having a bad one. I should be happy if this blessing were to be soon followed by that of a son equally promising, for Claremont has my best wishes that it may administer affluence to every succession of wise and good possessors. Your account of Edward gives me pleasure. The time will probably come when his French and German may be of public use, and I think he should continue to improve himself in both. It would be paying Benson but a niggardly compliment to say that Edward will learn no ill from him, for I know that virtue and humanity, as well as law, will always be found in his office.

The anecdote you mention of Edward is so far good; but the principle it manifests has two edges. Self-respect *augurs* well, for nothing good can grow in a soil which does not produce it. It must nevertheless be always managed and frequently pruned, especially in our democratic climate.

We have all been very sick, Mrs. Jay with an intermitting fever, which she caught two months ago, and which left her only eight days ago; the child, with a whooping-cough, teething, etc., is now out of danger; and myself, with an epidemic disorder called here the influenza, which reduced me very low. The summer has been an uncommon one; cold and almost perpetual rains have injured the fruits of the earth as well as the health of the inhabitants. There will be no *good* wine made in France this year, for the grapes will not be much more than half ripe. Fires, morning and evening, have not been very infrequent here during this and the last month. I have not yet met with any well ripened fruit, which I regret the more as there is great abundance and great variety of every kind. I am glad you raised some melons from the seed I sent. I hope they proved good; the seed was of the best I have ever tasted, and if yours were but ordinary, the soil or situation must have been to blame. I shall send over a supply of French seeds this fall. Would not the sandy ridge, between the westerly side of your house and the landing, be excellent for melons? The soil is warm, and there is choice of exposure.

You ask me when we shall meet. I wish it were in my power to answer this question with certainty, but it is not; all I can say is, that one of my first wishes is to return and to spend my days with a brother and sister, whom I send only love, and whose afflictions I earnestly desire to alleviate by every proof of fraternal affection. It might perhaps be in my power to pass a more splendid and easy life on *this* than on *that* side of the water, where the wrecks of the fortunes of the family afford no very flattering prospects. But as personal considerations ought to have no influence, I adhere to my first determination that the term of my absence shall depend entirely on public convenience, which in my opinion will not detain me longer than until the conclusion of the treaties which are to terminate the war.

Mrs. Jay assures you of her affection and respect. Be pleased to present our compliments and best wishes to your good family, and believe me to be, dear madam, with sincere esteem and attachment, your most obedient and humble servant,

JOHN JAY.

JAY TO JOHN ADAMS.

PARIS, September 1, 1782.

DEAR SIR:

I am this moment informed of a safe opportunity of conveying you a letter, and as such another may not soon offer, I must not omit it.

My opinion coincides with yours as to the impropriety of treating with our enemies on any other than an equal footing. We have told Mr. Oswald so, and he has sent an express to London to communicate it and to require further instructions.[1] He has not yet received an answer. Herewith enclosed is a copy of his commission. Mr. Vaughan has no public character. Mr. Fitzherbert is employed to talk about preliminaries with this Court. Nothing, I think, will be done until the return of Mr. Oswald's express. We shall then be enabled to form some judgment of the British Minister's real intentions. Adieu! I have only time to add that I am, with great esteem, your most obedient servant,

JOHN JAY.

MRS. JAY TO MRS. IZARD.

Mrs. Jay's compliments to Mrs. Izard. She is going this evening to the opera with the Marquis de la Fayette, who has given her the pleasure of inviting Mrs. Izard to be of the party, and Mrs. Jay is happy to offer Mrs. Izard a seat in her carriage.

Friday morning, September 5, 1782.

---

[1] Oswald's "Minutes of Conversation" with Franklin and Jay respecting the peace appear in full in Hale's "Franklin in France," vol. i., pp. 92–123.

MRS. IZARD TO MRS. JAY.

Mrs. Izard presents her Compliments to Mrs. Jay, and is extremely sorry that she can not do herself the pleasure of attending her to the Opera this evening ; she supped out last night, which is a thing so unusual with her, that she is paying for it by a bad head ache this morning. She is much obliged to Mrs. Jay for her kind offer of a seat in her Carriage.

Friday 5th Sept^{r.}

ROBERT R. LIVINGSTON TO JAY.

PHILADELPHIA, September 12th, 1782.

Dear Sir :

We yesterday received letters from Mr. Adams by Captain Smedley, who brought out the goods left by Commodore Gillon. These were the first advices, that had reached us from Europe since your short note of the 14th of May. You will easily believe, that this neglect is borne here with some degree of impatience, particularly at this interesting period when we learn that a negotiation for a peace has commenced, and that Mr. Grenville is in France upon that business. Mr. Adams's letters take no more notice of this important transaction, than if we were not interested in it ; presuming, probably, that we are fully informed from France. I may think improperly upon this subject, but I cannot be satisfied that a quarterly letter from our Minister is sufficient to give Congress the information, that is necessary for the direction of their affairs ; and yet this is much more than we receive. Some pay half yearly, and others offer only an annual tribute. Your last letter, properly so called, is dated in April ; Dr. Franklin's in March. This is the more mortifying, as want of time can hardly be offered as an excuse by our Ministers, who must eertainly have more leisure upon their hands than they know how to dispose of.

I congratulate you upon your arrival in France, where if your negotiations are not more successful than they have been in Spain, you will at least have some enjoyments, that will console you under your disappointments. Carleton has informed us, that Great Britain had agreed to yield us unconditional independence. I find that he has been too hasty in his opinion, and that the death of the Marquis of Rockingham has made a very material alteration in the system. That this inconsistency may be fully displayed, I would advise you to have the enclosed letter from Carleton and Digby published in Europe. Before the arrival of the packet, every disposition was made for the evacuation of Charleston, which was publicly announced. The tories have, in consequence of it, come out in crowds with the consent of General Leslie to solicit pardon. The works at Quarter House were burned. Whether the late intelligence will alter their determination I cannot say. High expectations have also been entertained of the evacuation of New York, where the royalists were in despair. Their hopes are again revived.

If the negotiations go on, let me beg you to use every means for procuring a direct trade with the West Indies. It is an object of the utmost importance to us. The exports of Philadelphia alone to the islands amounted before the war to three hundred thousand pounds ; they could not have been much less from New York ; they were considerable also from the Eastern States. We shall be very long in recovering the distress of the war, if we are deprived of this important commerce. It is certain, too, that the European powers who hold islands would find themselves interested in this intercourse, provided they exclude the introduction of manufactures, which might interfere with their own.

In proportion to the expense at which articles of the first necessity are furnished, must be the improvement, population, produce, and wealth of the islands, while the inhabitants of these States are compelled by law as well as allured by fashion and habit to receive their manufactures and luxuries from the mother country. She must reap the full benefit of such improvement, population, produce, and wealth. It may be said, that this check upon the exportation of provisions from the parent State would, by reducing the price of grain, discourage agriculture; to this I would observe, that it is extremely doubtful whether it would occasion such reduction; secondly, that if it did, it would be beneficial to the community. My doubt upon the first head arises from this consideration; if, as I maintain, the increased wealth and population of the islands occasioned an increased consumption of the manufactures of the mother country, the provisions that formerly fed the planters abroad are now consumed at home by the manufacturer, and the price of provisions stands where it did, with this clear advantage to the mother country, that by the cheapness of living on the islands, she has increased the number of subjects, who till the earth for her abroad, and by the same means has added to the people, who make her strength and riches at home.

My second position is grounded upon the competition, that prevails at this moment among the maritime manufacturing nations of Europe, France and England particularly. The nation that undersells its rival in foreign markets will sap the foundation of her wealth and power. The nation that can maintain its manufactures, and navigate its vessels at the cheapast rate, will undoubtedly enjoy this advantage, all things else being equal. It is obvious, that the price of labor is regulated by that of provisions, that manufacturers never earn more than a bare subsistence. If so, where provisions are cheap, manufactures can be carried on to most advantage. Of this, the East Indies are a striking proof. In proportion, too, to the price of provisions and the price of labor, which depends upon it, must be the expense of building and navigating ships. Both these advantages, where there is a concurrence, are therefore clearly in favor of the nation, that can reduce the price of provisions within her own kingdom.

But it may be said, that this reduction of the price of provisions, which seems so desirable in one view, may be found injurious in another; and that it is at least as expedient to encourage agriculture as manufactures. I agree in the principle, though not in the application. Going back to my first position, that the man who labors gets a bare subsistence, for the moment he does more, the number of laborers in that kind (provided his employment does not require uncommon skill) increases, and his labor is not more profitable, than that of the other laborers of the country. It will follow then, that so far as he consumes what he raises, the price will be entirely out of the question. If a bushel of grain a day is necessary for the support of his family, he will equally raise and equally consume that grain, whether it sells for a penny or a pound. But as there are other articles necessary for the use of his family, that he must purchase, this purchase can only be made by the excess of what he raises beyond his own consumption. If he purchases the manufactures of the country, and they rise in proportion to the value of provisions, it must be a matter of indifference to the husbandman, whether the price of the latter is high or low, since the same quantity will be necessary to purchase what his necessities demand in either case; unless indeed his provisions are carried to foreign markets, and the manufactures he wants imported, in which case the price of his grain will become an object of moment, and operate as an encouragement to agriculture. But it would also in the same proportion operate as a check on the manufactures, population, and navigation of the country. On the first, for reasons which have been already explained; on the second, because manufactures require more hands than agriculture; and on the third, because the expense of labor, which increases with the diminution of population, and the price of victualling the vessels employed in the transportation of their produce, will enable nations, who can maintain their subjects cheaper, to navigate their vessels at a lower rate, and of course to engross this branch of business, unless the laws of the State, such as acts of navigation, shall forbid, in which case those acts will operate so far as a discouragement upon agriculture; the advanced freightage being so much deducted from the husbandman's profit.

There are many collateral arguments to show the policy of this measure, even with reference to agriculture, arising out of the general positions I have stated, such as the advantage husbandmen find in a manufacturing country, in placing their weak or supernumerary children to trades, and procuring a number of hands on a short notice, at any of those critical periods, which so frequently occur in the culture of land, without being compelled to maintain them all the year, which increase their profit though they reduce the price of grain. But these are too extensive to take notice of here. I will conclude with some observations, which arise from the circumstances of the country with relation to Europe, which I trust will be found so important as to merit attention.

The commercial nations of Europe begin already to see, that the attention, which is almost universally afforded to the improvement of manufactures, must set bounds to their commerce, unless they can open new markets. Where are these new markets to be found but in America? Here the wishes and habits of the people will concur with the policy of the government, in encouraging the cultivation of their lands at the expense of manufactures. Both will continue to operate while we have a great wilderness to settle, and while a market shall be afforded for our produce. But if that market is shut against us; if we cannot vend what we raise, we shall want the means of purchasing foreign manufactures, and of course must from necessity manufacture for ourselves. The progress of manufactures is always rapid, when once introduced in a country where provisions are cheap, and the means of transportation so extremely easy as it is in America. I am fully persuaded, therefore, that it is the interest of a nation with whom present appearances promise us such extensive commerce as France, to give every encouragement to our agriculture, as the only means of keeping open this market for the consumption of their manufactures.

I meant to write a few lines on this subject, and I have written a treatise; it will however cost you no great trouble to read it, and may possibly afford you some useful hints.

Pigot is at New York with twenty-six sail of the line. The Marquis de Vaudreuil is at Boston with twelve, having lost the *Magnifique* in the harbor; Congress have presented his Most Christian Majesty with the *America*, a seventy-four built at Portsmouth. She was to have been commanded by Paul Jones. I wish heartily it were possible to give some employment to that brave officer.

The allied army is at present at Verplanck's Point, in good health and spirits. Where is the Marquis de Lafayette? We have impatiently expected him these four months. Present my compliments to him, General Du Portail, and Viscount de Noailles. Tell the last I congratulate him on his preferment, though it is with difficulty I rejoice at it, since it is to deprive us of the pleasure of seeing him again.

I have written you four private letters since the last I had from you.

I have the honor to be, Dear Sir,

ROBERT R. LIVINGSTON.

ROBERT R. LIVINGSTON TO JAY.

PHILADELPHIA, 17th Sepr., 1782.

DEAR SIR:

I have at length been favored with a private letter from you which gives me great pleasure, not only because it assures me of your health and that of Mrs. Jay, but because it is expressive of that friendship which I should be sorry to see lost in the ocean of politics in which we both have launched our barks.

I am sorry for the ill-health of my little god-daughter, but as the disorders she complains of are such as must necessarily be visited upon all the children of our Epicurean grandmother, I hope she bore them with becoming fortitude, and that she is happily freed from them before this. I thank you for the interest you have given me in her, and am not without prospects of being able ee'r long to return you the compliment.

I have not heard for some time from your family. Sir James, I suppose you know, is in Europe. I mentioned his misfortune in having been taken and carried into New York. What adds to that misfortune is that many people have attributed it to design.

I, for my part, acquit him of every thing but imprudence. His going to England has given more credit to the assertions of his enemies. The State of New York has made it the ground of a resolution for vacating his seat and electing Mr. Duane to it.

Benson has refused to take a seat in Congress, has lost his election to [the Legislature?], and is attentive to improve his fortune in the line of his profession. Hamilton has been elected in his place, and leaves for it the law, which he was just beginning to practice. . . .

I am just about to pay a visit to the banks of the Hudson, but have a thousand things to do first; the length of my journey must therefore shorten my letter, tho' it will lengthen my next by enabling me to speak of your friends. Adieu, my dear Sir, remember me affectionately to Mrs. Jay, and believe me to be what I most sincerely am, yours with undiminished friendship,

R. R. Livingston.

JAY TO PETER VAN SCHAACK.

Paris, 17th September, 1782.

Dear Sir :

Doctor Franklin sent me this morning your letter of 11th August last. I thank you for it. Aptitude to change in any thing never made a part of my disposition, and I hope makes no part of my character. In the course of the present troubles I have adhered to certain fixed principles, and faithfully obeyed their dictates, without regarding the consequences of such conduct to my friends, my family, or myself ; all of whom, however dreadful the thought, I have ever been ready to sacrifice, if necessary, to the public objects in contest.

Believe me, my heart has nevertheless been, on more than one occasion, afflicted by the execution of what I thought and still think was my duty. I felt very sensibly for you and for others, but as society can regard only the political propriety of men's conduct, and not the moral propriety of their motives to it, I could only lament your unavoidably becoming classed with many whose morality was convenience, and whose politics changed with the aspect of public affairs. My regard for you as a good old friend continued, notwithstanding. God knows that inclination never had a share in any proceedings of mine against you ; from such thorns no man could expect to gather grapes, and the only consolation that can grow in their unkindly shade is a consciousness of doing one's duty and the reflection that, as on the one hand I have uniformly preferred the public weal to my friends and connections, so on the other I have never been urged by private resentments to injure a single individual.   Your judgment and consequently your conscience differed from mine on a very important question ; but though, as an independent American, I considered all who were not for us, and you among the rest, as against us, yet be assured that John Jay did not cease to be a friend to Peter Van Schaack.   No one can serve two masters. Either Britain was right and America wrong, or America was right and Britain wrong.   They who thought Britain right were bound to support her, and America had a just claim to the services of those who approved her cause.   Hence it became our duty to take one side or the other, and no man is to be blamed for preferring the one which his reason recommended as the most just and virtuous.

Several of our countrymen indeed left and took arms against us, not from any such principles, but from the most dishonourable of human motives. Their conduct has been of a piece with their inducements, for they have far outstripped savages in perfidy and cruelty.   Against these men every American must set his face and steel his heart.   There are others of them, though not many, who, I believe, opposed us because they thought they could not conscientiously go with us. To such of them as have behaved with humanity I wish every species of prosperity that may consist with the good of my country.

You see how naturally I slide into the habit of writing as freely as I used to speak to you. Ah! my friend, if ever I see New York again, I expect to meet with "the shade of many a departed joy"; my heart bleeds to think of it. Where and how are your children? Whenever, as a private friend, it may be in my power to do good to either, tell me; while I have a loaf, you and they may freely partake of it. Don't let this idea hurt you. If your circumstances are easy, I rejoice; if not, let me take off some of their rougher edges.

Mrs. Jay is obliged by your remembrance, and presents you her compliments. The health of us both is but delicate. Our little girl has been very ill, but is now well. My best wishes always attend you, and be assured that, notwithstanding many political changes,

I remain, dear Peter,

Your affectionate friend and servant,

JOHN JAY.

JAY TO ROBERT R. LIVINGSTON.

PARIS, September 18, 1782.

DEAR SIR:

I send you herewith enclosed a copy of a translation of an important letter.[1] The original in French I have not seen, and at present is not accessible to me, though I shall endeavour to get a copy of it, in

[1] Marbois' letter to Vergennes opposing the American claim to the fisheries. See Jay to Livingston, November 17, 1782.

order the better to decide on the correctness of the translation. I am not at liberty to mention the manner in which this paper came to my hands. To me it appears of importance that it should for the present be kept a profound secret, though I do not see how that is to be done, if communicated to the Congress at large, among whom there always have been and always will be some unguarded members. I think, however, as I thought before, that your commissioners here should be left at liberty to pursue the sentiments of their country, and such of their own as may correspond with those of their country.

I am persuaded (and you shall know my reasons for it) that this Court chooses to postpone an acknowledgment of our independence by Britain, to the conclusion of a general peace, in order to keep us under their direction, until not only their and our objects are attained, but also until Spain shall be gratified in her demands to exclude everybody from the Gulf, etc. We ought not to let France know that we have such ideas. While they think us free from suspicion they will be more open, and we should make no further use of this discovery than to put us on our guard. Count de Vergennes would have us treat with Mr. Oswald, though his commission calls us colonies, and authorizes him to treat with any description of men, etc. In my opinion we can only treat as an independent nation, and on an equal footing. I am at present engaged in preparing a statement of objections in a letter to him, so that I have not time to write very particularly to you. The Spanish Ambassador presses me to proceed, but keeps back his powers. I tell him that an exchange of copies of our commissions is a necessary and usual previous step. This Court, as well as Spain, will dispute our extension to the Mississippi. You see how necessary prudence and entire circumspection will be on your side, and if possible secrecy. I ought to add that Dr. Franklin does not see the conduct of this Court in the light I do, and that he believes they mean nothing in their proceedings but what is friendly, fair, and honourable. Facts and future events must determine which of us is mistaken. As soon as I can possibly have time and health to give you details you shall have them. Let us be honest and grateful to France, but let us think for ourselves.

With great regard and esteem, I am, etc.,

JOHN JAY.

ROBERT R. LIVINGSTON TO JAY.

PHILADELPHIA, September 18th, 1782.

DEAR SIR:

Since closing the despatches you will receive with this, I was honored with yours of June. Nothing material having since occurred, I only write to enclose the annexed resolutions of Congress, on the subject of your powers for negotiating. I see by yours, that you entertain no hope of a speedy termination of that business, even though you were then unacquainted with the change that has since taken place in the administration, and which renders peace a more remote object. It has certainly wrought a great change here. The state of negotiations we are yet to learn, as neither you nor the Doctor have entered into that subject.

I hope my despatches by Mr Laurens, with the cyphers under his care, have reached you in safety, as very few either of your or Dr Franklin's letters, passed through the channel through which I usually receive them, come to me uninspected. Be pleased to acknowledge the receipt of my letters, that I may know which have reached you.

           I am, Dear Sir,

                ROBERT R. LIVINGSTON.

JAY TO ROBERT R. LIVINGSTON.

                PARIS, September 28, 1782.

DEAR SIR:

I have only time to inform you that our objections to Mr. Oswald's first commission have produced a second, which arrived yesterday. It empowers him to treat with the Commissioners of the *thirteen United States of America.* I am preparing a longer letter on this subject, but as this intelligence is interesting, I take the earliest opportunity of communicating it.

    With great regard and esteem, I am, etc.,

                    JOHN JAY.[1]

JAY TO ROBERT R. LIVINGSTON.

                PARIS, October 13, 1782.

DEAR SIR:

I hope my letter to you of the 18th of September, of which I also sent a duplicate, has come safe to hand, for it contained important matter, viz., a copy of a

---

[1] In a similar note of the same date, to John Adams, Jay added: "I have reasons for wishing that you would say nothing of this till you see me, which I hope and pray may be soon, very soon."

letter from M. Marbois to the Count de Vergennes against our sharing in the fishery.

This Court advised and persuaded us to treat with Mr. Oswald under his first commission. I positively refused.

Count d'Aranda will not or cannot exchange powers with me, and yet wants me to treat with him; this Court would have me do it, but I decline it.

I would give you details, but must not until I have an American to carry my letters from hence.

Mr. Oswald is well disposed. You shall never see my name to a bad peace, nor to one that does not secure the fishery.

I have received many long letters from you, which I am as busy in deciphering as my health permits.

M. de Lafayette is very desirous to give us his aid, but as we have a competent number of commissioners, it would not be necessary to give him that trouble.

I am, dear sir, with great esteem and regard, your most obedient servant,

JOHN JAY.

P. S.—General Duportail is to be the bearer of this. I believe he goes by order of the Court.

ROBERT MORRIS TO JAY.

MARINE OFFICE, PHILADELPHIA,
7th October, 1782.

SIR:

This letter will be delivered to you by Joshua Barney, Esqr. a Lieutenant in the Navy of the United States, and now commanding the Packet Ship *General Washington*.

This Young Gentleman is an active, gallant Officer who has already behaved well on many occasions, and I recommend him to your particular Notice and Attention from the Conviction that his Conduct will do honor to those by whom he is patronized and introduced.

I am, Sir, Your most obedient

humble Servant
ROB^{T.} MORRIS.

JAY TO ROBERT MORRIS.

PARIS, 13th October, 1782.

MY DEAR SIR :

Wherever and however occupied, I remember my friends, and always find my own satisfaction promoted when I have reason to think that I am conducing to theirs. This has led me to make your sons the subject of this letter. It is an interesting one to you, and therefore not indifferent to me.

On my arrival here I found them placed in a *pension* at Passy. My daughter was ill with a whooping-cough, and, lest your sons should catch it, we denied ourselves the pleasure of having them with us until after that obstacle had ceased. I have frequently seen them at Dr. Franklin's, as well as at my own house. They had promised to dine with us every Wednesday, but Mr. Ridley prolonged it to every other Wednesday. They are fine boys, and appear to possess a full share of natural talents. I am told that they have made a progress in French proportionate to the time they have been learning it. Of this I am not an adequate judge myself, and therefore must depend on the judgment of others. The *pension* at which they are has been, so far, well enough, but I think, with Mr. Ridley, that a better is to be wished for and to be sought. He is at present making the necessary inquiries, and I have every reason to believe that the trust you have reposed in him will be conscientiously and faithfully executed.

Mr. Ridley finds it difficult to decide on the expediency of carrying them to Geneva, and, from what I have heard, I think he has reason to entertain doubts on that head. As I have no materials to judge from but the report of others, and those perhaps not altogether well founded, it is difficult for me to form a decided opinion on the subject. I can only say that I have heard more against it than for it.

My opinion may perhaps seem singular, and the more so as it cannot be properly explained in the compass of a letter. I think the youth of every *free* civilized country should, if possible, be educated in it, and not permitted to travel out of it till age has made them so cool and firm as to retain their national and moral impressions. Connections formed at school and college have much influence, and are to be watched even at that period. If judiciously formed, they will often endure and be advantageous through life. American youth may possibly form proper, and perhaps useful, friendships in European seminaries, but I think not so *probably* as among their fellow-citizens, with whom they are to grow up, whom it will be useful for them to know and be early known to, and with whom they are to be engaged in the business of active life, and under the eye and direction of parents whose advice, authority, and example are frequently of more worth than the lessons of hireling professors, particularly on the subjects of religion, morality, virtue, and prudence.

The fine and some of the useful arts may doubtless be better acquired in Europe than America, and so may the living European languages; but when I consider that a competent knowledge even of these may be gained in our country, and that almost all of the more substantial and truly valuable acquirements may, in my opinion, with more facility and certainty be attained there than here, I do not hesitate to prefer an American education.

I fear that the ideas which my countrymen in general conceive of Europe are in many respects rather too high. If we should ever meet again, you shall know my sentiments very fully on that head.

But your sons are here, and what is to be done? Mr. Ridley is about doing what I think, with him, is the best thing that can at present be done, viz., to put them in one of the best *pensions* that can be found, and to give them the advantage of such extra tutors as may be requisite.

Perhaps further information may place Geneva in a more favourable light. You shall have frequent letters from me on this subject; and, while I remain here, you may be assured of my constant attentions to these promising boys.

I am, dear sir, with great esteem and regard,

Your affectionate friend and servant,

JOHN JAY.

JAY TO GOUVERNEUR MORRIS.

PARIS, 13th October, 1782.

DEAR MORRIS:

I have received your *festina lente* letter, but wish it had been at least partly in cipher; you need not be informed of my reasons for the wish, as by this time you must know that seals are, on this side of the water, rather matters of decoration than of use. It gave me, nevertheless, great pleasure to receive that letter, it being the first from you that had reached me the Lord knows when. I find you are industrious and, of consequence, useful; so much the better for yourself, for the public, and for our friend Morris, whom I consider as the pillar of American credit.

The king of Great Britain, by letters patent under the great seal, has authorized Mr. Oswald to treat with the commissioners of the *United States of America.* His first commission literally pursued the Enabling Act, and the authority it gave him was expressed in the very terms of that act, viz., to treat with the colonies, and with any or either of them, and any part of them, and with any description of men in them, and with any person whatsoever, of and concerning peace, etc.

Had I not violated the instructions of Congress their dignity would have been in the dust, for the French Minister even took pains not only to persuade us to treat under that commission, but to prevent the second by telling Fitzherbert that the first was sufficient. I told the Minister that we neither could nor would treat with any nation in the world on any other than on an equal footing.

We may and we may not have a peace this winter. Act as if the war would certainly continue. Keep proper garrisons in your strong posts and preserve your army sufficiently numerous and well appointed, until every idea of hostility and surprise shall have completely vanished.

I could write you a volume, but my health admits only of short intervals of application.

Present my best wishes to Mr. and Mrs. Morris and such other of our friends as may ask how we do.

I am, dear Morris, very much your friend,

John Jay.

PETER VAN SCHAACK TO JAY.

London, 15th Oct., 1782.

Dear Sir:

I will not attempt to describe my feelings upon the perusal of your very friendly letter. I consider it as a perfect picture, in which I can trace every well known feature of your character. Your unreserved commemoration of our old friendship, and assurance of its continuance; your kind inquiries into the situation of me and my children, and generous offers with respect to both them and myself; and your pathetic allusion to the melancholy scenes you will meet upon your return to New-York, melted my heart; and every idea of party distinction or political competition vanished in an instant!

The line you have drawn between your political character and your private friendships is so strongly marked, and will be so strictly attended to by me, that I hope our correspondence will not end here. Be assured, that were I arraigned

you may both again enjoy this invaluable blessing. Perhaps it would sound *equivocally* were I to express a wish that you would not attend so much to *public business*, but remember what Horace says of a wise and good man: " Ultra quam satis est, *virtutem* si petat *ipsam*." Your horse, I hope, is your only physician; and as to an apothecary, I hope you will not require even an ass. My health, which you kindly inquire after, was never better, saving the complaint in my sight, which, however, gives me no *pain*. The one eye is quite useless, and two years ago I got an attack upon the other; at that period, indeed, my friend, I wanted consolation; but I bless God I found resources in my mind which very soon prepared me with resignation for the worst.

As to my circumstances, my dear sir, they are quite easy; rendered so by the provision my good father-in-law made for my children: were they otherwise, I know no man who could sooner induce me to invade my maxim against incurring pecuniary obligations than yourself, for between the professions and actions of my friend John Jay, I never yet have known one instance of a variance. My spirits, too, are good; and I have a good circle of acquaintances, not only in town, but in the pleasant villages in its neigbourhood, where I frequently walk ten or twelve miles before dinner. Upon the whole, I believe few persons enjoy more social and convivial hours than I do; and though I do not so often partake of the " feast of reason, and the flow of soul," as I did at New-York, yet I ought rather to be thankful for my situation than to repine at my share of the public calamity, which has involved so many families in ruin.

My children (I acknowledge it gratefully) have been permitted to remain at Kinderhook; which, by-the-by, is become the Athens of the county of Albany; Harry is represented to me as a lively boy, and has been examined and approved at Yale College: I hope the poor fellow will not be reproached with the *malignity* of his father; on my part, I assure you I have often cautioned my friends to take care not to let him imbibe any political prejudices on account of any ill· usage he might possibly suppose I had received. I would not let him come to England, because I mean he should never leave America. If he has an American education, with a good share of the weighty bullion of American sense, I shall not regret his being unacquainted with the refinements of the Old World. Can you forgive me for dwelling so long on my private concerns? Your kind inquiries convince me you can. What a great theatre are you acting upon, and what a conspicuous part do you sustain! What a fund of information must you have collected; and, conscious of the rectitude of your measures, what must be your feelings upon the consummation! I have always considered you as one of the most formidable enemies of this country, but since what has happened, *has* happened, there is no man to whom I more cordially wish the glory of the achievement.

My respectful compliments to Mrs. Jay; and

Believe me, dear sir,

Your affectionate friend, and sincere well wisher,

PETER VAN SCHAACK.

EDWARD NEWENHAM TO JAY.

[PARIS] 18ᵗ Oct., 1782.

DEAR SIR:

Lady Newenham and my family return their warmest and most sincere thanks to you and your truly amiable Lady for your repeated kindness; we are concerned that we have it not (at present) in our power to make a full proof of the high respect which we have for your character. Perhaps it may yet be in our power to shew at least our endeavours to repay your friendship.

That America may be perfectly free, and as independent

as this kingdom, that her glorious Sons of Liberty may prosper, that the Virtues of her present patriots may descend to, and animate, their successors, and finally, that she may become, what her glorious perseverance justly entitles her to—a Great and Powerful Republic—is the constant prayer of my inmost soul. Time has not and shall not alter these principles; they are the result of a close investigation of the original and consequent conduct of quondam Great, but now Little Britain. I shall *never* forget the real happiness I enjoyed since my arrival here, in personaly seeing Dr. Franklin, his Grandson, M^r. Jay, the Marquiss La Fayette, that Patriotic Noble Roman—I say in seeing those whose Characters I have always revered. With these Sentiments, and the most Sincere respects, I have the Honor to be, Dear Sir,

Your most obliged and very aff^t. Humble Servt.

EDWARD NEWENHAM.

P. S.—All the Pictures, but one, shall have place in my Library. That one shall keep Royalty company in a suitable Apartment, where it is *hung* up these 9 years. Please to borrow Brutus and search Letters for the worthy Marquis to read.

GENERAL WASHINGTON TO JAY.

VERPLANCK'S POINT (ON THE HUDSON),
18th October, 1782.

DEAR SIR:

Not having received from your Excellency, during the last winter or summer, the acknowledgement of any letter, except of my public dispatches of October last, I apprehend that some private letters, which I have had the pleasure of addressing to you since that time, have miscarried. I resume my pen, therefore, to repeat the thanks which were contained in one of them, for the wine you had the goodness to present me with; and to assure you that I entertain the friendly sentiments towards you which I have ever experienced since our first acquaintance.

We have now passed another campaign, and no very important occurrence has intervened on this side the Atlantic. The evacuation of Charlestown was considered by General Greene, in his last letters to me, as an event which would certainly take place; and from other circumstances I am induced to believe it is effected by this time. Part of the garrison (the British troops) will probably go to the West Indies and the Germans to the northward. Admiral Pigot is now in New-York harbour, with twenty-six heavy ships, ready wooded and watered for sea; but the present circumstances, though somewhat equivocal, do not indicate that New-York will be abandoned this year; notwithstanding there have been many reports and conjectures of the kind some weeks ago.

The Marquis De Vaudruille is in Boston harbour with twelve sail of the line (three excepted, which are at Portsmouth), having unfortunately stranded and lost the *Magnifique* on entering that bay. But Congress have presented to his Most Christian Majesty the ship *America*, of 74 guns, built at Portsmouth, and now nearly fit for sea.

The changes in the British ministry, and the fluctuation of their councils, are the subjects of universal speculation. We wait with impatience to hear the result of the negotiations, and not being very sanguine in our expectations, endeavour to hold ourselves prepared for every contingency. I am certain it will afford you pleasure to know that our army is better organized, disciplined, and clothed, than it has been at any period since the commencement of the war. This you may be assured is the fact.

I shall always be happy to hear from you, especially at the present important crisis of European politics; and beg you will be persuaded, that with the warmest wishes and most respectful compliments to Mrs. Jay, I am, with sentiments of the highest regard and esteem,

Dear sir, your excellency's most obedient

And humble servant,

GEO. WASHINGTON.

EXTRACTS FROM JAY'S DIARY.[1]

21st October, 1782.—Visited Mr. Oswald ; he told me that a Mr. Pultney had within a few days arrived here to place his daughter (a rich heiress) in a convent ; that Mr. Pultney in confidence gave him the following anecdote, viz. : That in the latter part of last winter, or beginning of last spring, there was an Englishman of distinction here who, in conversation with a friend of Mr. Vergennes, expressed his regret that the affairs of America could not be so arranged as to lead to peace. The friend mentioned this to Vergennes, who agreed to admit the Englishman to an audience on the subject. Accordingly, the Englishman and his friend waited upon the minister, who, in the conference, offered to divide America with Britain, and in case the latter agreed to the partition, that the force of France and Britain should be used to reduce it to the obedience of the respective sovereigns. On parting, the minister said that in case this offer should not be accepted, he reserved to himself the right of denying all that he had said about it ; that this offer was refused, and that the friend in a letter to the

---

[1] See extracts under date June 23 and December 22, 1782.

Englishman had expressed his regret on the subject. Mr. Oswald told me further, that Mr. Pultney assured him that he received this information from the Englishman's own mouth. Mr. Oswald spoke handsomely of Mr. Pultney's character. I advised him to trace the matter further, and, if true, to get it properly authenticated, which he promised to do.

24th October.—Mr. Oswald told me he had received a courier last night; that our articles were under consideration; and that Mr. Strackey, Mr. Townshend's secretary, was on the way to confer with us about them; he further said, he believed *this court* had found means to put a spoke in our wheel. He consulted me as to the possibility of keeping Mr. Strackey's coming a secret. I told him it was not possible, and that it would be best to declare the truth about it, viz., that he was coming with books and papers relative to our boundaries.

Dined with Franklin. I found Mr. Rayneval there. Just after dinner, the Doctor informed me that Rayneval had sent him word, that he would dine with him to-day, and would be glad to see me there. I told the Doctor what I had heard from Oswald about Strackey; and that I thought it best not to say more to Rayneval than that we met difficulties, and that Oswald expected to receive instructions in a few days.

We retired with Rayneval. He asked how matters stood between us and Oswald. We told him that we could not agree about all our boundaries. We mentioned the one between us and Nova Scotia. He asked, what we demanded to the north. We answered, that Canada should be reduced to the ancient bounds. He then contested our right to those back lands, etc., etc.

He asked what we expected as to the fisheries. We said, the same right we had formerly enjoyed. He contested the propriety of that demand; adding some strictures on the ambition and restless views of Mr. Adams, and intimated that we might be contented with the coast fishery.

October 28th, Monday.—Mr. Adams was with me three hours this morning. I mentioned to him the progress and present state of our negotiation with Britain—my conjectures of the views of France and Spain, and the part which it appeared to me advisable for us to act. *He concurred with me in sentiment on all these points.*

JOHN VAUGHAN [1] TO JAY.

PHILADELPHIA, 3 Novr. 1782.

DEAR SIR :

I flatter myself some of the many letters I have had the pleasure of writing you have reached you, and made you acquainted with those sentiments of esteem and affection which have been awakened in my breast by the pleasing recollection of the kind attention paid to me by yourself and Mrs. Jay during my residence in Spain, and while you attended to this Continent by making me acquainted with some of the most agreeable and valuable characters on it. If my sincere thanks for the one and the other have not already reached you, please accept them at present with my

---

[1] See letter from Jay to Del Campo, November 3, 1781.

wishes that the situation of publick affairs may be such as to permit you to pay us a visit. There was a moment in which I flattered myself your journey to Paris was only a preparatory step towards it, and that you were soon to be the bearer of the welcome tidings of general peace. Unfortunately these appearances have daily become less promising. Britain still retains her pride, and harbors false hopes of partial accommodations; they were near expiring, but temperary successes seemed to have revived them, and I fear fresh struggles will be necessary to bring them to reason. Had Rockingham lived all had been well, but Shelburne seems to have pledged himself to humor the obstinate prejudices of his foolish master.

Independent of the chagrin these incidents must have occasioned you, I imagine you will be pleased with your trip to Paris, in which I doubt not Mrs. Jay will have joined you most heartily. It must appear to her a paradise after so long a residence at Madrid. Nothing but America will suit her now; she could not think of returning to Spain without the greatest regret; her friends here wish ardently to see her. I can particularly answer for the family at Elizabeth Town, which I had the pleasure of seeing last week, as does Peter Jay, who is very well and much grown. You will learn from Miss Livingston what is going to be done with him. Kitty has been long indisposed, but is now much better, and will, I hope, be soon perfectly well. The season here has been rather sickly, and we are told it has been equally so in Europe. I am sorry to find Mrs. Jay and yourself have been ranked among the invalids, but flatter myself the health of both is perfectly reestablished.

You will please to inform Mrs. Jay that I am not at all surprised at her attachment to her own country; its advantages are such as to captivate the affection of strangers who have no family ties in it. The rough beauties of nature far exceed what we generally see in Europe, and almost make us forget the want of the more polished beauties of art. Property is so easily acquired that every man may make himself independent and be master of his actions and sentiments—a circumstance which has of all others been the support of the people in the present revolution, made them rise superior to misfortune, and in the end insured success. A most unbounded field is open to every species of talents, and America is becoming the Asylum of liberty and receiving with open arms all whose generous minds cannot brook the oppression of more corrupted governments. With what pleasure we may contemplate the number of illustrious refugees who will, in seeking their own peace, serve to increase our knowledge and reputation ; if we add to these advantages those of more private and domestic nature, which in this country surpass those which any country in Europe can boast, we have but little to desire or wish for to the citizen. To a politician, how flattering the prospect which presents itself. The productions of this Country, its admirable situation for commerce, the impossibility of its being conquered whilst we are united, all mark it out for a great empire.

I am just returned from a three month's tour in the Country, in which I could have wished to have been accompanied by L^d. Shelburne and [?] They would have been surprised to see the Nationality which pervades every rank of people, and would never harbor an idea of its been possible to make a partial treaty with and recover the affections of a people whom their Armies have so cruelly treated. They would have found their former friends dead or tired out, they would have met only Americans who know England only as its bitterest enemy, who would have reproached them with the loss of their friends and relations, and the wanton destruction of their property, and whose Children had been taught to abhor the name of Britons. They would have found them well cloathed, well fed, and ready at a moment's warning to turn out against the enemy; they would have found them bearing with patience all the burdens and distresses incident to a new country which is the seat of war and whose commerce is entirely destroyed. The impossibility of conquest would have been self evident; they would have seen the folly of their past conduct, execrated their evil counsellors and own obstinacy, and have stooped to court the people they have affected to despise. I am sorry to say that party disputes have been carried to a great height in this State, owing to the endeavors of Constitutionalists to get a majority of their friends in the Assembly and Council in order that the present constitution might be preserved and their own exceptionable conduct escape [exposure]. They have however exhausted in vain every mean art to obtain this end. The representatives are in general such as worthy men and good patriots could wish. J. Dickenson, of Delaware state, is in the Council and it is imagined will be chosen president of this State. Our neighbours are not well pleased at his resigning the presidency over them in order to come here. Every effort is made use of to hinder his election; his faults are magnified and calumny has given him failings which never belonged to him. The papers teem with Satyres against him; but it is to be hoped that Newspaper abuse will not be the means of depriving us of his abilities at a period when they are so much wanted, especially as one Potter is opposed to him who can Scarce write his own name and must consequently be always the tool of a party.

Please remember me affectionately to M^rs. Jay and accept the most unfeigned assurances of esteem and regard from,

Your obedient and obliged humble Servant

J^no. VAUGHAN.

P. S.

M^r. Dickinson is chosen president } of the State. [Penna.]
General Ewing Vice president }

JAY TO ROBERT R. LIVINGSTON.[1]

PARIS, November 17, 1782.

DEAR SIR :

Although it is uncertain when I shall have an opportunity either of finishing or transmitting the long particular letter which I am now undertaking to write, I think the matter it will contain is too interesting to rest only in my memory, or in short notes, which nobody but myself can well unfold the meaning of. I shall, therefore, write on as my health will permit, and when finished shall convey this letter by the first prudent *American* that may go from hence to Nantes or L'Orient.

My reception here was as friendly as an American Minister might expect from this polite and politic Court; for I think they deceive themselves who suppose that these kinds of attentions are equally paid to their private as to their public characters.

Soon after the Enabling Act was passed I was shown a copy of it, and I confessed it abated the expectations I had formed of the intention of the British Ministry to treat in a manly manner with the United States, on the footing of an unconditional acknowledgment of their independence. The act appeared to me to be cautiously framed to elude such an acknowledgment, and, therefore, it would depend on future

---

[1] The papers relating to the peace negotiations of 1782–83 contain nothing more interesting or important than this report from Jay to Secretary Livingston. As detailing the steps leading up to the preliminary treaty with England and emphasizing the success of the American Commissioners it is especially valuable. A summary of views and criticisms expressed in regard to Jay's course in the negotiations is appended at the end of the volume.

contingencies, and on the terms and nature of the bargain they might be able to make with us.

Mr. Grenville, indeed, told the Count de Vergennes that his Majesty would acknowledge our independence unconditionally, but, on being desired to commit that information to writing, he wrote that his Majesty was *disposed* to acknowledge it. This had the appearance of finesse.

About this time, that is, in June last, there came to Paris a Mr. Jones and a Mr. Paradise, both of them Englishmen, the former a learned and active constitutionalist. They were introduced to me by Dr. Franklin, from whom they solicited recommendations for America. The story they told him was, that Mr. Paradise had an estate in the right of his wife in Virginia, and that his presence there had been rendered necessary to save it from the penalty of a law of that State respecting the property of absentees. Mr. Jones said he despaired of seeing constitutional liberty re-established in England, that he had determined to visit America, and in that happy and glorious country to seek and enjoy that freedom which was not to be found in Britain. He spoke in raptures of our patriotism, wisdom, etc., etc. On speaking to me some days afterwards of his intended voyage, he assigned an additional reason for undertaking it, viz., that his long and great friendship for Mr. Paradise had induced him to accompany that gentleman on an occasion which, both as a witness and a friend, he could render him essential services in Virginia.

I exchanged three or four visits with these gentlemen, and, in the meantime, was informed that Mr. Jones was a rising character in England, that he had refused a very lucrative appointment in the Indies, and had, by his talents, excited the notice of men in power.

In conversing one morning with this gentleman on English affairs, he took occasion to mention the part he had taken in them, and, at parting, gave me two pamphlets he had published.

The first was a second edition of " An Inquiry into the Legal Mode of Suppressing Riots," etc., first published in 1780, to which was added " A Speech on the Nomination of Candidates to Represent the County of Middlesex, on the 9th of September, 1780." And this second edition contained also a letter, dated the 25th of April, 1782, from Mr. Jones to Mr. Yeates, the Secretary to the Society for Constitutional Information, of which Mr. Jones is a member. The other was " A Speech to the Assembled Inhabitants of Middlesex and Surrey, etc., on the 28th of May, 1782."

As it appeared to me a little extraordinary that a gentleman of Mr. Jones' rising reputation and expectations should be so smitten with the charms of American liberty as " to leave all and follow her," I began, on returning to my lodgings, to read these pamphlets with a more than common degree of curiosity, and I was not a little surprised to find the following paragraphs in them.

In his letter to Mr. Yeates of last April he says: " My future life shall certainly be devoted to the support of that excellent constitution which it is the object of your society to unfold and elucidate, and from this resolution, long and deliberately made, no prospects, no connections, no station here or abroad, no fear of danger or hope of advantage to myself, shall ever deter or allure me."

He begins his essay on suppressing riots by saying : "It has long been my opinion that, in times of national adversity, those citizens are entitled to the highest praise who, by personal exertions and active valor, promote, at their private hazard, the general welfare."

In his speech of last April are these paragraphs. In the first, speaking of his being sick, he says : "It would not prevent my attendance, for, in health or in sickness, I am devoted to your service.   I shall never forget the words of an old Roman, Ligarius, who, when the liberties of his country were in imminent danger, and when a real friend to those liberties was condoling with him on his illness at so critical a time, raised himself from his couch, seized the hand of his friend, and said : 'If you have *any business worthy of yourselves, I am well.*'

"Since I have risen to explain a sudden thought, I will avail myself of your favourable attention and hazard a few words on the general question itself. Numbers have patience to hear who have not time to read.   And, as to *myself, a very particular and urgent occasion, which calls me some months from England,* will deprive me of another opportunity to communicate my sentiments until the momentous object before us shall be made certainly attainable through the concord, or forever lost and irrecoverable through the disagreement, of the nation."

To make comments on these extracts would be to waste time and paper. On reading them I became persuaded that Mr. Paradise and American liberty were mere pretences to cover a more important errand to America, and I was surprised that Mr. Jones' vanity should so far get the better of his prudence as to put such pamphlets into my hands at such a time.

I pointed out these extracts to Dr. Franklin; but they did not strike him so forcibly as they had done me. I mentioned my apprehensions also to the Marquis de Lafayette, and I declined giving any letters either to Mr. Paradise or to Mr. Jones.

I am the more particular on this subject, in order that you may the better understand the meaning of a paragraph in my letter to you of the 28th of June last, where I inform you " that, if one may judge from appearances, the Ministry are very desirous of getting some of their emissaries into our country, either in an avowed or in a private character; and, all things considered, I should think it more safe not to admit any Englishman in either character within our lines at this very critical juncture."

Mr. Jones and Mr. Paradise went from hence to Nantes in order to embark there for America. Some weeks afterwards I met Mr. Paradise at Passy. He told me Mr. Jones and himself had parted at Nantes, and that the latter had returned directly to England.

How this happened I never could learn. It was a subject on which Mr. Paradise was very reserved. Perhaps the sentiments of America, on General Carleton's overtures, had rendered Mr. Jones' voyage unnecessary; but in this I may be mistaken, for it is mere conjecture.

On the 25th of July, 1782, the King of Great Britain issued a warrant, or order, directed to his Attorney or Solicitor-General.

A copy of this warrant was sent by express to Mr. Oswald, with an assurance that the commission should be completed and sent him in a few days. He communicated this paper to Dr. Franklin, who, after showing it to me, sent it the Count de Vergennes. The Count wrote to the Doctor the following letter on the subject.

[Translation.]

" I have received, Sir, the letter of to-day, with which you have honored me, and the copy of the powers which Mr. Oswald communicated to you. The form in which it is conceived, not being that which is usual, I cannot form my opinion on the first view of it. I am going to examine it with the greatest attention, and, if you will be pleased to come here on Saturday morning, I shall be able to confer about it with you and Mr. Jay, if it should be convenient for him to accompany you.

" I have the honor to be, &c.

" DE VERGENNES.

" VERSAILLES, August 8th, 1782."

On the 10th of August we waited upon the Count de Vergennes, and a conference between him and us on the subject of Mr. Oswald's commission ensued.

The Count declared his opinion that we might proceed to treat with Mr. Oswald under it as soon as the original should arrive. He said it was such a one as we might have expected it would be, but that we must take care to insert proper articles in the treaty, to secure our independence and our limits against all future claims.

I observed to the Count that it would be descending from the ground of independence to treat under the description of Colonies. He replied, that names signified little; that the King of Great Britain's styling himself the King of France was no obstacle to the King of France's treating with him; that an acknowledgment of our independence, instead of preceding, must in the natural course of things be the effect of the treaty, and that it would not be reasonable to expect the effect before the cause. He added, that we must be mindful to exchange powers with Mr. Oswald, for that his acceptance of our powers, in which we were styled Commissioners from the United States of America, would be a tacit admittance of our independence. I made but little reply to all this singular reasoning. The Count turned to Dr. Franklin and asked him what he thought of the matter. The Doctor said he believed the commission would do. He next asked my opinion. I told him that I did not like it, and that it was best to proceed cautiously.

On returning, I could not forbear observing to Dr. Franklin that it was evident the Count did not wish to see our independence acknowledged by Britain

until they had made all their uses of us. It was easy
for them to foresee difficulties in bringing Spain into
a peace on moderate terms, and that if we once found
ourselves standing on our own legs, our independence
acknowledged, and all our other terms ready to be
granted, we might not think it our duty to continue
in the war for the attainment of Spanish objects. But,
on the contrary, as we were bound by treaty to continue the war till our independence should be attained,
it was the interest of France to postpone that event
until their own views and those of Spain could be
gratified by a peace, and that I could not otherwise
account for the Minister's advising us to act in a
manner inconsistent with our dignity, and for reasons
which he himself had too much understanding not to
see the fallacy of.

The Doctor imputed this conduct to the moderation
of the Minister, and to his desire of removing every
obstacle to speedy negotiations for peace. He observed, that this Court had hitherto treated us very
fairly, and that suspicions to their disadvantage
should not be readily entertained. He also mentioned our instructions, as further reasons for our
acquiescence in the advice and opinion of the Minister. A day or two afterward I paid a visit to Mr.
Oswald, and had a long conversation with him respecting his commission. On the resignation of Mr.
Fox many reports to the prejudice of Lord Shelburne's sincerity on the subject of American independence had spread through France as well as
through Great Britain. His Lordship, fearful of

their effect on the confidence with which he wished
to inspire the American Commissioners, conveyed by
Mr. Benjamin Vaughan to Dr. Franklin an extract of
certain instructions to Sir Guy Carleton, of which
the following is a copy, viz. :

"*June 25th*, 1782. It has been said, that 'great effects might
be obtained by something being done *spontaneously* from
England.' Upon this and other considerations, his Majesty
has been induced to give a striking proof of his royal magnanimity and disinterested wish for the restoration of peace,
by commanding his Majesty's Ministers to direct Mr. Grenville, *that the independence of America should be proposed by
him in the first instance, instead of making it the condition of
a general peace.*

"I have given a confidential information to you of these
particulars, that you may take such measures as shall appear to you most advisable for making a direct communication of the substance of the same, either immediately
to Congress, or through the medium of General Washington, or in any other manner, which you may think most
likely to impress the well-disposed parts of America with
the fairness and liberality of his Majesty's proceedings in
such great and spontaneous concessions.

"The advantages, which we may expect from such concessions are, that America, once apprised of the King's
disposition to acknowledge the independence of the thirteen
States, and of the disinclination in the French Court to
terminate the war, must see that it is from this moment to
be carried on with a view of negotiating points, in which
she can have no concern, whether they regard France, or
Spain and Holland at the desire of France; but some of
which, on the contrary, may be in future manifestly injurious
to the interests of America herself.

"That if the negotiation is broken off, it will undoubtedly

be for the sake of those powers, and not America, whose object is accomplished the instant she accepts of an independence, which is not merely held out to her in the way of negotiation by the executive power, but a distinct unconditional offer, arising out of the resolutions of Parliament, and therefore warranted by the sense of the nation at large.

"These facts being made notorious, it is scarce conceivable that America, composed as she is, will continue efforts under French direction, and protract the distresses and calamities, which it is well known that war has subjected her to. It is to be presumed, that from that moment she will look with jealousy on the French troops in that country, who may from allies become dangerous enemies.

"If, however, any particular States, men, or description of men, should continue against the general inclination of the Continent devoted to France, this communication will surely detect their views, expose their motives, and deprive them of their influence in all matters of general concern and exertion. You will, however, take particular care in your manner of conducting yourselves, not only that there should not be the smallest room for suspicions of our good faith and sincerity, but that we have no view in it of causing dissensions among the colonies, or even of separating America from France upon terms inconsistent with her own honor. You must therefore convince them, that the great object of this country is, not merely peace, but reconciliation with America on the noblest terms and by the noblest means."

In the course of the before-mentioned conversation with Mr. Oswald I reminded him that the judgment and opinion of America respecting the disposition and views of Britain towards her must be determined by facts and not by professions. That the Enabling

Act, and the commission granted to him in pursuance of it, by no means harmonized with the language of these instructions to Sir Guy Carleton. That, unless the offers and promises contained in the latter were realized by an immediate declaration of our independence, America would naturally consider them as specious appearances of magnanimity, calculated to deceive and disunite them, and, instead of conciliating, would tend to irritate the States. I also urged, in the strongest terms, the great impropriety, and, consequently, the utter impossibility, of our ever treating with Great Britain on any other than an equal footing, and told him plainly that I would have no concern in any negotiation in which we were not considered as an independent people.

Mr. Oswald, upon this, as upon every other occasion, behaved in a candid and proper manner. He saw and confessed the propriety of these remarks ; he wished his commission had been otherwise, but was at a loss how to reconcile it to the King's dignity to make *such* a declaration immediately after having issued *such* a commission. I pointed out the manner in which I conceived it might be done ; he liked the thought, and desired me to reduce it to writing. I did so, and communicated it to Dr. Franklin, and, as we corrected it, is as follows, viz. :

" George III, &c. to Richard Oswald, greeting. Whereas by a certain act, &c. [here follows the Enabling Act].

" And whereas, in pursuance of the true intent and meaning of the said act, and to remove all doubts and jealousies, which might otherwise retard the execution of the same, we

did, on the   day of   instruct Sir Guy Carleton,
&c. our General, &c. to make known to the people of the
said Colonies, in Congress assembled, our royal disposition
and intention to recognise the said Colonies as independent
States, and as such, to enter with them into such a treaty
of peace as might be honorable and convenient to both
countries.

"And whereas further, in pursuance of the said act, we
did on the   day of   authorise and commission
you, the said Richard Oswald [here follows the commis-
sion]. Now, therefore, to the end that a period may be put
to the calamities of war, and peace, and commerce, and mutual intercourse the more speedily restored, we do hereby,
in pursuance of our royal word, for ourselves and our successors, recognise the said thirteen Colonies as free and independent States. And it is our will and pleasure, that you
do forthwith proceed to treat with the Commissioner or
Commissioners already appointed, or to be appointed for
that purpose by the Congress of the said States, and, with
him or them only, of and concerning the objects of your
said commission, which we do hereby confirm, and that this
declaration be considered by you as a preliminary article to
the proposed treaty, and be in substance or in the whole
inserted therein, or incorporated therewith. And it is our
further will and pleasure, that, on receiving these presents,
which we have caused to be made patent, and our great seal
to be hereunto affixed, you do deliver the same to the said
Commissioner or Commissioners, to be by him or them
transmitted to the Congress of the United States of America, as an earnest of the friendship and good will, which we
are disposped to extend to them. Witness, &c. 15th of
August, 1782."

Mr. Oswald approved of the draft and said he
would recommend the measure to the Minister. The

next day, however, he told me that he had an instruction which he thought enabled him to make the declaration ; but that it would be necessary to obtain the previous consent of the Minister for that purpose. He then read to me the fourth article of his instructions, of which the following is a copy, viz. :

" In case you find the American Commissioners are not at liberty to treat on any terms short of independence, you are to declare to them, that you have our authority to make that cession ; our ardent wish for peace disposing us to purchase it at the price of acceding to the complete independence of the thirteen colonies."

He said he would immediately despatch a courier to London, and would press the Ministry for permission to acknowledge our independence without further delay, which he accordingly did.

At this time the commission under the great seal had arrived, and Dr. Franklin and myself went to Versailles to communicate that circumstance to the Count de Vergennes, and (agreeably to our instructions) to inform him of what had passed between Mr. Oswald and us.

The Count and myself again discussed the propriety of insisting, that our independence should be acknowledged previous to a treaty. He repeated, that it was expecting the effect before the cause, and many other similar remarks, which did not appear to me to be well founded. I told the Count, that a declaration of our independence was in my opinion a matter of very little consequence ; that I did not consider our independence as requiring any aid or validity from British acts; and provided that nation treated us as she treated other nations, viz., on a footing of equality, it was all that I desired. He differed with me also in this opinion. He thought an explicit acknowledgment of our independence in treaty very necessary, in order to prevent our being exposed to further claims. I told him we should always have arms in our hands to answer those claims; that I considered mere paper fortifications as of but little consequence; and that we should take care to insert an article in the treaty, whereby the King of Great Britain should renounce all claims of every kind to the countries within our limits.

The Count informed us he had delayed doing business with Mr. Fitzherbert, until we should be ready to proceed with Mr. Oswald, and that he expected to see him the next day or the day after.

Mr. Fitzherbert went the next day to Versailles, and immediately despatched a courier to London.

The answer of the British Ministry to Mr. Oswald is contained in the following extract of a letter to him from Mr. Townshend, dated Whitehall, September 1, 1782:

" SIR:

" I have received and laid before the King your letters of the 17th, 18th, and 21st ultimo, and I am commanded to signify to you, his Majesty's approbation of your conduct, in communicating to the American Commissioners the fourth article of your instructions; which could not but convince them, that the negotiation for peace, and the cession of independence to the Thirteen United Colonies, were intended to be carried on and concluded with the Commissioners in Europe.

" Those gentlemen, having expressed their satisfaction concerning that article, it is hoped they will not entertain a doubt of his Majesty's determination to exercise in the fullest extent the powers with which the act of Parliament has invested him, by granting to America, full, complete, and unconditional independence, in the most explicit manner, as an article of treaty."

When Mr. Oswald communicated this letter to me, I did not hesitate to tell him, that his Court was misled by this, for that the language of Mr. Townshend corresponded so exactly with that of the Count de Vergennes, and was at the same time so contrary to that of the instructions to Sir Guy Carleton, as to be inexplicable on any other principle. I also told him I suspected that the courier despatched by Mr. Fitzherbert on his return from Versailles had been the means of infusing these ideas. He smiled, and after a little pause said ; why, Count de Vergennes told Mr. Fitzherbert, that my commission was come and that he thought it would do, and therefore they might now go on, and accordingly they did go on to discuss certain points, and particularly that of Newfoundland.

Mr. Oswald did not deny or contradict the inference I drew from this, viz., that Mr. Fitzherbert, struck by this conduct of Count de Vergennes, and finding that the commission given to Mr. Oswald was deemed sufficient by him, thought it his duty directly to inform his Court of it, and thereby prevent their being embarrassed by our scruples and demands on a point on which there was so much reason to think that our allies were very moderate.

For my own part, I was not only persuaded that this was the case, but also that the ill success of Mr. Oswald's application was owing to it.

These considerations induced me to explain to him what I supposed to be the natural policy of this Court on the subject, and to show him that it was the interest of Britain to render us as independent on France as we were resolved to be on her. He soon adopted the same opinion, but was at a loss to see in what manner Great Britain, considering what had just passed, could consistently take further steps at present. I told him that nothing was more easy, for that the issuing of another commission would do it. He asked me if he might write that to the Ministry; I told him he might; he then desired, in order to avoid mistakes, that I would give it to him in writing, which I did as follows, viz. :

"A commission [in the usual form] to Richard Oswald to treat of peace or truce with Commissioners, vested with equal powers by and on the part of the United States of America, would remove the objections to which his present one is liable, and render it proper for the American Commissioners to proceed to treat with him on the subject of preliminaries."

I then reminded him of the several resolutions of Congress, passed at different periods, not to treat with British Commissioners on any other footing than that of absolute independence, and also intimated that I thought it would be best to give him our final and decided determination not to treat otherwise in writing, in the form of a letter. He preferred this to a verbal answer, and the next day I prepared the following draft of such a letter :

JAY TO RICHARD OSWALD.

Sir :

It is with regret that we find ourselves obliged, by our duty to our country, to object to entering with you into negotiations for peace on the plan proposed. One nation can treat with another nation only on terms of equality, and it cannot be expected that we should be the first and only servants of Congress who would admit doubts of their independence.

The tenor of your commission affords matter for a variety of objections, which your good sense will save us the pain of enumerating. The journals of Congress present to you unequivocal and uniform evidence of the sentiments and resolutions of Congress on the subject, and their positive instructions to us speak the same language.

The manner of removing these obstacles is obvious, and, in our opinion, no less consistent with the dignity than the interest of Great Britain. If the Parliament meant to enable the King to conclude a peace with us on terms of independence, they necessarily meant to enable him to do it in a manner compatible with his dignity, and, consequently, that he should previously regard us in a point of view that would render it proper for him to negotiate with us. What this point of view is you need not be informed.

We also take the liberty of submitting to your consideration how far his Majesty's now declining to take this step would comport with the assurances lately given on that subject, and whether hesitation and delay would not tend to lessen the confidence which those assurances were calculated to inspire.

As to referring an acknowledgment of our independence to the first article of a treaty, permit us to remark that this implies that we are not to be considered in that light until after the conclusion of the treaty, and our acquiescing would be to admit the propriety of our being considered in another light during that interval. Had this circumstance been attended to, we presume that the Court of Great Britain would not have pressed a measure which certainly is not delicate, and which cannot be reconciled with the received ideas of national honour.

You may rest assured, sir, of our disposition to peace on reasonable terms, and of our readiness to enter seriously into negotiations for it, as soon as we shall have an opportunity of doing it in the only manner in which it is possible for one nation to treat with another, viz., on an equal footing.

Had you been commissioned in the usual manner, we might have proceeded ; and as we can perceive no legal or other objection to this, or some other such like expedient, it is to be wished that his Majesty will not permit an obstacle so very unimportant to Great Britain, but so essential and insuperable with respect to us, to delay the re-establishment of peace especially, and in case the business could be but once begun, the confidence we have in your candour and integrity would probably render the settling all our articles only the work of a few hours.

We are, etc.

I submitted this draft to Dr. Franklin's consideration. He thought it rather too positive, and therefore rather imprudent, for that in case Britain should remain firm, and future circumstances should compel us to submit to their mode of treating, we should do it with an ill grace after such a decided and peremptory refusal. Besides, the Doctor seemed to be much perplexed and fettered by our instructions to be guided by the advice of this Court. Neither of these considerations had weight with me, for as to the first I could not conceive of any event which would render it proper and therefore possible for America to treat in any other character than as an independent nation; and, as to the second, I could not believe that Congress intended we should follow any advice which might be repugnant to their dignity and interest.

On returning to town, Mr. Oswald spoke to me about this letter. I told him that I had prepared a draft of one, but that on further consideration, and consulting with Dr. Franklin, we thought it best not to take the liberty of troubling his Court with any arguments or reasonings which without our aid must be very evident to them.

He appeared disappointed, and desired me to let him see the draft. I did. He liked it. He requested a copy of it, but as I doubted the propriety of such a step, I told him I would consider of it, and give him an answer the next day.

It appeared to me, on further reflection, that no bad consequences would arise from giving him a copy of this paper; that, though unsigned, it would nevertheless convey to the Ministry the sentiments and opinions I wished to impress, and that if finally they should not be content to treat with us as independent, they were not yet ripe for peace or treaty with us; besides, I could not be persuaded that Great Britain, after what the House of Commons had declared, after what Mr. Grenville had said, and Sir Guy Carleton been instructed to do, would persist in refusing to admit our independence, provided they really believed that we had firmly resolved not to treat on more humble terms.

I gave him a copy, and also copies of the various resolutions of Congress which evince their adherence to their independence. These papers he sent by express to London, and warmly recommended the issuing a new commission to remove all further delay. This matter was not communicated to the Count de Vergennes, at least to my knowledge or belief, by either of us.

I might now enumerate the various expedients proposed by the Count de Vergennes and the Marquis de Lafayette to reconcile our difficulties. Such as Mr. Oswald's writing a letter to us, signifying that he treated with us as independent, etc., etc. But as our independence was indivisible, there could not easily be contrived a half-way mode of acknowledging it, and therefore any method of doing it short of the true and proper one could not bear examination.

Being convinced that the objections to our follow-ing the advice of the Count de Vergennes were un-answerable, I proposed to Dr. Franklin that we should state them in a letter to him, and request his answer in writing, because, as we were instructed to ask and to follow his advice on these occasions, we ought always to be able to show what his advice was.

The Doctor approved of the measure, and I under-took to prepare a draft of such a letter.

I must now remind you of what some of my former letters informed you, viz., the propositions made to me by the Count d'Aranda on the part of Spain. It is necessary that I should in this place go into that detail, because they will be found in the sequel to be strongly connected with the subject more immediately under consideration.

On my arrival at Paris in June last, it being doubt-ful whether if I made a visit to Count d'Aranda he would return it, I thought it most advisable to avoid that risk, and to write him the following letter:

JAY TO COUNT D'ARANDA.

PARIS, June 25, 1782.

SIR:

On leaving Madrid his Excellency, the Count de Florida Blanca, informed me that the papers relative to the objects of my mission there had been trans-mitted to your Excellency, with authority and instruc-tions to treat with me on the subject of them.

I arrived here the day before yesterday, and have the honour to acquaint your Excellency of my being ready to commence the necessary conferences at such time and place as your Excellency may think proper to name.

Your Excellency's character gives me reason to hope that the negotiation in question will be conducted in a manner agreeable to both our countries, and permit me to assure you that nothing on my part shall be wanting to manifest the respect and consideration with which I have the honour to be, etc.

JOHN JAY.

The following is a copy of the Count's answer:

[Translation.]

PARIS, June 27th, 1782.

SIR:

I have the honour to reply to your note of the 25th, informing me of your happy arrival at this Court. I shall also have the honour to receive you, when you shall intimate that it is proper, and whenever you will inform me of your intention, so that I may expect you at whatever hour shall be most convenient to you.

I shall be pleased to make your acquaintance, and to assure you of the respect with which I have the honour, &c.

THE COUNT D'ARANDA.

It having been intimated to Dr. Franklin that if we paid a visit to Count d'Aranda it would be returned, we waited on him on the 29th of June. He received us in a friendly manner, and expressed his wishes that closer connection might be formed between our countries on terms agreeable to both.

He returned our visit the next day, and gave us an invitation to dine with him a few days afterwards. On that day I was taken sick, and continued so for many weeks, nor, indeed, am I yet perfectly recovered from the effects of that illness, having a constant pain in my breast, and frequently a little fever.

Hence it happened that I did not meet Count d'Aranda on business till a month afterwards, when, agreeably to a previous appointment, I waited upon him.

He began the conference by various remarks on the general principles on which contracting nations should form treaties, on the magnanimity of his sovereign, and on his own disposition to disregard trifling considerations in great matters. Then opening Michell's large map of North America, he asked me what were our boundaries; I told him that the boundary between us and the Spanish dominions was a line drawn from the head of Mississippi, down the middle thereof to the thirty-first degree of north latitude, and from thence by the line between Florida and Georgia.

He entered into a long discussion of our right to such an extent, and insisted principally on two objections to it. 1st. That the western country had never belonged to, or been claimed as belonging to, the ancient colonies. That previous to the last war it had belonged to France, and after its cession to Britain remained a distinct part of her dominions, until by the conquest of West Florida and certain posts on the Mississippi and Illinois it became vested in Spain.

2dly. That supposing the Spanish right of conquest did not extend over *all* that country, still that it was possessed by free and independent nations of Indians, whose lands we could not with any propriety consider as belonging to us. He therefore proposed to run a longitudinal line on the east side of the river, for our western boundary ; and said that he did not mean to dispute about a few acres or miles, but wished to run it in a manner that would be convenient to us ; for though he could never admit the extent we claimed, yet he did not desire to crowd us up to our exact limits.

As it did not appear to me expedient to enter fully into the discussion of these objections until after he had marked the line he proposed, I told him I would forbear troubling him with any remarks on the subject until the points in controversy should be reduced to a certainty ; and therefore I desired him to mark on the map the line he proposed, and to place it as far to the west as his instructions would possibly admit of. He promised to do it, and to send me the map with his proposed line marked on it in a day or two.

I then gave him a copy of my commission, and showed him the original. He returned it to me with expressions of satisfaction, and then changed the subject by desiring me if, after receiving his map and examining his lines, I should find it in any respect inconvenient, that I would mark such other line on it as would, in my opinion, be more agreeable to America, assuring me that he had nothing more at heart than to fix such a boundary between us as might be satisfactory to both parties. I told him that on receiving his map I would take all that he had said into consideration, and take the earliest opportunity of acquainting him with my sentiments respecting it. I then observed that I hoped his powers to treat were equal with mine. He replied that he had ample powers to confer, but not to sign any thing without previously communicating it to his Court, and receiving their orders for the purpose; but, to my surprise, he did not offer to show me any powers of any kind.

A few days afterwards he sent me the same map, with his proposed line marked on it in red ink. He ran it from a lake near the confines of Georgia, but east of the Flint River, to the confluence of the Kanawha with the Ohio, thence round the western shores of Lakes Erie and Huron, and thence round Lake Michigan to Lake Superior.

On the 10th of August I carried this map to the Count de Vergennes, and left it with him. Dr. Franklin joined with me in pointing out the extravagance of this line; and I must do him the justice to say that in all his letters to me, and in all his conversations with me respecting our western extent, he has invariably declared it to be his opinion that we should insist upon the Mississippi as our western boundary, and that we ought not, by any means, to part with our right to the free navigation of it.

The Count de Vergennes was very cautious and reserved; but M. Rayneval, his principal secretary, who was present, thought we claimed more than we had a right to.

Having thus clearly discovered the views of Spain, and that they were utterly inadmissible, I had little hope of our ever agreeing, especially as the Mississippi was, and ought to be, our *ultimatum.*

It was not long before I had another interview with M. Rayneval. He asked me whether I had made any progress in my negotiations with the Count d'Aranda. I told him that the Count had not yet shown me any powers from his Court to treat. He expressed surprise that I should have any difficulties on that head, especially considering the public as well as private character of that nobleman. I replied that I was very sensible of the respectability both of his public and private character, but neither the one nor the other authorized him to negotiate treaties with the United States of America, and, consequently, that his Court would be at liberty to disavow all his proceedings in such business ; that it was my duty to adhere to the forms usual in such cases, and that those forms rendered it proper for Ministers to exchange copies of their commissions before they proceeded on the business which was the object of them.

The Count d'Aranda was very urgent that I should mark on his map some line or other to the eastward of the Mississippi, to which we could agree ; and on the 26th of August we had another conference on these subjects. I told him frankly that we were bound by the Mississippi, and that I had no authority to cede any territories east of it to his Catholic Majesty, and that all I could do relative to it was to transmit his proposition to Congress for their consideration.

He affected to be much surprised that I should have no discretionary authority on that subject, and observed that he had supposed I was a Minister Plenipotentiary. I told him that few Ministers Plenipotentiary had discretionary power to transfer and cede to others the countries of their sovereigns. He denied that the countries in question were our countries, and asked what right we had to territories, which manifestly belong to free and independent nations of Indians. I answered that those were points to be discussed and settled between us and them ; that we claimed the right of pre-emption with respect to them, and the sovereignty with respect to all other nations. I reminded him that Mexico and Peru had been in the same predicament, and yet that his Catholic Majesty had had no doubts of his right to the sovereignty of those countries.

He then desired me to write him a letter on the subject, in order that he might with the greater accuracy convey my sentiments to his Court.

On the 4th of September, I received the following letter from M. de Rayneval :

[Translation.]

Versailles, September 4th, 1782.

Sir,

I should be glad to have a conversation with you on the subject of the boundaries in regard to Spain, but it is impossible for me to go to Paris for this purpose. You would oblige me, if you would have the goodness to come to Versailles to-morrow morning. It will give me great pleasure to see you at dinner. Meanwhile I have the honour, &c.　　　　　　　　　　　Rayneval.

I accordingly waited upon M. de Rayneval. He entered into a long disquisition on our claims to the western country. It is unnecessary to repeat in this place what he said on those subjects, because I shall insert in this letter a copy of a paper which at my request he wrote to me on them. That paper will speak for itself. You will be at no loss to form a judgment of the mode in which he proposed to reconcile us, by what he called a conciliatory line. We discussed very freely the propriety of my objecting to proceed with the Count d'Aranda; and among other reasons which induced him to think I ought to go on was my having already conferred with him on those subjects. My answer to this was obvious, viz., that though I had heard Count d'Aranda's propositions, yet that I had offered none of any kind whatever.

On the 6th of September, M. de Rayneval wrote me, the following letter :

M. DE RAYNEVAL TO JAY.

[Translation.]

VERSAILLES, September 6th, 1782.

I have the honour, Sir, to send you as you desired me, my personal ideas on the manner of terminating your discussions about limits with Spain. I hope they will appear to you worthy to be taken into consideration.

I have reflected, Sir, on what you said to me yesterday of the Spanish Ambassador's want of powers. You cannot in my opinion urge that reason to dispense treating with that Ambassador, without offending him, and without contradicting the first step you have taken towards him.

This reflection leads me to advise you again to see the Count d'Aranda, and to make him a proposition of some sort or other on the object in question. That which results from my memoir appears to me the most proper to effect a reasonble conciliation ; but it is for you to judge whether I am mistaken, because you alone have a knowledge of the title, which the United States can have to extend their possessions at the expense of nations, whom England herself has acknowledged to be independent.

As to the rest, Sir, whatever use you may think proper to make of my memoir, I pray you to regard it at least as a a proof of my zeal, and of my desire to be useful to the cause of your country.

I have the honour to be, with perfect consideration, yours, &c., &c.

RAYNEVAL.

P. S. As I shall be absent for some days, I pray you to address your answer to M. Stenin, Secretary to the Council of State, at Versailles.

I must desire you not to let the perusal of the following memoir make you forget the postscript of the above letter, for in the sequel you will find it of some importance.

M. de Rayneval's Memoir respecting the Right of the United States to the Navigation of the Mississippi.

[Translation.]

" The question between Spain and the United States of North America is, how to regulate their respective limits towards the Ohio and the Mississippi. The Americans pretend, that their dominion extends as far as the Mississippi, and Spain maintains the contrary.

" It is evident, that the Americans can only borrow from England the right they pretend to have to extend as far as the Mississippi ; therefore, to determine this right, it is proper to examine what the Court of London has thought and done on this head.

"It is known, that before the treaty of Paris, France possessed Louisiana and Canada, and that she considered the savage people, situated to the east of the Mississippi, either as independent, or as under her protection.

"This pretension caused no dispute ; England never thought of making any, except as to the lands situated towards the source of the Ohio, in that part where she had given the name of Alleghany to that river.

"A discussion about limits at that time took place between the Courts of Versailles and London, but it would be superfluous to follow the particulars ; it will suffice to observe, that England proposed in 1755 the following boundary. It set out from that point where the river de Boeuf falls into the Ohio, at the place called Venango ; it went up this river towards lake Erie as far as twenty leagues, and setting off again from the same place, Venango, a right line was drawn as far as the last mountains of Virginia, which descend towwards the ocean. As to the savage tribes situated between the aforesaid line and the Mississippi, the English Minister considers them as independent ; from whence it follows, that according to the very propositions of the Court of London, almost the whole course of the Ohio belonged to France, and that the countries situated to the westward of the mountains were considered as having nothing in common with the Colonies.

"When peace was negotiated in 1761, France offered to make a cession of Canada to England. The regulation of the limits of this Colony and Louisiana was in question. France pretended that almost the whole course of the Ohio made a part of Louisiana, and the Court of London, to prove that this river belonged to Canada, produced several authentic papers ; among others, the chart which M. Vaudreuil delivered to the English commandant when he abandoned Canada. The Minister of London maintained at the same time, that a part of the savages situated to the eastward of the Mississippi were independent, another part under its protection, and that England had purchased a part from the five Irequois nations. The misfortunes of France cut these discussions short; the treaty of Paris assigned the Mississippi for the boundary between the possessions of France and Great Britain.

" Let us see the dispositions, which the Court of London has made in consequence of the treaty of Paris.

" If they had considered the vast territories situated to the eastward of the Mississippi as forming part of their ancient Colonies, they would have declared so, and have made their dispositions accordingly. So far from any such thing, the King of England, in a proclamation of the month of October, 1763, declares in a precise and positive manner that the lands in question are situated between the Mississippi and the ancient *English establishments*. It is, therefore, clearly evident, that the Court of London itself, when it was as yet sovereign of the Thirteen Colonies, did not consider the aforementioned lands as forming part of these same Colonies; and it results from this in the most demonstrative manner, that they have not at this time any right over these lands. To maintain the contrary, every principle of the laws of nature and nations must be subverted.

" The principles now established are as applicable to Spain as to the United States. This power cannot extend its claims beyond the bounds of its conquests. She cannot therefore, pass beyond the Natchez, situated towards the thirtyfirst degree of latitude; her rights are, therefore, confined to this degree; what is beyond, is either independent or belonging to England; neither Spain nor the Americans can have any pretensions thereto. The future treaty of peace can alone regulate the respective rights.

" The consequence of all that has been said is, that neither Spain nor the United States has the least right of sovereignty over the savages in question, and that the transactions they may carry on as to this country would be to no purpose.

" But the future may bring forth new circumstances, and this reflection leads one to suppose, that it would be of use that the Court of Madrid and the United States should make an eventual arrangement.

" This arrangement may be made in the following manner. A right line should be drawn from the eastern angle of the Gulf of Mexico, which makes the section between the two Floridas, to Fort Toulouse, situated in the country of the Alabamas ; from thence the river Loneshatchi shou. be ascended, from the mouth of which a right line should b drawn to the Fort or Factory Quenassee ; from this last place, the course of the river Euphaseè is to be followed till it joins the Cherokee ; the course of this last river is to be pursued to the place where it receives the Pelisippi ; this last to be followed to its source, from whence a right line is to be drawn to Cumberland river, whose course is to be followed until it falls into the Ohio. The savages to the westward of the line described should be under the protection of Spain ; those to the eastward should be free, and under the protection of the United States ; or rather, the Americans may make such arrangements with them, as is most convenient to themselves. The trade should be free to both parties.

" By looking over the chart we shall find, that Spain would lose almost the whole course of the Ohio, and that the establishments, which the Americans may have on this river, would remain untouched, and that even a very extensive space remains to form new ones.

" As to the course and navigation of the Mississippi, they follow with the property, and they will belong, therefore, to the nation to which the two banks belong. If then, by the future treaty of peace, Spain preserves West Florida, she alone will be the proprietor of the course of the Mississippi from the thirtyfirst degree of latitude to the mouth of this river. Whatever may be the case with that part which is beyond this point to the north, the United States of America can have no pretensions to it, not being masters of either border of this river.

"As to what respects the lands situated to the northward of the Ohio, there is reason to presume that Spain can form no pretensions thereto. Their fate must be regulated with the Court of London."

I did not return M. Rayneval any answer to his letter, nor any remarks on his memoir, but the first time I saw him afterwards I told him, I had received his letter and memoir he had done me the honour to write, and that I should send a copy of it to our Secretary for Foreign Affairs.

As both the letter and memoir were *ostensibly* written by him in a private character, it did not appear to me expedient or necessary to enter into any formal discussions with him on those subjects.

The perusal of this memoir convinced me,

1st. That this Court would, at a peace, oppose our extension to the Mississippi.

2dly. That they would oppose our claim to the free navigation of that river.

3dly. That they would *probably* support the *British* claims to all the country above the 31st degree of latitude, and *certainly* to all the country north of the Ohio.

4thly. That in case we should not agree to divide

with Spain in the manner proposed, that then this Court would aid Spain in negotiating with Britain for the territory she wanted, and would agree that the residue should remain to Britain.

In my opinion, it was not to be believed that the first and confidential Secretary of the Count de Vergennes would, without his knowledge and consent, declare such sentiments, and offer such propositions, and that, too, in writing. I therefore considered M. Rayneval as speaking the sentiments of the Minister, and I confess they alarmed me, especially as they seemed naturally to make a part of that system of policy, which I believed induced him rather to postpone the acknowledgment of our independence by Britain to the conclusion of a general peace, than aid us in procuring it at present.

You will now be pleased to recollect the postscript to M. Rayneval's letter.

On the 9th of September I received certain information that on the 7th M. Rayneval had left Versailles, and was gone to England ; that it was pretended he was gone into the country, and that several precautions had been taken to keep his real destination a secret.

A former page in this letter informs you that a little before this, Mr. Oswald had despatched a courier with letters, recommending it to his Court to issue a new commission, styling us *United States*, and that I had agreed to prepare a letter to the Count de Vergennes, stating our objections to treat with Mr. Oswald under his present one.

This, therefore, was a period of uncertainty and suspense, and whatever part Britain might take, must necessarily be followed by very important consequences. No time was, therefore, to be lost in counteracting what I supposed to be the object of M. Rayneval's journey. But before I enter into that detail, I must here insert a copy of the letter which I wrote to the Count d'Aranda, agreeably to his request herein before-mentioned :

JAY TO COUNT D'ARANDA.

PARIS, September 10, 1782.

SIR :

Agreeably to your Excellency's request, I have now the honour of repeating in writing, that I am not authorized by Congress to make any cession of any countries belonging to the United States, and that I can do nothing more respecting the line mentioned by your Excellency, than to wait for and to follow such instructions as Congress, on receiving that information, may think proper to give me on that subject.

Permit me, nevertheless, to remind your Excellency that I have full power to confer, treat, agree, and conclude with the Ambassador or Plenipotentiary of his Catholic Majesty, *vested with equal powers*, of and concerning a treaty of amity and commerce and of alliance, on principles of equality, reciprocity, and mutual advantage.

I can only regret that my overtures to his Excellency, the Count de Florida Blanca, who was *ex of-*

ficio authorized to confer with me on such subjects, have been fruitless.

It would give me pleasure to see this business begun, and I cannot omit this opportunity of assuring your Excellency of my wish and desire to enter upon it as soon as your Excellency shall be pleased to inform me that you are authorized and find it convenient to proceed.   I have the honour to be, etc.

JOHN JAY.

To this letter, the Count returned the following answer:

[Translation.]

SIR:

I have the honour to reply to your note of yesterday, that I am furnished with ample instructions from my Court, and am authorized by it to confer and treat with you on all points on which you may be instructed and authorized to treat by your constituents.

As soon as you communicate your propositions, they will be examined, and I will submit to you my observations on them, in order that we may be able to agree on both sides.

I have the honour to be, &c.

THE COUNT D'ARANDA.

On the same day, viz. the 10th of September, a copy of a translation of a letter from M. Marbois to the Count de Vergennes, against our sharing in the fishery, was put into my hands.   Copies of it were transmitted to you, enclosed with my letter of the 18th of September, of which a duplicate was also forwarded.

I also learned from good authority, that on the morning of M. Rayneval's departure the Count d'Aranda had, contrary to his usual practice, gone with *post horses* to Versailles, and was two or three hours in conference with the Count de Vergennes and M. Rayneval before the latter set out.

All these facts taken together led me to conjecture, that M. Rayneval was sent to England for the following purposes :

1st. To let Lord Shelburne know that the demands of America, to be treated by Britain as independent previous to a treaty, were not approved or countenanced by this Court, and that the offer of Britain to make that acknowledgment in an article of the proposed treaty was in the Count's opinion sufficient.

2dly. To sound Lord Shelburne on the subject of the fishery, and to discover whether Britain would agree to divide it with France to the exclusion of all others.

3dly. To impress Lord Shelburne with the determination of Spain to possess the exclusive navigation of the Gulf of Mexico, and of their desire to keep us from the Mississippi ; and also to hint the propriety of such a line as on the one hand would satisfy Spain, and on the other leave to Britain all the country north of the Ohio.

4thly. To make such other verbal overtures to Lord Shelburne, as it might not be advisable to reduce to writing, and to judge from the general tenor of his Lordship's answers and conversation whether it was probable that a general peace, on terms agreeable to France, could be effected, in order if that was not the case an immediate stop might be put to the negotiation.

Having after much consideration become persuaded that these were M. Rayneval's objects, I mentioned his journey to Mr. Oswald, and after stating to him the first three of these objects, I said everything respecting them, that appeared to me necessary ; but at the same time with a greater degree of caution than I could have wished, because I well knew it would become the subject of a long letter to the Ministry. On reflecting, however, how necessary it was, that Lord Shelburne should know our sentiments and resolutions respecting these matters, and how much better they could be conveyed in conversation than by letter ; and knowing also that Mr. Vaughan was in confidential correspondence with him, and he was and always had been strongly attached to the American cause, I concluded it would be prudent to prevail upon him to go immediately to England.

I accordingly had an interview with Mr. Vaughan, and he immediately despatched a few lines to Lord Shelburne, desiring that he would delay taking any measures with M. Rayneval until he should either see or hear further from him.

Mr. Vaughan agreed to go to England, and we had much previous conversation on the points in question, the substance of which was :

That Britain, by a peace with us, certainly expected other advantages than a mere suspension of hostilities, and that she doubtless looked forward to cordiality, confidence, and commerce.

That the manner as well as the matter of the proposed treaty was therefore of importance, and that if the late assurances respecting our independence were not realized by an unconditional acknowledgment, neither confidence nor peace could reasonably be expected ; that this measure was considered by America as the touchstone of British sincerity, and that nothing else could abate the suspicions and doubts of her good faith which prevailed there.

That the interest of Great Britain, as well as that of the Minister, would be advanced by it ; for, as every idea of conquest had become absurd, nothing remained for Britain to do, but to make friends of those whom she could not subdue ; that the way to do this was by leaving us nothing to complain of, either in the negotiation or in the treaty of peace, and by liberally yielding every point essential to the interests and happiness of America; the first of which points was, that of treating with us on an equal footing.

That if the Minister really meant to make peace with us, it was his interest to make us believe so, and thereby inspire us with a certain degree of confidence, which could no otherwise be obtained ; that his enemies charged him with insincerity on this very point, and that it must be useful to him to convince all the world that such a charge was groundless.

That it would be vain to amuse themselves with expectations from the affected moderation of France on this head ; for that America never would treat on any but an equal footing, and, therefore, although such expectations might cause delay, they would ultimately be fruitless.

That a little reflection must convince him, that it was the interest and consequently the policy of France to postpone if possible the acknowledgment of our independence to the very conclusion of a general peace, and by keeping it suspended until after the war, *oblige us by the terms of our treaty, and by regard to our safety, to continue in it to the end.*

That it hence appeared to be the obvious interest of Britain immediately to cut the cords which tied us to France, for that, though we were determined faithfully to fulfil our treaty and engagements with this Court, *yet it was a different thing to be guided by their or our construction of it.*

That among other things we were bound not to make a separate peace or truce, and that the assurance of our independence was avowed to be the object of our treaty. While therefore Great Britain refused to yield this object, we were bound, as well as resolved, to go on with the war, although perhaps the greatest obstacles to a peace arose neither from the demands of France nor America. Whereas that object being conceded, we should be at liberty to make peace the moment that Great Britain should be ready to accede to the terms of France and America, without our being restrained by the demands of Spain, with whose views we had no concerns.

That it would not be wise in Great Britain to think of dividing the fishery with France and excluding us, because we could not make peace at such an expense, and because such an attempt would irritate America still more, would perpetuate her resentments, and induce her to use every possible means of retaliation by withholding supplies in future to the fishery, and by imposing the most rigid restraints on a commerce with Britain.

That it would not be less impolitic to oppose us on the point of boundary and the navigation of the Mississippi:

1st. Because our right to extend to the Mississippi was proved by our charters and other acts of government, and our right to its navigation was deducible from the laws of nature, and the consequences of revolution, which vested in us every British territorial right. It was easy therefore to foresee what opinions and sensations the mere attempt to dispossess us of these rights would diffuse throughout America.

2dly. Because the profits of an extensive and lucrative commerce, and not the possession of vast tracts of wilderness, were the true objects of a commercial European nation.

That by our extending to the Mississippi to the west, and to the proclamation bounds of Canada to the north, and by consenting to the mutual free navtion of our several lakes and rivers, there would be an inland navigation from the Gulf of St. Lawrence to that of Mexico, by means of which the inhabitants west and north of the mountains might with more ease be supplied with foreign commodities, than from ports on the Atlantic, and that this immense and growing trade would be in a manner monopolized by

Great Britain, as we should not insist that she should admit other nations to navigate the waters that belonged to her. That therefore the navigation of the Mississippi would in future be no less important to her than to us, it being the only convenient outlet, through which they could transport the productions of the western country, which they would receive in payment for merchandise vended there.

That as to retaining any part of the country, or insisting to extend Canada, so as to comprehend the lands in question, it would be impolitic for these further reasons. Because it would not be in their power either to settle or govern that country ; that we should refuse to yield them any aid, and that the utmost exertions of Congress could not prevent people from taking gradual possession of it, by making establishments in different parts of it. That it certainly could not be wise in Britain, whatever it might be in other nations, thus to sow the seeds of future war in the very treaty of peace, or to lay in it the foundation of such distrusts and jealousies as on the one hand would forever prevent confidence and real friendship, and on the other naturally lead us to strengthen our security by intimate and permanent alliances with other nations.

I desired Mr. Vaughan to communicate these remarks to Lord Shelburne, and to impress him with the necessity and policy of taking a decided and manly part respecting America.

Mr. Vaughan set off the evening of the 11th of September. It would have relieved me from much anxiety and uneasiness to have concerted all these steps with Dr. Franklin, but on conversing with him about M. Rayneval's journey, he did not concur with me in sentiment respecting the objects of it, but appeared to me to have a great degree of confidence in this Court, and to be much embarrassed and constrained by our instructions.

Nothing now remained to be done but to complete the letter we had agreed to write to the Count de Vergennes, stating our objections to treat with Mr. Oswald under his present commission. I accordingly prepared the following draft of such a letter, and it was under Dr. Franklin's consideration, when the news of our success in England rendered it unnecessary :

JAY'S LETTER TO COUNT DE VERGENNES.

SIR :

The question, whether we ought to exchange copies of our respective commissions with Mr. Oswald, and proceed to business with him under his, is not only important and consequential in itself, but derives an additional degree of weight from the variance subsisting between your Excellency's sentiments and our own on that subject.

The respect due to your Excellency's judgment, our confidence in the friendship of our good and great ally, and the tenor of our instructions from Congress, all conspire to urge us to lay before your Excellency a full state of the facts and circumstances which create our objections to treating with Mr. Oswald under the commission in question.

We flatter ourselves that in the course of this discussion some light will be cast upon the subject, and it gives us pleasure to reflect that our objections will be reviewed by a Minister, possessed of candour to acknowledge their force on the one hand, and talents to detect and discover to us their fallacy on the other.

It appears to us unnecessary to premise that on the 4th day of July, 1776, the representatives of the then late Thirteen United Colonies, in Congress assembled, did in the name and by the authority of the good people of those Colonies, and for the reasons in that act specified, "solemnly publish and declare that the said United Colonies were and of right ought to be *free and independent States*, that they were absolved from all allegiance to the British Crown, and that all political connection between them and the State of Great Britain was and ought to be totally dissolved ; and that as *free and independent States*, they had *full power* to levy war, *conclude peace*, contract alliances, establish commerce, and to do all other acts and things which independent nations ought of right to do. And for the support of that declaration, with a firm reliance on the protection of Divine Providence, they did mutually pledge to each other their lives, their fortunes, and their *sacred honour*."

This declaration was immediately ratified by the legislative acts of the different States, all of whom have ever since so uniformly abided by it that the authority of the King of Great Britain has never from that day to this extended over more ground in that country than was from time to time under the feet of his armies.

The United States also bound themselves to each other by a solemn act of confederation and perpetual union, wherein they declare, " that the style of the Confederacy should be, *the United States of America,*" and by it they vested *in Congress* the sole and *exclusive* right and power of determining on *peace* and war, of sending and receiving Ambassadors, and entering into *treaties* and alliances.

Thus becoming of right, and being in fact free, sovereign, and independent States, their representatives in Congress did on the 15th day of June, 1781, grant a commission to certain gentlemen (of whom we are two) *in their name* to confer, treat, and conclude, with the Ambassadors, Commissioners, etc. *vested with equal powers* relating to the re-establishment of peace, etc.

On the 25th of July, 1782, his Britannic Majesty issued a commission under the great seal of his kingdom to Richard Oswald, reciting in the words following, " that whereas by an act passed in the last session of Parliament, entitled ' An Act to enable his Majesty to conclude a peace or truce with certain Colonies in North America,' therein mentioned, it recited, that it is essential to the *interest, welfare, and prosperity* of Great Britain, and the *Colonies and Plantations* of New Hampshire, Massachusetts Bay, etc. [naming the thirteen], that peace, intercourse, trade, and commerce should be restored between them, therefore, and for a full manifestation of our earnest wish and desire, and of that of *our Parliament* to put an end to the calamities of war, it is enacted, that it should and might be lawful for us to treat, consult of, agree and conclude with any Commissioner or Commissioners, named or to be named, *by the said Colonies or Plantations*, or with any body or bodies, corporate or politic, or any assembly or assemblies, *or description of men or any person whatsoever*, a peace or truce with said Colonies or Plantations, *or any of them*, or any *part or parts thereof*, any law, act or acts of Parliament, matter or thing to the contrary in anywise notwithstanding." The commission then proceeds to appoint and authorize Mr Oswald to treat, etc. in *the very words of the act.*

We do not find ourselves described in this commission as the persons with whom Mr. Oswald is authorized to treat.

Nations, particularly corporations, mercantile companies, and indeed every private citizen, in every country, have their titles, their styles, their firms, and their additions, which are necessary to their being known in the law ; that is to say, the law of nations requires that national acts shall give to every sovereign and nation its proper political name or style, in the same manner as the municipal law of the land will only take notice of corporations, companies, and even private citizens by their proper names and legal descriptions.

When the United States became one of the nations of the earth, they published the style or name by which they were to be known and called, and as on the one hand they became subject to the law of nations, so on the other they have a right to claim and enjoy its protection, and all the privileges it affords.

Mr. Oswald's commission is a formal, national act, and no nation not mentioned or properly described in it can consider him properly authorized to treat with them. Neither the United States of America, nor Commissioners appointed by *them*, are mentioned in it, and therefore we *as their servants* can have no right to treat with him.

We are apprised the word *Colonies* or Plantations of New Hampshire, etc. in *North America*, conveys to the reader a geographical idea of the country intended by the commission, and of the manner of its first settlement, but it conveys no political idea of it, except perhaps a very false one, viz. as dependent on the British Crown; for it is to be observed, that the words *Colonies or Plantations* have constantly been used in British acts of Parliament, to describe those countries while they remained subject to that Crown, and the act holds up that idea in a strong point of light when it declares, "*that it is essential to the interest, welfare, and prosperity of the Colonies or Plantations* of New Hampshire, etc., that peace, etc., should be restored, etc." For as independent States our interests, welfare, and prosperity were *improper objects for the Parliamentary discussion and provision of Great Britain.*

The United States cannot be known, at least to their Commissioners by any other than *their present*, *proper, political name,* for in determining whether Mr. Oswald's commission be such as that we ought to treat with him under it, we must read it with the eyes, and decide upon it with the judgment, of *American Ministers* and not of private individuals.

But admitting that the studied ambiguity of this commission leaves every reader at liberty to suppose that we are or are not comprehended in it, nay supposing it to be the better construction that we are, still in our opinion it would ill become the dignity of Congress to treat with Mr. Oswald under it.

It is evident that the design of the commission was, if possible, to describe the United States, the Congress, and their Commissioners, by such circumlocutory, equivocal, and undeterminate words and appellations, as should with equal propriety apply to the Thirteen States considered as British Colonies and territories, or as independent States, to the end that Great Britain might remain in a capacity to say that they either had the one or the other meaning, as circumstances and convenience might in future dictate.

As Congress have no doubts of their own independence, they cannot with propriety sanctify the doubts of others, and, therefore, cannot admit the sufficiency or decency of any commission that contains them.

It being well known, that the United States have vested in Congress the exclusive right to make peace, this commission, by authorizing Mr. Oswald to treat with them *separately*, and even with parts of them, and with any person or persons whatsoever, offers such open and direct violence to the honour and prerogatives of Congress as to be better calculated to excite their resentment than their acquiescence. Nor can we conceive it very decent in Great Britain to expect that Congress, after having so long firmly and uniformly maintained the rights of independence, should now consent to deviate from that character by negotiating with her for peace, in any other capacity than the one in which they have carried on the war with her.

It seems agreed on all hands, that the commission does not acknowledge us to be independent, and though the King of Great Britain consents to make it the *first article* of the proposed treaty, yet, as neither the first nor the last article of the treaty can be of validity till the conclusion of it, can it be reasonably expected that we should consent to be viewed during all that interval as British subjects, there being no middle capacity or character between subjection and independence? Neither Congress nor their servants, if so inclined, have a right to suspend the independence of the United States for a single moment, nor can the States themselves adopt such a measure, while they remember the solemn manner in which they pledged to each other their lives, their fortunes, and their *sacred honour*, to support their independence.

It gives us pleasure to find that these inferences and conclusions from the general nature and rights of independence stand confirmed by the express acts and declarations of Congress on the subject, and in whatever view these acts may be regarded by others they must be considered as authoritative by their servants.

So early as the 17th of July, 1776, Congress resolved, " That General Washington, in refusing to receive a letter said to be sent by Lord Howe, addressed to ' George Washington, Esq.,' acted with a dignity becoming his station, and, therefore, that this Congress do highly approve the same, and *do direct* that no letter or message be received on any occasion whatever from the enemy by the Commander-in-chief, or others, the commanders of the American army, but such as shall be directed to them in the characters they respectively sustain."

We conceive that the reason of this resolution extends with at least equal force to *civil* officers, and particularly to Commissioners appointed to treat of peace with Great Britain.

On the 5th of September, 1776, Congress resolved, " That General Sullivan be requested to inform Lord Howe that this Congress, *being the representatives of the free and independent States of America*, cannot with propriety send any of its members to confer with his Lordship in their *private* characters, but that ever desirous of establishing peace on reasonable terms, they will send a committee of their body to know whether he has any authority to treat with persons *authorized by them* for that purpose in behalf of *America*, and what that authority is ; and to hear such propositions as he shall think fit to make respecting the same ; that the President write to General Washington and acquaint him that it is the opinion of Congress no proposals for making peace between Great Britain and the United States of America *ought to be received or attended to,* unless the same be made in writing, and addressed to the representatives of the said States in Congress, or *persons authorized by them,* and if application be made to him by any of the commanders of the British forces on that subject, that he inform them that these United States, who entered into the war only for the defence of their lives and liberties, will cheerfully agree to peace on reasonable terms, *whenever such* shall be proposed to them in MANNER AFORESAID."

These resolutions were passed at a time when the United States had formed no alliances, and when the formidable and hostile army had just arrived to invade their country. If such, therefore, were their sentiments, and such their resolutions, at so early, so dangerous, and doubtful a period, there certainly is reason to presume that the fortitude which influenced them has not been abated by the present aspect of their affairs.

On the 22d of November, 1777, Congress resolved, " That all proposals of a treaty between the King of Great Britain or any of his Commissioners and the United States, *inconsistent with the independence* of the said States, or with such treaties or alliances as may be formed under their authority, *will be rejected by Congress.*"

We cannot consider the present proposals to treat with us in a character *below independence to be consistent with it.*

Among other objections *unanimously* made by Congress, on the 22d of April, 1778, to certain bills of the British Parliament, then about to be passed into laws to enable the King of Great Britain to appoint Commissioners to treat, etc., is the following, viz. :

" Because the said bill purports that the Commissioners therein mentioned may treat with *private individuals*, a measure highly derogatory to *national honor*."

Mr. Oswald's commission contains a similar clause, and, consequently, is liable to the same objections.

The Congress did also, on the same day, *unanimously* declare, "that these United States cannot with propriety hold any conference or treaty *with any Commissioners* on the part of Great Britain, unless they shall, *as a preliminary thereto*, either withdraw their fleets and armies, or else *in positive and express terms acknowledge the independence of the said States*." Neither of these alternatives has as yet been complied with.

On the 6th of June, 1778, the Congress ordered their President to give an answer in the following words to the Commissioners appointed under the British acts of Parliament before mentioned viz.:

" My Lord,

" I have had the honour to lay your Lordship's letter of May the 27th, with the acts of the British Parliament enclosed, before Congress, and I am instructed to acquaint your Lordship, that they have already expressed their sentiments upon bills not essentially different from those acts, in a publication of the 22d of April last.

"Your Lordship may be assured that when the King of Great Britain shall be seriously disposed to put an end to the unprovoked and cruel war waged against these United States, Congress will readily attend to such terms of peace as may consist with the *honour of independent nations*, the interest of their constituents, and the sacred regard they mean to pay to treaties."

"The honour of an *independent nation* forbids their treating in a *subordinate* capacity."

On the 17th of June, 1778, Congress in another letter to the same Commissioners, *unanimously* join in saying:

"Nothing but an earnest desire to spare the further effusion of human blood could have induced them to read a paper containing expressions so disrespectful to his Most Christian Majesty, the good and great ally of these States, or to *consider* propositions so derogatory to the honour of an independent nation.

"The acts of the British Parliament, the commission from your sovereign, and your letter, suppose the people of these States to be subjects of the Crown of Great Britain, and are founded on an *idea of dependence*, which is utterly *inadmissible*.

"I am further directed to inform your Excellencies that Congress are inclined to peace, notwithstanding the unjust claims from which this war originated, and the savage manner in which it has been conducted. They will therefore be ready to enter *upon the consideration* of a treaty of peace and commerce not inconsistent with treaties already subsisting, *when* the King of Great Britain shall demonstrate a sincere disposition for that purpose. The only solid proof of this disposition will be an explicit acknowledgment of the independence of these States, or the withdrawing his fleets and armies."

On the 11th of July, 1778, the British Commissioners again endeavoured to prevail upon Congress to treat with them on the humiliating idea of dependence. And on the 18th day of the same month Congress came to the following resolution, viz :

" Whereas Congress, in a letter to the British Commissioners of the 17th June last, did declare that they would be ready to *enter into the consideration* of a treaty of peace and commerce not inconsistent with treaties already subsisting, *when* the King of Great Britain should demonstrate a sincere disposition for that purpose, and that the only solid proof of this disposition would be an *explicit acknowledgment of the independence* of these States, or the withdrawing his fleets and armies ; and whereas neither of these alternatives has been complied with, therefore resolved, that no answer be given to the letter of the 11th instant from the British Commissioners."

We find Congress still adhering to the same resolutions and principles, and in pursuance of them lately directing General Washington to refuse Sir Guy Carleton's request of a passport for one of his family to carry despatches from him to Congress. The late resolutions of the different States on that occasion show how exactly the sense of the people at large corresponds with that of their representatives in Congress on these important points.

To our knowledge, there is not a single instance in which Congress have derogated from the practice and conduct of an independent nation. All their commissions, as well *civil* as *military*, are and always have been in that style. They have treated with France and the States-General of the United Provinces, and those powers have treated with them on an equal footing. What right, therefore, can Britain have to demand that we should treat in a different manner with her? Or with what propriety can we pay marks of respect and reverence to our enemies, which we never have paid to our friends ; friends, too, who are at least equal to her in power and consideration ; nor can we forbear observing, that the second article of our treaty of alliance with his Most Christian Majesty declares, " That the essential and direct end of the present defensive alliance is, to maintain effectually the *liberty, sovereignty, and independence absolute and unlimited,* of the said United States as, well in matters of *government* as of commerce."

Hence it appears, that not only the regard due to our own dignity, but also to the dignity of our great ally, and the faith of treaties, forbid our receding in the least from the rights of *that sovereignty and independence,* the support of which forms the *direct end* of our alliance.

But although the United States as an independent nation can regard Great Britain in no other light than they would any other kingdom or state with

whom they may be at war, yet we can easily perceive that Great Britain has stronger objections than
other nations can have to treating with us as *independent*. But these objections, however strong, are
more proper subjects for their deliberations whom
they affect, than for ours, whom they do not respect.
Britain may amuse herself with, and therefore be
embarrassed by doubts of, our title to independence,
but we have no such doubts, and therefore cannot be
perplexed or influenced by them.

Other nations owe their origin to causes similar
to those which gave birth to ours, and it may not be
useless to inquire how they conducted themselves
under similar circumstances.

The tyranny of Philip II. of Spain made his subjects
in the Low Countries declare themselves independent ; a long and cruel war ensued, which was suspended by a truce for twelve years, and afterwards
concluded by a definitive treaty of peace.

History bears honourable testimony to the wisdom
and fortitude of that nation during that interval, and
we think the following detail is so interesting, and so
applicable to the case of our country in general, and
particularly to the point in question, that we cannot
forbear requesting your Excellency to peruse it :

On the 26th of July, 1581, the United Provinces,
by a formal act, declared that Philip II. had forfeited
his right to the sovereignty of those Provinces, and
that consequently they were independent.

On the last of June, 1584, the King of France sent
an Ambassador (le Sieur Pruneaul) to Holland, and

he in writing represented to the States assembled at Delft, that his Majesty had understood that they desired to treat with him, and that he had thought proper to inform them that they should let him know on what terms they proposed to do it, with many reasons to induce the Provinces to come into such treaty.

Queen Elizabeth did nearly the same thing by her letter of the last of October, 1584, which she sent to her Ambassador *Davidson.*

The Deputies of the States soon after, by their order, returned thanks to the Queen, and informed her that they had resolved to accept the King of France for Prince of the country in the same manner as Charles V. had been, but on condition to retain their rights and privileges.

On the 3d of January, 1585, the States despatched Deputies to make this offer to the King of France. Spain remonstrated against their being *admitted to an audience*, calling them rebels, etc.

To this remonstrance the King of France gave an answer which does the highest honour to his magnanimity.

On the 13th of February, 1585, the deputies had an audience of the King, and afterwards of the Queen Mother.

On the 8th of March, 1585, the King gave for answer to the Deputies, that he could not at present accept their offer nor assist them ; complained greatly of the violence done him by the Spaniards and Guises, and desired them to provide for their own defence, until such time as he should be in quiet with his own subjects, and promised to recommend them to the Queen of England.

On the 6th of June, 1585, the States-General resolved to transfer the sovereignty to the Queen of England, on lawful and reasonable conditions, or to treat with her to take them under her protection, or to obtain more aid and assistance from her.

On the 9th of July, 1585, they had an audience of the Queen at Greenwich, and offered to her the sovereignty, etc.

The Queen declined to accept the sovereignty or undertake the perpetual protection of the United Provinces, but on the 10th of August, 1585, she entered into a formal treaty with them to afford aid, etc.

On the 16th of October, 1587, the States made a declaration to their Governor Leicester on the subject of some differences between them, in which they say : " And as by divers acts, and particularly by a certain letter, which he wrote on the 10th of July to his secretary Junius (as is said), the authority of these States is drawn into doubt, they think it proper to make a more ample declaration, containing a deduction of the rights of the States, which they are bound by oath to maintain. *For in case they had not been well founded in the sovereignty of the Provinces, they could not have deposed the King of Spain, nor have defended themselves against his power. Nor would they have been able to treat with their Majesties of France and England,* nor to have transferred the government to your Excellency," etc., etc.

On the 3d of September, 1587, the Earl of Leicester, by order of the Queen, intimated to them the propriety of negotiating for peace, for it seems the King of Denmark had privately sounded the King of Spain on that subject.

The States answered : " That they had never given any such commission to the King of Denmark, nor ever thought of it ; but, on the contrary, they had observed to the Earl of Leicester, in the year 1586, on his leaving Holland, and on his speaking to them about making peace, that there was *nothing so dangerous and injurious in their condition as to speak or treat of peace,* and that it was one of the *old finesses of Spain ;* that neither a long war, the damages suffered, nor force, nor the unexpected deaths of their chiefs had been able to hinder their doing their duty, nor make them recede one step from that foundation of constancy on which they were fixed ; but that seeing the honourable weapons which were left them, viz., firmness and resolution, they were sufficiently powerful to surmount their difficulties in the same manner as the virtue of the Romans had made them triumph over Carthage." They also reminded the Earl that, by pretext of treating of peace on a former occasion, they had lost Artois, Hainault, and other countries. That the treaties at Ghent and Bruges, which were prior to their independence, had cost the lives of more than a hundred thousand persons ; that negligence and false security were always the consequences of such negotiations.

On the 30th of October, 1588, the Queen again

proposed entering into negotiations for peace, and they again refused.

In 1590 and 1591, the Emperor endeavoured to persuade the United Provinces to enter into negotiations, by the mediation of his good offices for a *reconciliation* with the King of Spain. And on the 7th of April, 1592, they gave a formal answer to the Emperor, containing their reasons for declining his proposal; on this occasion they struck a medal representing a Spaniard offering peace to a Zealander, who points to a snake in the grass, with these words, "*latet anguis in herba.*"

On the 6th of May, 1594, the Archduke of Austria sent a letter to the States on the same subject, and received the like answer, accompanied with a full statement of their reasons for it.

In the same year the United Provinces sent Ambassadors to Denmark, and received others from King James of Scotland, who desired them to send some persons on their behalf to assist at the baptism of his son, and to renew ancient treaties, etc.

On the 31st of October, 1596, the King of France entered into a treaty of alliance with the United Provinces against Spain.

On the 9th of August, 1597, the Emperor by his Ambassador, then at The Hague, proposed to the States to treat of peace. They refused, *alleging that they had been lawfully separated from the dominion of the King of Spain, and had formed alliances with England, France, etc.*

On the 15th of October, 1597, Ambassadors from

the King of Denmark arrived at The Hague, among other things to dispose the States to peace. On the 24th of October, the States gave them a long answer, recapitulating their reasons for refusing to negotiate.

On the 2d of November, 1597, the King of France, having been offered advantageous terms of peace by Spain, hinted his pacific inclinations to the States. They earnestly dissuaded him from making either *peace* or *truce*. The King, nevertheless, began to treat under the mediation of the Pope, etc.

The States sent Ambassadors to France with instructions dated 13th of January, 1598, to dissuade the King from peace, and to take measures with France against Spain for the ensuing campaign.

On the 2d of May, 1598, peace was concluded between France and Spain, at Vervins.

In treating of the articles of this peace, the Deputies of France declared that they could not proceed to conclude it unless the Queen of England and the United Provinces, who were allied with his Christian Majesty, were received and admitted to the treaty. To which the Deputies of the King of Spain answered, that from the commencement of the conferences they had declared that *they were ready and content to* receive and treat with the Deputies of the said Queen and Provinces, and that they had resided long enough in that place to give them time to come there if they had been so pleased ; and it was concluded and agreed that if in six months the Deputies of the said Queen and United Provinces should come with sufficient powers, and declare themselves willing to treat of peace, they should there be received, and for that purpose the Deputies of the King of Spain should be at Vervins, or such other place as by common consent of parties should be agreed upon ; and at the instance of the Deputies of his Christian Majesty, it was further agreed, that there should be a cessation of arms and hostilities between his Catholic Majesty, the Queen of England, and the United Provinces for two months, to be computed from the day on which the said Queen and Provinces should inform the Archduke of Austria that they accepted the said cessation, etc.

On the 6th of May, 1598, the King of Spain conveyed the Low Countries and Burgundy to his daughter Isabella Clara Eugenia on certain conditions, the first of which was, to marry Albert, the Archduke of Austria.

On the 29th of June, 1598, the Queen of England, by her Ambassador Sir Francis Veer, addressed the States on the subject of the late peace between France and Spain, and left it to *their choice* to accede or continue the war. They resolved not to treat of peace.

The Archduke expressed his astonishment that the Queen should assist his *rebellious subjects*, on which she desired the King of France to tell him that alliances with the States of the Low Countries was not a new thing ; that they had not *recognized him* for their sovereign, and that though she respected him as the brother of the Emperor and Archduke of Austria, yet as the Lieutenant of the King of Spain she held him as an enemy.

On the 16th of August, 1598, the Queen of England entered into a new convention with the United Provinces, confirming the treaty of 1585, with certain other stipulations.

On the 28th of August, 1598, the Archduke wrote a letter to the States-General, to persuade them to accept him for their sovereign. To this letter they resolved *not to give any answer*.

On the 13th of September, 1598, Philip II., King of Spain, died. In the year 1599, the Emperor again commissioned Ambassadors to persuade the United Provinces to treat of peace, etc. The States, in their answer of the 2d of December, 1599, refused to treat, because, among other reasons, "the insolence of the Archduke and Infanta was such, that although they knew very well that they could claim no right to the said United Provinces under the beforementioned donation, or by any other title, yet so it was, that by placards, by public and notorious libels, and by indecent and unjust acts, which they could never excuse, they held them for rebels."

On the 7th of June, 1600, the States, in their answer to another application to the Emperor, said, among other things, that the Archduke had "treated the inhabitants barbarously, proclaiming those to *be rebels who had nothing to do with him*, and that well considering all these things, they had good reason to judge that it would neither be consistent with their honour nor their interest to acknowledge the Archduke, or treat either with him or with Spain."

On the 3d of April, 1603, the Queen of England died.

On the accession of James the Archduke immediately sent Nicholas Schossy to sound the King on
the subject of peace, and the next year sent Count
Arembergh there for the same purpose.   King James
sent Rudolph Winwood to inform the States that the
Archduke had proposed to him to treat of peace, but
that he would do nothing till he had informed them
of it, and should be advised of their inclinations.

On the 30th of July, 1603, the Kings of France
and England concluded a treaty of confederation,
principally for the defence of the United Provinces
against the King of Spain.   This treaty was secret.

In May, 1604, conferences for a peace were opened
at London between the Deputies of Spain and the
Archduke on the one part, and those of England on
the other.

The Spaniards requested the King to mediate a
peace between the Archduke and the United Provinces *on reasonable and equal terms*.   The English
answered that it was not their business, and that they
could treat together without saying any thing of the
United Provinces.

On the 28th of August, 1604, peace was concluded
between Spain and the Archduke on the one part,
and England on the other.

On the last of May, 1605, the States, in answer to
the propositions for peace made by the Emperor, Elec-
tors, Princes, and States of the empire, say : "That
they had been legally discharged from their oaths to
the late King of Spain ; insomuch that all impartial
Kings, Princes, and States did at present acknowledge

and hold the Low Countries for a *free State*, qualified to govern itself in form of a republic, or to choose another Prince.

" That as to what they had been advised, viz., to enter into any treaty, contrary to the free government right, which they had obtained, and which they still enjoyed, they considered it as *contrary to God, their honour, and their safety.*"

About the end of February, 1607, there came from Brussels to Holland, as Deputy from the Archduke, the Commissary-General of the minor brothers, whose father had formerly been well acquainted with the Prince of Orange.

He came to learn the reasons which had prevented the propositions of the Sieur Horst from being successful. After speaking often in private with Prince Maurice, he came to The Hague, where he also had an audience of Prince Maurice, to whom he said that it was not the intention of his Highness *either to better or to lessen his right by any treaty of truce, but to treat with the States in the state in which they were.* And on being given to understand that the Archduke *must acknowledge the State for a free State before they would enter into any treaty*, he undertook to bring the Archduke to consent to it, in order to avoid the effusion of blood. On the 9th he went in Prince Maurice's boat to Antwerp, and returned on the 17th of March to The Hague, and did so much that both parties finally agreed to come to some mutual treaty, agreeable to the conditions of the following declaration, viz.:

" The Archdukes have found it proper to make the following declaration, offer, and presentation *to the States-General of the United Provinces of the Low Countries.*

" That the Archdukes, having nothing more at heart than to see the Low Countries and the inhabitants thereof delivered from the miseries of war, declare, by these presents, and with mature deliberation, that they are content to treat with the States-General of the United Provinces, in quality, and as holding them *for free Countries, Provinces, and States, to which their Highnesses pretend nothing,* either by way of perpetual peace, or truce, or cessation of arms for twelve, fifteen, or twenty years, at the election of the said States, and on reasonable conditions " ; then follow certain propositions for a truce, etc., and afterwards a condition, " That the States agree to the aforesaid provisional truce in eight days after the delivery of these presents, and shall make a declaration to their Highnesses in writing, before the 1st of September next ensuing, touching the principal treaty aforesaid of truce or cessation of arms, with the time and place which they may have chosen. Done at Brussels, under the signatures and the seal of their Highnesses, the 13th of March, 1607."

To this declaration and offer the States answered : " That the States-General, in quality of and as free States, Countries, and Provinces, over which their Highnesses have nothing to pretend, and being equally desirous of nothing more than to consent to a Christian, honourable, and sure issue to, and deliverance from the miseries of this war, after mature deliberation, and with the advice of his Excellency, and of the Council of State, *have accepted* the said declaration of the Archdukes *to regard their United Provinces as free Countries, to which their Highnesses have nothing to pretend,* and also a truce for eight months, etc., etc. Their Highnesses further promising to obtain and deliver to the said States-General within three months next ensuing, the agreement of the King of Spain touching the treaty, under all the necessary renunciations and obligations, as well general as special."

On the last of June, 1607, the King of Spain ratified the truce, but *omitted an acknowledgment of their independence.*

The States-General, on the 9th and 11th of August, " declared these ratifications to be imperfect both in substance and in form." The Archduke promised to procure a more complete one.

On the 18th of September, 1607, the King of Spain made a new ratification *containing the acknowledgment in question,* but declaring that the said ratification should be void, unless the peace or truce in contemplation should take place.

To this condition the States made strong objections.

On the 2d of November, 1607, the States made various remarks on the ratification. They *absolutely refused to accept, and protested against the condition* contained in it, but offered to proceed on the footing of the declaration, *provided* the States should be firmly assured that nothing would be proposed either on the part of the Archduke or of the King *contrary to the same*, or prejudicial to the State or government of the United Provinces, and provided also that the Archduke did send his Deputies to The Hague fully authorized, etc., within ten days after the receipt of that answer.

On the 10th of November the States-General adjourned to take the sense of their constituents on the subject of the ratification, and agreed to meet again on the 10th of December.

On the 24th of December, 1607, they wrote to the Archduke that, under the *protest and declaration* contained in the answer of the 2d of November, they were content to enter into conferences with his Deputies at The Hague, and proposed to prolong the truce a month or six weeks.

On the 7th of January the answer of the Archduke arrived, in which he calls the States " *très chers et bons amis.*" He observed that he had learned from their letter, of the 24th of December, the resolution they had taken to enter into conferences with his Deputies about peace, and, in the meantime, to prolong the truce for a month or six weeks.

That, as to the first point, he had appointed for the said conferences the same persons whom he had before employed, and that they should set out the 15th of January, and that, as to the truce, he was content to prolong it for six weeks.

On the 6th of February, 1608, the Deputies of the States and those of the Archduke had their first meeting to exhibit their respective credentials. The

Deputies of the Archduke produced two, one from him, and the other from the King of Spain.

On the 8th of February, 1608, the Deputies of both parties had their second meeting. Those of the States asked the others if they were fully instructed (*enchargés*) *to acknowledge the United Provinces to be free Provinces and Countries, and to treat with them in that capacity*, to which they explicitly (*rondement*) answered *yes*. The Dutch Deputies thereupon asked, why then the Archduke retained the arms and name of the said Provinces. They then replied, that it ought not to seem strange, for that the King of Spain retained the title of King of Jerusalem, the King of France that of King of Navarre, and the King of England retained the arms and title of France.

On the 11th of February, 1608, they met again ; the Deputies of the States presented to the others an article which they had drawn up, by which the " Provinces were declared to be free, and that the King of Spain and the Archdukes relinquished all their pretensions to the sovereignty of the said Provinces, etc., as well for themselves as for their successors and heirs, *with the name and arms*."

The others received the article, and took time to consider of it, on which the meeting was adjourned. They immediately despatched a courier with a copy of it to Brussels, and received an answer on the 13th. They complained, however, to the Ambassadors of France and Great Britain, etc., of the States being *so precise* in that article.

On the 13th of February, 1608, in the afternoon, the Deputies again assembled, and those of the Archduke *consented to the article as it was drawn up*, with reserve, nevertheless, that in case all the other points should be agreed upon, *they hoped* the States would do something for the King of Spain and the Archduke respecting the Indies, etc.

On the 15th of February they again met ; they agreed on the points of amnesty and oblivion ; but on treating of reciprocal free trade and navigation to each other's ports and countries, the Deputies of the Archduke declared that they did not mean to comprehend in that free trade, *the navigation to the Indies* and all the fortresses there, but, on the contrary, that all the subjects of these countries should *forthwith desist therefrom*. The Dutch Deputies opposed *this strongly and firmly*, saying that it would prejudice the liberty of the Provinces and *the free use of the sea*, and, therefore, that they were not authorized to relinquish it. The others continued firm in their demand, and after long debates the Deputies separated.

On the 19th, 23d, and 27th of February, and 4th of March, 1608, the Deputies met, but, except debating, did nothing, both parties continuing firm and resolved not to cede any thing.

The Deputies of Spain, finding they could not carry the point as to the Indies, declared, at length, that they would consult together on a proposition to make a truce for some years respecting the navigation, and that they were ready to go on to the other points, and try to agree upon some of them.

On the 7th of March they exchanged heads of articles for consideration. On the 11th and 12th of March they again met, and had fruitless debates about a *free navigation to the Indies, etc.* The Marquis Spinola proposed that the subject should be divided, and that two sets of propositions should be prepared, one for the navigation in Europe and the other for the Indies.

On the 17th of March they again met, and the Dutch Deputies offered to the others two sets of propositions, as had been proposed ; they received them for consideration ; but, after debate, they declared that they could not agree to them, and that they must make a journey to Spain for further instructions ; for this reason the truce was prolonged to the end of May.

The truce was continued from time to time, and sundry fruitless meetings held ; but, on the 20th of August, 1608, the Deputies assembled ; " the Spanish ones declared that they had lately received full instructions on the several points in question, viz., *that the King and Archduke were content to quit the sovereignty of the United Provinces ;* but that he required two points to be yielded by the States by way of compensation, viz., the re-establishment of the Roman Catholic religion in every place in the Provinces, and that they should immediately *desist from all navigation both to the East and West Indies.*"

The Dutch Deputies reported this to the States-

General. On the 25th of August the States-General made a long and spirited declaration on the subject of this report, resolving against negotiating any longer, and they ordered a copy of it to be delivered to the Spanish Deputies.

On the 27th of August, 1608, the Ambassadors of France and England, etc., came to the States-General and endeavoured to prevail upon them to agree to a long truce.

On the 30th of August, the States expressed their readiness to agree to a long truce, provided the adverse party " would *so absolutely acknowledge them for free countries, as that it should not be questioned after the expiration of the truce;* that otherwise they could not listen to a truce."

On the 3d of September the Spanish Deputies said they had no instructions to treat of truce, in acknowledging the United Provinces to be absolutely free, and *permitting the navigation to the Indies,* but that they had sent the proposition to Brussels, in order to have further instructions.

On the 7th of September they received an answer from Brussels, and they declared that they had no instructions to agree to a long truce with the States, on condition to acknowledge them to be States absolutely free, and without comprehending the re-establishment of the Roman religion, and the relinquishment of *all navigation to the Indies,* but that the Archduke would send the proposition to Spain, from whence he might expect an answer by the end of September.

They then proposed either to wait for the answer of Spain, or continue the present truce for seven years, observing that it had been made with an express declaration to hold the United Provinces for free countries, and that as to the trade to the Indies, the Archduke would promise to *get it ratified by the King of Spain for that space of time.*

The States unanimously rejected this new proposition, but gave them the time they had demanded for the answer of Spain. On the 28th of September the Spanish Deputies applied to the Ambassadors of France, etc., to ask ten days more from the States. The Ambassadors agreed to do it *in the name of the Deputies*, but they declined it.

On the last of September they took their leave.

The States-General became possessed by accident of the instructions given to Spinola and the other Deputies; they were signed by the Archdukes, and dated at Brussels the 6th of January, 1608. They were thereby instructed to insist on the free exercise of the Roman Catholic religion.

As to independence the instructions say :

" As to the subject of liberty, since you know what we have granted, make no difficulty of arranging it as they wish ; doing or saying nothing in opposition, which may make them suspect that we desire to revoke our declaration on that point, as we are determined to abide by it in all respects."

These instructions also directed them to insist that the States should renounce, and entirely and absolutely desist from, the trade of the East and

West Indies, and should agree to punish those who might undertake such voyages, etc., etc.

On the departure of the Spanish Deputies, the Ambassadors of France and Great Britain endeavoured to prevail upon the States-General to listen to a truce, and proposed to their consideration certain articles which they had prepared. The States, after much deliberation, agreed to enter into further negotiations on the subject.

On the 25th of March, 1609, the Deputies of both parties met at Antwerp, and on the 9th of April following, a truce for twelve years was concluded upon. It was forthwith ratified by the States and the Archdukes, and published on the 14th of April.

On the 7th of July, 1609, at Segovia, the King of Spain explicitly and without reserve ratified this truce, viz. :

"His Majesty having seen the contents of the articles of truce and capitulation, which his dear and well beloved brothers, the Archdukes Albert and Isabella Clara Eugene have sent him, concerning the truce granted in the name of his Majesty by his representative, and in that of their Highnesses by themselves to the States-General of the United Provinces of the Low Countries, and having maturely considered it, declares that he applauds, approves, confirms, and ratifies the said truce, in so much as concerns him, etc."

The first article of this truce was in the words following :

"First, the abovementioned Archdukes declare, in

their own name and in that of the King, that they are content to treat with the said States-General of the United Provinces in the character of, and holding them for a free country, estates, and provinces, over which they have no claims, and to make a truce with them in the name and under the character above described; and this they do on the conditions hereinafter described and declared by these presents."

On the 30th of January, 1648, a treaty of peace was concluded between Spain and the United Provinces.

The full powers or commission given by the King of Spain to his plenipotentiaries for making this peace were dated near two years before, viz., 7th of June, 1646, and they show clearly that he negotiated with those Provinces as with independent States, on that occasion.

The tenor of this commission is very different from that of Mr. Oswald. The following is an extract from it:

" All the powers which are concerned in this war, having by common consent chosen the city of Munster as a place of holding the Congress and the negotiations for the peace aforesaid, we have thought proper to name plenipotentiaries there to treat with the States of the free Provinces of the Low Countries, or with their Ambassadors and Plenipotentiaries, authorized and deputed for this purpose, etc."

From this detail it appears that the Dutch ever after their declaration of independence in July, 1581, uniformly treated with the neighbouring nations on an *equal footing*, and also that they constantly and firmly refused to negotiate either for truce or peace with Spain until she consented to treat with them in *like manner*.

We forbear engaging your Excellency's time and attention by the application of these facts and conclusions to the case of our country. We are persuaded that the similarity between the two will not escape your discernment, and that we shall not be thought singular in our opinion that the example of the United Provinces merits at least in these respects the imitation as well as the approbation of the United States of America.

But, Sir, we not only think it inconsistent with the dignity of the United States to treat with Britain in the humiliating manner proposed, but also that it would be repugnant to their interest.

The respect of other nations is undoubtedly of importance to America; but, Sir, if she ceases to respect herself, how can she expect to be respected by others?

America has taken and published noble and manly resolutions to support her independence at every hazard. She has hitherto done it, and would it be for her interest to quit the ground for which she has lost so much of her blood, merely to accommodate herself to the high-blown pride of an enemy? Sir, the very proposition carries with it insult, and therefore bears strong marks of *insincerity*.

But suppose that the United States should descend from their present ground of equality, in order to treat with Mr. Oswald, and that our negotiations should be *fruitless.* In what an awkward situation should we then be? We should find ourselves betrayed, by our too great pliancy and our too great desire of peace, to the ridicule of our enemies, the contempt of other nations, and the censure of our own minds. What a page would this make in history!

As to Mr. Oswald's offer to make an acknowledgment of our independence the first article of our treaty, and your Excellency's remark that it is sufficient, and that *we are not to expect the effect before the cause*, permit us to observe, that by the *cause*, we suppose, is intended the *treaty*, and by the *effect*, an acknowledgment of our independence. We are sorry to differ from your Excellency, but, really, Sir, we cannot consider an acknowledgment of our independence as a subject to be treated about; for while we feel ourselves to be independent in fact, and know ourselves to be so of right, we can see but one cause from whence an acknowledgment of it can flow as an effect, viz., *the existence and truth of the fact.* This cause has long existed and still exists, and therefore we have a right to expect that Great Britain will treat with us being what we are, and not as what we are not. To treat about this matter would be to suppose that our independence was incomplete until they pronounced it to be complete. But we hold it to be complete already, and that as it never did, so it never will or must, depend in the least degree on their will and pleasure. To us there appears to be a wide distinction between their acknowledging the United

States to be independent, and their renouncing their pretended though troublesome claims ; the former, being a pre-existing fact, cannot depend upon, and therefore is not a proper subject for, a treaty ; but to renounce or not to renounce a claim, whether good or bad, depends on the will of him who makes and prosecutes it ; and, therefore, like other matters of interest and convenience, is a proper subject for bargains and agreements between those who trouble their neighbours with such claims, and their neighbours who are troubled by them ; and who, for the sake of peace, may choose to continue the lawsuit, unless their future quiet is secured by a quit claim.

———

I think it was on the 24th of September that I was informed of the intention of the British Court to give Mr. Oswald such a new commission as had been recommended.

On the 26th of September, I went to pay a visit to the Count de Vergennes at Versailles. I found the Marquis de Lafayette in the antechamber, and the Ambassador of Spain shortly after entered. After some common conversation, the Ambassador asked me when we should proceed to do business. I told him as soon as he should do me the honour of communicating his powers to treat. He asked me whether the Count de Florida Blanca had not informed me of his being authorized. I admitted that he had, but observed that the usual mode of doing business rendered it proper that we should exchange certified copies of our respective commissions. He said that could not be expected in our case, for that Spain had not yet acknowledged our independence. I replied that we had declared it, and that France, Holland, and Britain had acknowledged it. Here the Marquis de Lafayette took up the subject, and it continued between him and the Ambassador till the Count de Vergennes came in. The Marquis told the Ambassador, among other things, that it would not be consistent with the dignity of France for her ally to treat otherwise than as independent. This remark appeared to me to pique the Count d'Aranda not a little.

The Count de Vergennes, on coming in, finding the conversation earnest, inquired whether we could not agree. The Ambassador stated my objections. The Count said I certainly ought to treat with the *Ambassador*, and that it was proper we should make a treaty with Spain in the same manner that we had done with France. I told him I desired nothing more; and that the commission to M. Gerard, and the reason assigned by this Court to the King of Great Britain for entering into alliance with us, pointed out both the manner and the principles which were observed and admitted on that occasion. The Count did not seem pleased with my allusion to the communication made of our alliance to England. He observed, that Spain did not deny our independence, and he could perceive no good reason for my declining to confer with the Ambassador about a treaty, without saying any thing about our independence, an acknowledgment of which would naturally

be the effect of the treaty proposed to be formed. I
told the Count that, being independent, we should
always insist on being treated as such, and, therefore,
it was not sufficient for Spain to forbear denying our
independence while she declined to admit it, and that
notwithstanding my respect for the Ambassador, and
my desire of a treaty with Spain, both the terms of
my commission and the dignity of America forbade
my treating on any other than an *equal footing.*

The Count carried the Ambassador into his cabinet,
and when he retired I was admitted.

The Count commenced the conversation by explaining the reason of sending M. Rayneval to England, which he said was that, by conversing with
Lord Shelburne about peace and matters connected
with it, he might be able to judge whether a pacific
disposition really prevailed in the British Court, and,
therefore, whether any dependence might be placed
in his Lordship's professions on that head ; that he
was satisfied with M. Rayneval's report, and that he
believed that Lord Shelburne was sincerely desirous
of peace.

A few words then passed about Mr. Oswald's new
commission ; the Count observing, in general terms,
that as it removed our former objections we might
now go on to prepare our preliminaries.

The conversation next turned to our negotiation
with Spain, and to her claims east of the Mississippi.
Nothing new passed on the first topic ; as to the latter, the Count made only some very general remarks,
such as that he hoped we should, on conferring fur-

ther about the matter, approach nearer to each other ; that those limits ought to be settled, and while they remained in contest a treaty with Spain could not reasonably be expected ; that as soon as we should agree upon those points, Count d'Aranda would have a further or more formal commission to conclude the treaty, etc.

I remarked that these claims of Spain were of recent date, for that on my first arriving in Spain the Count de Florida Blanca told me that the success of my mission would probably turn upon one single point, viz., the cession of our rights to the navigation of the river Mississippi ; from which, as well as from their subsequent and uniform demands on that head, it was evident that they then considered that river as our boundary ; for it would have been very strange indeed that they should insist on our forbearing to navigate a river whose waters washed no part of our country, and to which we could not, of consequence, have any pretence of claim.

The Count smiled, but avoided making any direct reply ; he hoped we should, nevertheless, agree, and that we must endeavour to approach and meet each other. I told him I could not flatter myself with such expectations while Spain continued her claims to those countries, for that we should be content with no boundary short of the Mississippi.

I went from the Count's to M. Rayneval's chamber, for I had not seen him since his return from England. He gave me the same reason for his journey which I had just received from the Count. We then talked of his memoir and the Spanish negotiation. He said much in favour of the conciliatory line he had proposed, and of the advantages of placing the Indian nations on the *west* side of it, under the *protection* of Spain, and those on the *east*, under that of the United States; that the rights of those nations would be thereby secured, and future disputes between us and Spain avoided. I replied that, so far as our claims might affect those Indian nations, it was a matter solely between us and them; and that, admitting them to be independent, they certainly had a right to choose their own protectors; and, therefore, that we could have no right, without their knowledge or consent, to choose for them. I also made the same remark to him respecting the recency of these Spanish claims which I had just before done to Count de Vergennes. He said it was a subject which Count de Florida Blanca had not understood, and imputed their former ideas of our extending to the Mississippi to their ignorance respecting those matters; hence it became evident from whom they had borrowed their present ideas.

On the 27th of September Mr. Vaughan returned here from England with the courier that brought Mr. Oswald's new commission, and very happy were we to see it. Copies of it have already been sent to you, so that I will not lengthen this letter by inserting it here; nor wil! I add any thing further on this head at present, than to assure you that Mr. Vaughan greatly merits our acknowledgments.

The next thing to be done was to prepare and

draw up the proposed articles. They were soon completed and settled between us and Mr. Oswald, by whom they were sent to his Court, with letters declaring his opinion that they ought to be accepted and agreed to ; but they differed with him in opinion.

These articles, for very obvious reasons, were not communicated to the Count de Vergennes.

Mr. Oswald did not receive any opinion from his Court relating to our articles until the 23d of October, when letters from the Minister informed him that the extent of our boundaries and the situation of the tories, etc., caused some objections, and the Minister's Secretary was on the way here to confer with us on those subjects.

On the 24th of October I dined at Passy with Dr. Franklin, where I found M. Rayneval. After dinner we were in private with him a considerable time. He desired to know the state of our negotiation with Mr. Oswald. We told him that difficulties had arisen about our boundaries, and that one of the Minister's Secretaries was coming here with papers and documents on that subject. He asked us what boundaries we claimed. We told him the river St. John to the east, and ancient Canada, as described in the proclamation, to the north. He contested our right to such an extent to the north, and entered into several arguments to show our claim to be ill founded. These arguments were chiefly drawn from the ancient French claims, and from a clause in the proclamation restraining governors from making grants in the Indian country, etc.

He inquired what we demanded as to the fisheries.
We answered that we insisted on enjoying a right in
common to them with Great Britain. He intimated
that our views should not extend further than a coast
fishery, and insinuated that pains had lately been
taken in the Eastern States to excite their apprehensions and increase their demands on that head. We
told him that such a right was essential to us, and
that our people would not be content to make peace
without it ; and Dr. Franklin explained very fully
their great importance to the Eastern States in particular. He then softened his manner and observed
that it was natural for France to wish better to us
than to England ; but as the fisheries were a great
nursery for seamen, we might suppose that England
would be disinclined to admit others to share in it,
and that for his part he wished there might be as few
obstacles to a peace as possible. He reminded us,
also, that Mr. Oswald's new commission had been
issued posterior to his arrival in London.

On the 26th of October Mr. Adams arrived here,
and in him I have found a very able and agreeable
coadjutor.

When I began this letter I did not flatter myself
with being able to write this much before Captain
Barney would leave us ; and I now find myself too
much exhausted to proceed with further details, and
must therefore refer you to the letters you will receive
from Mr. Adams and Dr. Franklin.

The same reason also prevents my writing to you
and Mr. Morris on other subjects by Captain Barney,

and I hope the length of this letter, and the disagreeable state of my health, will apologize for my not writing even to my own family by this opportunity.

I am sensible of the impression which this letter will make upon you and upon Congress, and how it will affect the confidence they have in this Court. These are critical times, and great necessity there is for prudence and secrecy.

So far and in such matters as this Court may think it their interest to support us, they certainly will, but no further, in my opinion.

They are interested in separating us from Great Britain, and on that point we may, I believe, depend upon them ; but it is not their interest that we should become a great and formidable people, and therefore they will not help us to become so.

It is not their interest that such a treaty should be formed between us and Britain as would produce cordiality and mutual confidence. They will, therefore, endeavour to plant such seeds of jealousy, discontent, and discord in it as may naturally and perpetually keep our eyes fixed on France for security. This consideration must induce them to wish to render Britain formidable in our neighbourhood, and to leave us as few resources of wealth and power as possible.

It is their interest to keep some point or other in contest between us and Britain to the end of the war, to prevent the possibility of our sooner agreeing, and thereby keep us employed in the war, and dependent on them for supplies. Hence they have favoured, and will continue to favour, the British demands as to matters of boundary and the tories.

The same views will render them desirous to continue the war in our country as long as possible, nor do I believe they will take any measures for our repossession of New York, unless the certainty of its evacuation should render such an attempt advisable. The Count de Vergennes lately said that there could be no great use in expeditions to take places which must be given up to us at a peace.

Such being our situation, it appears to me advisable to keep up our army to the end of the war, even if the enemy should evacuate our country ; nor does it appear to me prudent to listen to any overtures for carrying a part of it to the West Indies, in case of such an event.

I think we have no rational dependence except on God and ourselves, nor can I yet be persuaded that Great Britain has either wisdom, virtue, or magnanimity enough to adopt a perfect and liberal system of conciliation. If they again thought they could conquer us they would again attempt it.

We are, nevertheless, thank God, in a better situation than we have been. As our independence is acknowledged by Britain, every obstacle to our forming treaties with neutral powers and receiving their merchant ships is at an end, so that we may carry on the war with greater advantage than before, in case our negotiations for peace should be fruitless.

It is not my meaning, and therefore I hope I shall not be understood to mean, that we should deviate in the least from our treaty with France ; our honour and our interest are concerned in inviolably adhering to it. I mean only to say that if we lean on her love of liberty, her affection for America, or her disinterested magnanimity, we shall lean on a broken reed, that will sooner or later pierce our hands, and Geneva as well as Corsica justifies this observation.

I have written many disagreeable things in this letter, but I thought it my duty. I have also deviated from my instructions, which, though not to be justified, will, I hope, be excused on account of the singular and unforeseen circumstances which occasioned it.

Let me again recommend secrecy, and believe me to be, dear sir, etc.[1]

JOHN JAY.

P. S.—I have neither seen nor heard any thing of Mr. Laurens, nor of the cipher you mention to have sent by him.

---

[1] Additional papers relating to the treaty, including Livingston's reply to Jay's letter as above, and Jay's further explanation of his course, July 19, 1783, will appear in the order of their dates in Vol. III. of the present series.